SOLAR ARCHITECTURE

The Direct Gain Approach

TIMOTHY E. JOHNSON
Massachusetts Institute of Technology

An Energy Learning Systems Book
McGRAW-HILL BOOK COMPANY

New York, St. Louis, San Francisco, Auckland, Bogota, Hamburg, Johannesburg, London, Madrid,
Mexico, Montreal, New Delhi, Panama, Paris, Sao Paulo, Singapore, Sydney, Tokyo, Toronto

For Neil and Eric

Library of Congress Cataloging in Publication Data

Johnson, Timothy Edward.
  Solar architecture.

  (An Energy learning systems book)
  Includes index.
  1. Solar houses.   2. Solar energy — Passive
systems.   3. Architecture and solar radiation.
I. Title.   II. Series.
TH7414.J63   728'.047   81-20941

ISBN 0-07-032598-7

123456789 KPKP 898765432

Contents

Acknowledgments

*J*ust ten years ago, I met Day Chahroudi who envisioned the day when buildings would make their own exquisit climate through natural processes. He called these buildings "biospheres" because, like living cells, their specialized skins would selectively admit and reject energy to produce comfortable interiors. That idea proved to be a great influence in my work and in the writing of this book.

Some of the information in this book comes from my students, who being good students, taught their teacher. I am especially appreciative of Charles Benton, Stephen Hale, and James Rosen who helped me refine the design methods appearing here.

I am grateful to Robert Entwistle for his vigorous support and guidance in the ways of writing books. Many thanks also to Marilyn Entwistle for interpreting my rough drawings.

Chapter 1

Introduction

REDISCOVERING THE GLASS HOUSE

"Fuel savings with Glass." "The most exciting architectural news in decades." These optimistic words are not from today, but from more than forty years ago when Chicago architect George Fred Keck demonstrated that homes could be heated directly by the sun. Keck first demonstrated passive solar heating at the 1933-34 Chicago Century of Progress Exposition with his all-glass "Crystal House." (See Figure 1.1.) The structure overheated during sunny Chicago winters, but the experience prepared Keck for more important work. The next year, Libbey-Owens Ford commercially introduced hermetically sealed, double-plate glass. Keck and others realized for the first time that glass could insulate. The 1941 Hugh Duncan residence in Flossmoor, Illinois (See Figure 1.2), resulted from Keck's marriage of this glass technology and direct-gain solar principles.

In the age before air conditioning, Keck was most interested in designing not only for thermal comfort, but also for visual and aesthetic comfort. He acknowledged, in passing, the intrinsic fuel savings that were a part of passive solar heating. Nevertheless, a *Chicago Tribune* reporter coined the phrase "solar home" when describing his work. In 1942 Keck teamed up with a builder of prefabricated houses to produce "Green's Ready-Built Homes." Some of these one story homes were built on poured concrete slab foundations. In most cases, throw rugs were used to partially cover the tile floor finishes. Fuel bills were only reduced by 30 percent because the floor slab was not properly insulated and no nighttime insulation was

1

Figure 1.1 George Keck's "Home of Tomorrow" at the 1933 Chicago Century of Progress Exposition (Courtesy of Hedrich-Blessing and Keck and Keck, Architects)

used in the windows. But Keck was selling the "picture window," sun tempering, natural daylighting, and a new style of postwar living made possible by an advance in window technology. Many of Keck's ideas survived the postwar period, but rapidly declining fuel prices opened the way for low-cost mechanical heating and air conditioning substitutes.

WHAT THIS BOOK IS ABOUT

More than forty years later we are faced with a similar advance in technology, but this time the technical advance encompasses a whole range of building products in addition to windows. This book explores those technologies and how to apply them to residential design. As used here, the term "residential" covers many building types, from single-family, detached structures to townhouses and high-rise apart-

Figure 1.2 The Duncan Residence, 1941, Flossmoor, Illinois (Courtesy of Keck and Keck, Architects)

ments. Although the importance of fuel savings is much greater today, Keck's criteria for living — comfort — is still foremost. Structures are built not to save energy, but to tastefully provide shelter, security, and comfort. For this reason, the bulk of this book (Chapters 4-8) shows how to design for thermal and visual comfort using direct-gain solar design methods that will accept new technologies.

Comfort begins outdoors at the building site. The site is the transition zone between indoors and out, where a certain amount of buffering and tempering is necessary to modify local outdoor conditions (the microclimate). Careful site design can extend the moderate spring and fall seasons by creating sun traps with natural and man-made materials. Similarly, wind velocities can be reduced in the winter to lower building heat losses, and increased during the summer to promote natural ventilation. The site can be designed to become a large, natural solar collector that warms the outdoor air in winter without overheating during the summer. This not only promotes enjoyment of the site, but also it reduces building thermal loads up to 15 percent. Chapter 4 shows how this can be done by careful use of vegetation, land forms, building orientation, and view.

Solar architectural design basics are introduced in Chapter 3. The underlying principles of solar availability, heat flow, glare, and natural daylighting are given in useable form.

What we really learn from is history. The successful direct-gain solar-heated residences of today are based on the successes and failures of the past. This book starts with the lessons of the 1940s and moves into some of today's examples. We applied two criteria in selecting the examples: technical excellence and/or beauty. Also, these examples were chosen because they hint at the delightful kind of spaces that can be built using direct-gain principles and the new, high performance solar building products.

Chapter 2

Modern Historical Precedent

We have learned about building direct gain structures from the ancients. The Romans used solar energy to heat some of their public bathing spaces and, of course, the American Indians of the Southwest showed us how to use the sun to heat adobe and rock shelters. Despite the impact these and other ancient buildings have had on solar heating, the modern examples teach us more because they are based in our culture. The few examples in this chapter are not meant to represent the range of possible responses to the sun, but instead are chosen because they represent the generic approaches to direct-gain solar architecture.

EARLY BUILDINGS HEATED DIRECTLY BY THE SUN
The Duncan Residence, Flossmoor, Illinois by George Keck — 1941

Like other architects before him, Keck was interested in bringing the outdoors in by using glass and space to soften the boundary between indoors and outdoors. Keck heightened this approach by tastefully placing most of the glass on the south side for solar heating while preserving comfort. (See Figure 1.2.)

Overhangs were added to the south-facing windows to exclude the summer sun while admitting warmth from the low winter sun. Figure 2.1 shows how Keck carefully proportioned the overhang width and window height according to this solar criteria. The two photographs show the stages of sun penetration at two critical times of the year, September 21 (Figure 2.2) and December 21 (Figure 2.3) at ap-

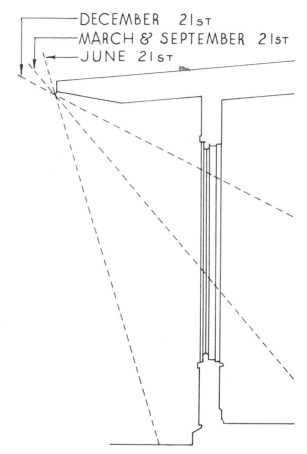

Figure 2.1 Overhang design for the Duncan Residence (Courtesy of Keck and Keck, Architects)

proximately 10:30 A.M. Notice in the winter the sun just reaches the masonry that forms the north wall of the living area. This mass and the masonry floor store the solar energy for later use at night. Tests performed by the Illinois Institute of Technology and published in *Architectural Forum* in August, 1943, showed the sun provided approximately 15 percent of the heating requirements. This is remarkable, considering the house did not have floor slab insulation and had only 2 inches of insulation in the roof and walls (the building also suffered from poorly caulked windows). The house overheated on sunny winter days, but this was due mainly to poor temperature regulation of the radiantly heated 4-inch thick floor slab. Keck correctly finished the floor with a light colored masonry veneer to help reflect some of the sunlight to the rear brick wall.

Figure 2.2 The Duncan living area on September 21 (Courtesy of Keck and Keck, Architects)

Figure 2.3 The Duncan living area on December 21 (Courtesy of Keck and Keck, Architects)

Figure 2.4 St. George's School, Wallasey, England

The natural daylighting provided by the south windows proved to be comfortable and glare-free for the Duncans, except that snow cover caused excessive glare. The house showed skeptics that double glazing could provide more heat than it loses in the Chicago area climate.

St. George's School, Wallasey, England, by Edward Morgan – 1962

The heating requirements for a school are not closely related to a residence, because heat from the school lights and students contributes significantly to the heating load, whereas a residence does not experience a comparably large internal gain. However, the building in Figure 2.4 demonstrates the sound use of many direct-gain heating principles that also apply to multiple family housing where concrete block or slab construction is common. The exterior view shows a two story, double glazed, 230 foot by 27 foot south wall. Summer sun is excluded with seasonally placed blinds which fit between the two layers of glass spaced 2 feet apart. The floors, walls, and ceiling are all at least 7-inch thick concrete. The roof and walls are externally insulated with 5 inches of expanded polystyrene. The building is extremely tight to keep air seepage to a minimum.

The interior photo (Figure 2.5) shows a typical second story art room on a sunny day. All the surfaces are exposed light colored concrete, except that the floor is a concrete slab veneered with vinyl-asbestos tile. Morgan guaranteed the sunlight would reach this entire heat storing mass by building a light diffuser in the south window. The inner light of glass is patterned to break up the sunlight and send it in all directions. The light colored wall and ceiling surfaces repeatedly reflect the light. The surfaces are not perfectly white, but absorb about 20 percent of the solar energy. Part of the light is absorbed each time it bounces, until 90 percent of the

Figure 2.5 A second story art room at St. George's.

light that passes the window is absorbed in the interior. A limited view to the outside is provided by clear glass in the lower sections of the window. The building suffers from glare problems on sunny days when the sun's rays turn the diffusing window into a brilliant white, luminous field. Daily thermal fluctuations are usually less than ±2°F because so much mass is participating. The building has never required auxiliary heat, but researchers have determined that nearly half the seasonal heating energy comes from the incandescent bulbs and the occupants.

One must remember the climate in England is mostly cloudy, so Morgan probably was not overly concerned with the relatively rare sunny day glare conditions. Diffuse solar radiation filtering through the clouds can provide significant solar heating in this case, since the outdoor air temperatures in England rarely go below 40°F. Even on cloudy days, the diffusing window increases the light penetration and the amount of mass participating in storing the solar energy. This happens because a cloudy sky is brighter near the zenith, therefore, the filtered sunlight has a prominent direction to it which can be redirected by the tiny ribs cast into the window.

Figure 2.6   Climator house, Skovde, Sweden.

Morgan defied all architectural practice in England at the time by building with interior mass. For years after his death, researchers tried to understand why his building works as well as it does. Now that we know, we can only marvel at his genius.

RECENT DIRECT-GAIN EXAMPLES

The Climator House, Skovde, Sweden, by H. Heineman — 1978

One must turn to other means of storing solar energy when distributed masonry is not available for thermal storage, as is the case for most single family residences. The 1300-square-foot Climator house was one of the first residences designed on the solar heating principles demonstrated by MIT Solar Building No. 5. Figure 2.6 shows south facing windows filled with upside-down, reflectorized venetian blinds. The blinds are designed to target solar energy on the ceiling where it is stored as shown in Figure 2.7. The Swedish design uses a grid of metal pans in the ceiling to support thin pouches of phase change material. The phase change material stores great amounts of heat in only a ¾-inch thickness as it melts at a constant phase change temperature of 74°F. The ceiling temperature is kept low on sunny days by the melting thermal storage material. Since the ceiling cannot get hot, the room cannot overheat, so thermal comfort is maintained on days that would drive normal room air temperatures into the mid-eighties. Reflecting louvers decrease glare by simply removing bright patches of sunlight from the floor. The ceiling must be dark

Figure 2.7 The living room in the Climator house.

to absorb the solar energy. A variety of dark colors, such as earth tones or greens, can be used. The floor must be light to compensate for the reduced internal reflectance. Heineman showed how a tastefully designed space can remain pleasant in the face of a dark ceiling.

Tests performed by Lund University showed the demonstration house gained 30 percent of its seasonal heating requirements from the sun without the use of nighttime thermal shutters over the windows. This is comparable to the contribution gained from typical flat plate collectors installed in the same Swedish climate. The house envelope and slab were insulated to Swedish standards far more stringent than United States minimum property standards.

The Sarno Residence, Boylston, Massachusetts by Gerald Sarno — 1979

This house was designed to use the new selective transmitting glass (discussed later in this book) that insulates twice as well as ordinary double glazing. Unfortunately the special glass was not available at the completion date, so hermetically sealed double glazing was used instead. Figure 2.8 shows the house seen from the south on a mid-November day at about 1:30 P.M. The two story high southeast glass brings morning sun into the kitchen and eating area, while the southwest glass seen behind the cluster of birch trees heats the living room and study above on the second floor. All the glass is shaded by birch trees in the summer so overhangs are not necessary. Figure 2.9 shows the living room looking southeast and Figure 2.10 shows the living room looking west. Solar energy is stored in the massive rock fireplace on the northwest wall and heavy ¾-inch Mexican floor tile on top of 1-inch-thick concrete. Normally this would not be enough exposed mass to do the job, but the heavy wooden post-and-beam construction brings the mass up to an appropriate level. Although the naturally finished cedar walls and ceilings are darker than usual, the large amount of glass on the two faces of the living area easily brighten the space. Contrast glare from the large window is minimized by the nearby stand of deciduous trees. The trees obscure much of the bright sky which would normally make the south view intolerably bright. Direct sight lines to the sun are cut off by the "interior overhang" that forms a balcony over the living area.

The living room air temperature peaks at approximately 75°F on a sunny winter afternoon. The 3900-square-foot house has 6 inches of fiber glass in the walls, and 12 inches of foam in the roof. The nearby trees retard heat loss by sheltering the house from the wind. Approximately 2½ cords of wood were used as auxiliary heat in 1979. Nighttime insulation is not used on the windows. This sometimes causes discomfort due to the radiation heat loss from the body to the windows, but this uncomfortable feeling can be overcome by using the new glass for which the house was designed. The use of glass in this design is architecturally correct. The woods and rock outcroppings are continued inside by the cedar veneers and the boulders used to form the fireplace. The line between indoors and outdoors has been dramatically softened by glass in this most unusual space.

Figure 2.8 The Sarno Residence, Boylston, Massachusetts.

Figure 2.9 Facing southeast in the Sarno living room.

Figure 2.10   Facing west in the Sarno living room.

The Orringer Residence, Duxbury, Massachusetts, by Allen & Mahone — 1980

The open plan first floor living area of this 1690-square-foot residence is almost completely surrounded by masonry (Figure 2.11) which acts as the thermal storage element. The brick east and west walls bear precast concrete floor and ceiling slabs. The concrete ceiling is exposed, and the slab floor is veneered with dark colored tile. The brick flue and arch visible in the photo serve to divide the living and dining area and also to support the ceiling slab. The weather skin of the building is 2 foot by 4 foot construction filled with R-11 fiberglass batt and sheathed with 1 inch of Styrofoam®. The basement ceiling is insulated with R-19 fiberglass batt to prevent the heat stored in the floor slab from leaking uselessly into the basement. The first floor south-facing windows (Figure 2.12) equal nearly 25% of the floor area. Lined fabric shades are drawn over the windows at night to reduce the heat loss through the windows.

Most of the early solar heated residences, such as the adobe structures in New Mexico, also have exposed dark colored interior masonry which overheats on sunny

Figure 2.11 The living area in the Orringer Residence.

Figure 2.12 The Orringer Residence

winter days even though the outside air temperature drops to 20°F. Yet the wintertime indoor air temperature in this house rarely exceeds 75°F. Both types of houses bring sunlight directly down onto dark colored floors and both have dark masonry walls. The difference is that the adobe structures have lightweight wood deck ceilings, and this house has a massive concrete ceiling. Even though the masonry ceiling never receives direct or reflected sunlight, it still acts as a storage element because of infrared coupling. Figure 6.1 shows that large areas of secondary mass parallel to the floor can reduce temperature swings by up to 30%.

This house saves about 35% on its heating bill. Once the nighttime insulation is improved, nearly 45% of the heat needed to heat a conventional house of this size will be supplied by the sun. Higher savings are not possible because of the relatively small south facing glass area used on the second floor (Figure 2.12) and because several north facing rooms are not in radiation contact with the south windows. Notice eyebrow overhangs are used on each floor to block summer sun.

The brick arch work in this home give it a delightful Mediterranean feeling that complements the ever-changing southern view overlooking a seaside salt marsh.

Interest in solar heated low-rise and high-rise multiple family housing is beginning to increase. All the principles demonstrated in the above examples can be used in multiple family dwellings. Less window area is required though, since the thermal loads are reduced by the presence of common walls. However, light distribution is more difficult because floor plans tend to have narrow dimensions parallel to the windows. Chapter 6 covers many of the solar heating issues confronted in higher density living.

REFERENCE

1. K. Botti and J. Perlin, *The Golden Thread, 2500 Years of Solar Architecture and Technology*, Van Nostrand Reinhold Co., New York, 1980.

Chapter 3

Solar Architecture Fundamentals

The sun is constantly moving in the sky as a result of the earth's rotation and planetary orbit. This motion partially determines the solar energy available for collection. The amount of solar energy reaching the earth's surface is related to (1) the earth-sun distance, (2) the distance the sun's rays travel through the atmosphere, (3) the angle these rays strike an intercepting surface, and (4) the time the sun is above the horizon. This chapter begins by examining the sun's motion as experienced at a given site.

The amount of energy available at the earth's surface is also affected by the local weather. Atmospheric conditions affect the proportion of direct, diffuse, and reflected solar radiation that strikes the earth. Various means of accounting for these effects are discussed in the section on solar radiation later in this chapter.

Collected solar energy is subtly converted into useful room heat by many complex heat transfer processes. Our discussion of heat flow which follows will unravel the relevant principles that determine our thermal comfort. The chapter ends with daylighting fundamentals that lead to glare minimization and visual comfort.

SOLAR AVAILABILITY

The sun has always been used to light and heat buildings. Shafts of warming sunlight colorfully light interiors and strengthen our primal ties to the outdoors. These natural benefits can be increased to the point of supplying all of a building's heating and daytime lighting needs by designing a building's orientation, proportions, and materials to take advantage of the sun's path.

More solar energy is available in December at noon that in June due to the earth's elliptical orbit. The earth is 3.1 million miles closer to the sun in December than in June. This difference in distance brings 7.0 percent more solar energy into the upper atmosphere during northern winters. Also, during the winter the atmosphere is clearer than in the summer due to the low humidity. So although the sun's rays must travel through more atmosphere in the winter because the sun's path is closer to the horizon, more solar radiation is available for collection due to the increased atmospheric transparency and the closer proximity of the sun.

The earth does become cold because the sun's rays strike the ground more obliquely in the winter when the earth's axis tilts 23½° away from the sun. When the sun's rays strike an object obliquely, the solar radiation is spread over a larger area and less energy is available for absorption. The earth's atmosphere is not heated directly by the sun; the air acquires heat by wafting over ground warmed by the sun. As the winter solar absorption rate drops, the amount of heat available for transfer to the air drops, which brings on the season's cold weather. Also, the duration of solar exposure is reduced in the winter. When the northern hemisphere is tipped away from the sun, the North Pole is constantly dark. Slightly less than half of the same hemisphere is in sunlight near the equator. Thus, the day length becomes shorter as one moves towards the dark North Pole. When the snows arrive, most of the solar energy is reflected back to outer space. This reduces even further the energy absorbed by the earth.

The situation for a *vertical*, south facing surface is exactly the opposite. The rays from the low winter sun strike a vertical surface more directly, infusing it with more energy. Any accumulated snow will increase further the collected energy, since more solar energy is reflected to the vertical surface. Although the winter solar exposure time is less, the winter sun spends more time in front of a south facing vertical surface than it does in the summer. All these wintertime effects combine to produce nearly ¾ of the energy collected by an equal area of flat ground in the summer at mid-latitudes. This large wintertime collection potential for vertical, south facing windows is the reason direct-gain solar heating works.

SOLAR POSITION

The sun's apparent motion is, of course, quite predictable. The path of the sun, as seen by an observer at 40° north latitude, is shown schematically in Figure 3.1. At the equinox, the sun always rises and sets exactly in the east and west, respectively, as seen from every point on the earth. The noon altitude of the sun (the angle above the horizon) on the equinox is always equal to 90° minus the latitude of the site. For example, the altitude at noon on March 21 at 40°N latitude is 50°. At noon on the summer solstice, the sun is 23½° higher than at noon on the equinox. During the winter solstice, the sun is 23½° lower at noon than at the equinox. The

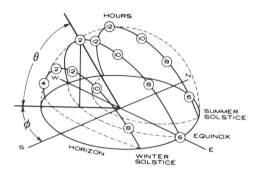

Figure 3.1 The sun's path across the sky at three different times of the year. θ is the altitude, ϕ is the azimuth. (From Anderson: The Solar Home Book, Cheshire Books)

winter sun rises south of east, and during the summer, the sun rises north of east. Knowledge of the sun's movement is necessary for calculating the effectiveness of summer shading schemes and for estimating the amount of solar energy intercepted by arbitrarily oriented surfaces.

The sun's movement as observed at various latitudes can be more accurately depicted with projections as shown in the sun path diagrams in Figure 3.2. The sun's path is projected onto a horizontal plane as a series of elliptical curves where the horizon is shown as the outer circle and the observer is at the center. The inner concentric circles mark the sun's altitude in 10° increments. The radial lines are used to measure the sun's *azimuth*, the angle the sun's projection makes in plan relative to true south.

Each elliptical curve is the projection of the sun's path on the twenty-first day of the month, designated by the Roman numerals. The curves that intersect the sun path curves at right angles show the time in Arabic numerals. For example, the sun's position at 40°N at 10:00 A.M. on December 21 is altitude 20°, azimuth 30°.

The times used on these charts are *solar times*, not local times. Solar time is the time that would be given by a sun dial oriented true south (solar noon is when the sun reaches its maximum altitude). The length of a day (measured from solar noon to solar noon) is not uniform throughout the year because of the earth's nonuniform motion around the sun. This can skew the solar time with respect to local time, which is measured with clocks moving at a uniform rate. Also, if the observer is not exactly on the time meridian for his time zone, his local time will be shifted further.

To find the corresponding solar time for a local time, apply the following procedure:

1. Subtract one hour from the local time if daylight savings time is in effect.

2. Determine the correction for the earth's nonuniform movement, called the *equation of time* (ET), from Figure 3.3, according to the day of the year.

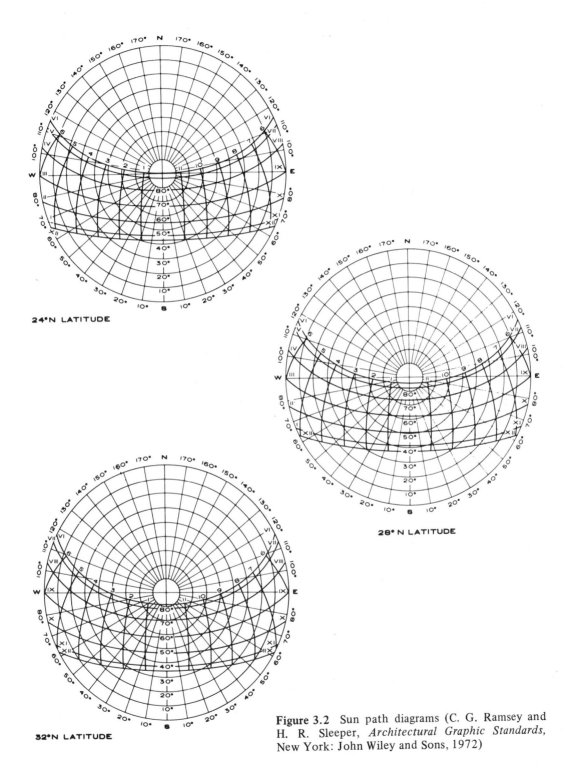

24°N LATITUDE

28° N LATITUDE

32°N LATITUDE

Figure 3.2 Sun path diagrams (C. G. Ramsey and H. R. Sleeper, *Architectural Graphic Standards,* New York: John Wiley and Sons, 1972)

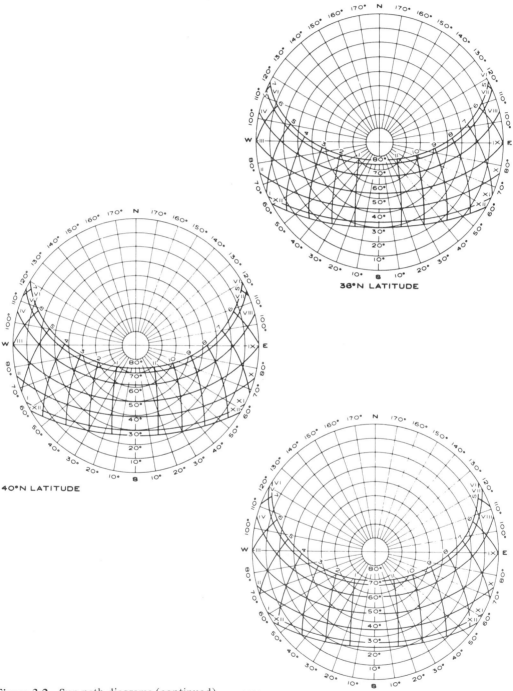

Figure 3.2 Sun path diagrams (continued)

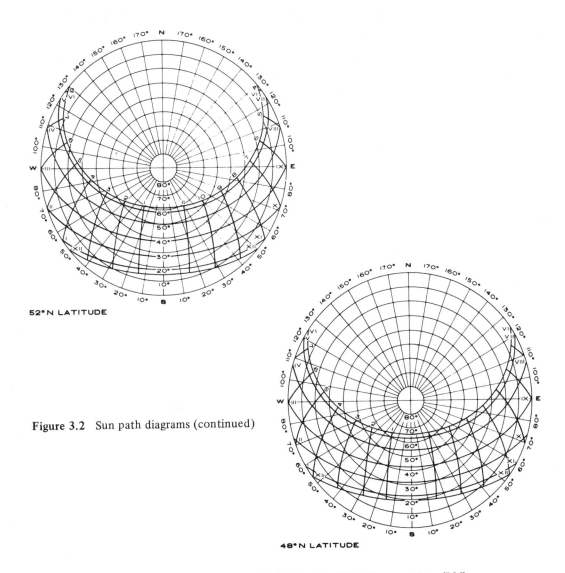

52°N LATITUDE

48°N LATITUDE

Figure 3.2 Sun path diagrams (continued)

3. Use the longitude of the site (L) and the longitude of the time meridian (LM) for the site's time zone (from Table 3.1) in the following equation for determining solar time:

$$\text{Solar time} = \text{ET} + 4 \text{ minutes/degree} \times (\text{LM}° - \text{L}°) + \text{local time}$$

This procedure can be used in reverse to find the site's true north-south line on a sunny day by noting the position of a vertical post's shadow at noon. Determining true north-south from compass bearings is not always reliable due to the influences of hidden ferrous material or nearby metal structures. The procedure for finding a true north-south line is as follows:

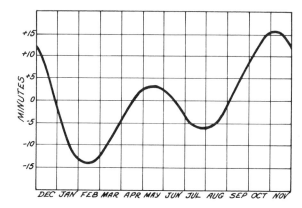

Figure 3.3   Equation of time (from Libbey-Owens-Ford, sun angle calculator)

1. Use a carpenter's level to locate a horizontal patch of ground.
2. Drive a tall stake at an angle into the ground and hang a plumb bob off the exposed end so the tip of the bob hangs just above the levelled ground.
3. Find the local time when solar noon occurs using the following relation:

$$\text{Local time} = 12:00 - ET - 4 \text{ minutes/degree } (LM - L)$$

4. At this time, drive a small stake into the levelled ground at the point marked by the shadow cast by the top of the plumb bob string. The line formed by the small stake and the point on the ground below the plumb bob is the true north-south line.

True north-south orientation of a building is essential when using horizontal shading devices such as overhangs or louvers, since small deviations (greater than $8°$) markedly reduce their effectiveness. Energy collection effectiveness is not as sensitive to deviations from true south. The seasonal solar energy incident on a vertical surface is not decreased by more than 5 percent by deviations as large as $30°$ off south.

TABLE 3.1   U.S. Time Meridians

Zone	Position	Standard Meridian (Longitude)
+4	Atlantic	60°W
+5	Eastern	75°W
+6	Central	90°W
+7	Mountain	105°W
+8	Pacific	120°W

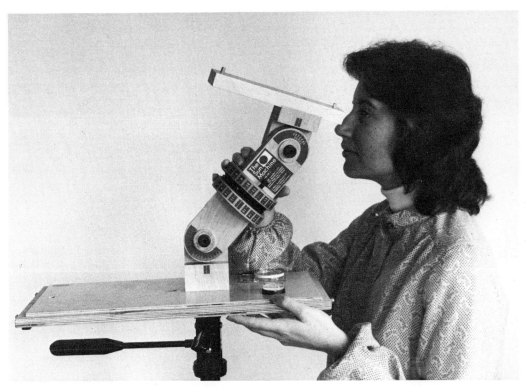

Figure 3.4   An example of a sun path finder (Courtesy of Teamworks, Cambridge, MA)

Once south has been located, it is necessary to determine if the sun is ever obstructed by site features. There are several sun path finders out on the market for this purpose; one is shown in Figure 3.4. The machine is set up by facing the major axis of the machine to the south and by rotating one of the machine's axes to the site's latitude. A sun path can be simulated by selecting a day on a second machine axis and sighting over the "barrel" of the rotatable arm while swinging an arc. The observer would be in shadow if a tree, hill, or building is seen through the instrument's sights. One can measure how many hours the observation point is obscured by the target for any day of the year. All the expected window locations on the site must be checked in this manner.

The same instrument can also be used to check for desirable summer shading by tree canopies. For winter heating applications, some shading is tolerable. No hard-and-fast rule can be applied for the permissible amount of shading, but normally the site should not be shaded for more than one third of the day for more than one fifth of the heating season. Site-specific criteria will help the user reach a decision on this matter. If one merely wants to see if a totally unobstructed view of the sun is available, then the charts shown in Figure 3.5 can be used for the named

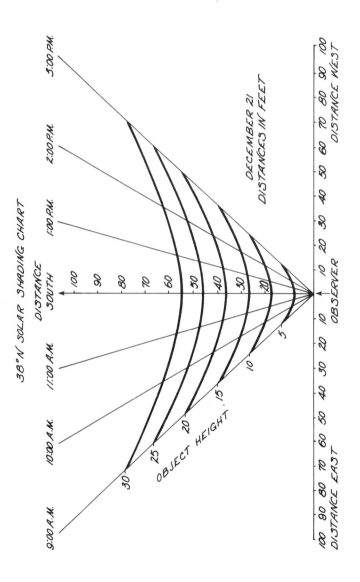

Figure 3.5   Solar shading charts

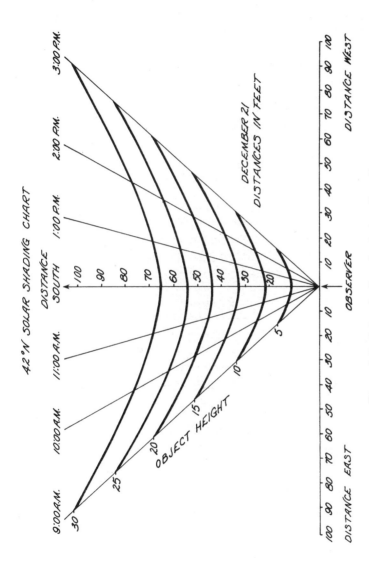

Figure 3.5 Solar shading charts (continued)

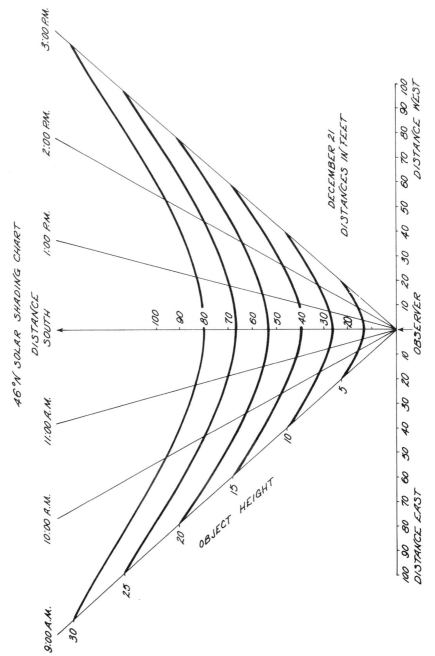

Figure 3.5 Solar shading charts (continued)

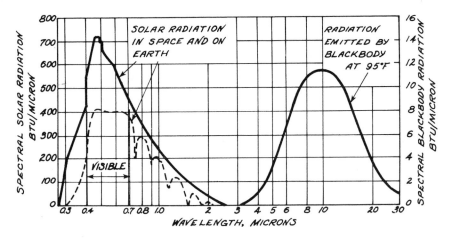

Figure 3.6 Solar and room temperature blackbody radiation spectrums

latitutdes. The charts show the boundaries for obstructions of given heights that are just out of shadow distance on December 21 for an observer at a relative height of 0 (zero) ft at point **A** on the chart. For example, the second closest curve to point **A** shows the boundary for shadow-free placement of objects 10 ft taller than the observer at point **A**. Any 10 foot object placed closer to the observer will cause a shadow at point **A** for part of the day. The radial edge lines show the azimuth angles at 9:00 a.m. and 3:00 p.m. angles. Solar collection outside these hours is usually not productive.

SOLAR RADIATION

All light produces heat when it strikes an absorbing surface. Solar energy is particularly energetic in this respect because of the sun's extremely high temperature, yet most of the energy content in sunlight lies outside the visible region, as shown in Figure 3.6. The near infrared region of the solar spectrum contains approximately 49 percent of the available energy. Fortunately, glass and other glazing products are fairly transparent to this short wave infrared energy, so most of the heating energy available in the solar spectrum gets past a window.

The amount of solar radiation that enters the earth's atmosphere (known as the *solar constant*) is 429.2 BTU/ft² hr. This figure does vary slightly throughout the year due to the earth's elliptical orbit, but this variation is inconsequential when compared to other effects. The incoming radiation is thinned down by the intervening atmosphere to 295 BTU/ft² hr by the time it reaches sea level. Figure 3.7 shows how the radiation is winnowed by the atmosphere on a typical partly cloudy day at mid-latitude. Each arrow depicts a path the sun's energy could follow, and the arrow's width is proportional to its energy content. More than 40 per-

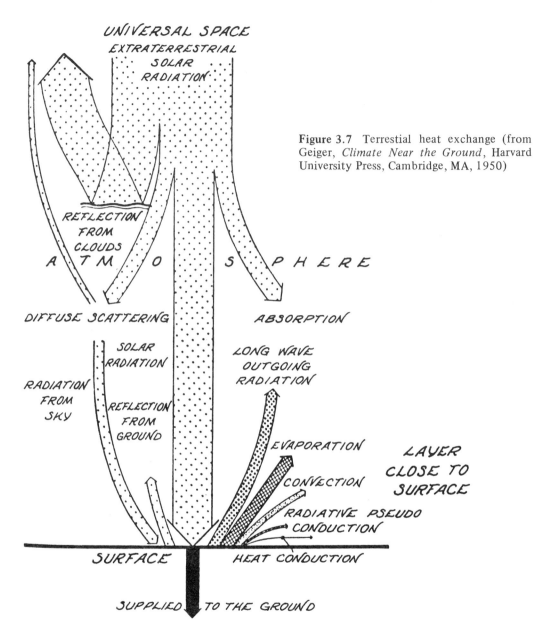

UNIVERSAL SPACE
EXTRATERRESTRIAL SOLAR RADIATION

Figure 3.7 Terrestial heat exchange (from Geiger, *Climate Near the Ground*, Harvard University Press, Cambridge, MA, 1950)

REFLECTION FROM CLOUDS

A T M O S P H E R E

DIFFUSE SCATTERING

ABSORPTION

SOLAR RADIATION

LONG WAVE OUTGOING RADIATION

RADIATION FROM SKY

REFLECTION FROM GROUND

EVAPORATION

CONVECTION

LAYER CLOSE TO SURFACE

RADIATIVE PSEUDO CONDUCTION

SURFACE

HEAT CONDUCTION

SUPPLIED TO THE GROUND

HEAT TRANSPORT BY:

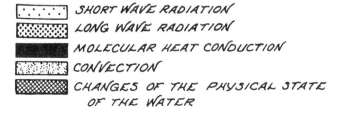

SHORT WAVE RADIATION
LONG WAVE RADIATION
MOLECULAR HEAT CONDUCTION
CONVECTION
CHANGES OF THE PHYSICAL STATE OF THE WATER

Table 3.2 Monthly Clear Day Insolation Data for South Facing Vertical Surfaces with 20% Ground Reflectance at Various Latitudes (BTU/ft^2 day)*

| 21st day | LATITUDE | | | | |
	24°	32°	40°	48°	56°
January	1928	1908	1821	1538	1072
February	1676	1816	1871	1828	1672
March	1249	1484	1669	1790	1827
April	733	1003	1249	1473	1647
May	502	727	979	1230	1445
June	461	633	875	1137	1376
July	499	714	955	1203	1423
August	711	971	1202	1417	1580
September	1211	1427	1595	1698	1716
October	1635	1753	1789	1728	1549
November	1891	1870	1780	1502	1044
December	1955	1908	1724	1349	738

*Based on ASHRAE data.

cent of the incoming radiation is reflected back to outer space by the average layer of clouds. Some radiation also is lost by absorption in the upper atmosphere. A small amount is scattered by the atmosphere to produce a diffuse component of solar radiation at the earth's surface. The rest of the energy enters as beam, or direct solar energy. Some of the beam sunlight is reflected by the ground to contribute to the diffuse radiation. On a *clear* day, the diffuse radiation will contribute between 10 and 20 percent of the total incoming radiation that strikes a *vertical* south facing surface. The high figure is used in urban areas where suspended atmospheric particles cut down the beam component while increasing the scattering effect, and the low figure is used in the desert regions. Outside city limits, usually 16 percent of the clear day radiation is diffuse.

Table 3.2 gives clear day daily radiation totals for south facing vertical surfaces at various latitudes with a ground reflectance of 20 percent. Hourly and daily radiation totals for other ground reflectances and surface orientations at arbitrary latitudes may be found by using the TI-59 calculator program published in Appendix 1. The radiation totals shown in Table 3.2 are for days which have high atmospheric clearance. The computer program allows for downward variation of the atmospheric clearance to model radiation totals in urban areas where pollution and suspended particle levels are high. Also, the diffuse component of the total insolation figure is given by this program.

Normally designers think of gathering direct sunlight for heating purposes, but diffuse radiation is also an important source of heat that can be tapped with new kinds of windows discussed in Chapter 5. The amount of diffuse and reflected radiation striking any vertical surface is nearly the same at any instant, because light is diffusely reflected by the ground (most ground materials have a matte surface), and diffuse radiation from the sky is evenly distributed around the compass points of the sky vault. So north walls get approximately as much diffuse radiation as south walls.

The absolute amount of diffuse radiation available on a cloudy day varies with the weather; on average, the amount of diffuse radiation intercepting a vertical surface is 11 percent of the clear day radiation striking a south facing vertical surface. This translates, for example, into an average figure of approximately 170 BTU/dayft^2 on March 21 for an observer at mid-latitudes. This figure drops during the winter when the days are shorter.

Any given cloudy day radiation total could vary as much as 50 percent either side of this figure. It is difficult to quantify the radiation available on an average cloudy day since there are so many types of clouds. The given figure represents an average taken at a Boston site in March with an Epply pyranometer.

The average amount of solar radiation available at a given site is, of course, somewhere between the cloudy day level and the clear day level. The seasonal solar intake for a particular building design can then be estimated from this figure. One way to determine this figure is to measure the radiation at a site over 10 to 30 years and average it. Unfortunately, only a handful of United States weather stations have been recording insolation data for more than 10 years. Researchers overcome the lack of measurements by using weighting methods to transfer the limited data to other United States sites, depending on locally measured cloud cover conditions. Needless to say, the weightings chosen are controversial. The latest generally accepted list of average insolation data for 300 United States cities is found in Appendix 2. The table gives the average daily hemispheric solar radiation on a horizontal surface for each month. Also, monthly average temperatures and monthly degree days are given for each location. Finally, the amount of daily total solar radiation incident on a vertical south facing surface is given. This figure uses an assumed ground reflectance of 30 percent and a correlation based on latitude and declination. The TI-59 program in Appendix I is used to find average daily total solar radiation on surfaces with arbitrary orientations and ground reflections. The same program also gives the average diffuse and beam component of the total incident radiation. This breakdown can be important when glazing transmission characteristics for diffuse and beam radiation are vastly different. Generally, diffuse radiation strikes vertical windows at a daily average angle of incidence equal to 60°, independent of the season. (*Angle of incidence* is the angle between a ray of light striking a surface and a perpendicular to that surface.) Average daily incident angles for beam radiation at various latitudes are given in Table 5.2.

ORIENTATION AND SHAPE

A simple rectangular building receives varying amounts of solar radiation depending upon its orientation and shape. For most homes, it is desirable to maximize solar exposure in the winter and minimize it in the summer.

Seasonal solar performance is never optimal with a square plan. The optimum shape for a residence of similar roof area is a rectangle with the major axis lying in

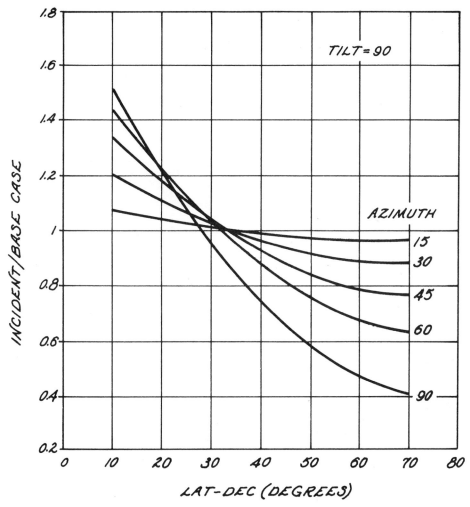

Figure 3.8 Seasonal effects of azimuth on incident solar radiation for a vertical wall at various latitudes. Declination at the winter solstice = –23½°, at Equinox = 0° (from D. Balcomb, *Passive Solar Design Handbook*, NTIS, Springfield, VA, 1979)

the east-west direction. Although this increases the wall's conduction losses in winter and the conducted heat gains in the summer because of the added perimeter, the additional solar performance more than compensates for the additional losses. All shapes elongated on the north-south axis fail to match the performance of even the square plan.

Figure 3.8 shows the variation in seasonal solar intake for a vertical wall at varying angles away from south. A 22° variation from due south lowers the seasonal intake by about 3 percent, and a 10° variation makes little difference in available solar energy. Solar intake for a vertical curvilinear wall with its major axis running

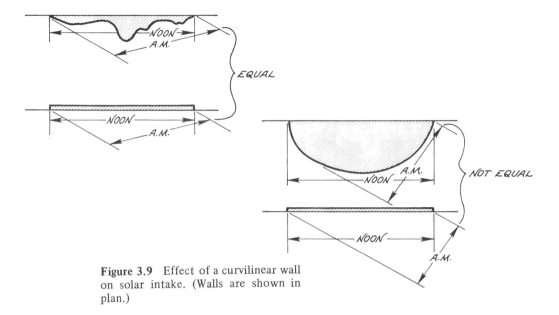

Figure 3.9 Effect of a curvilinear wall on solar intake. (Walls are shown in plan.)

east-west rarely exceeds the intake for a plane wall running east-west. Figure 3.9 shows this graphically. The upper figure shows that the width of the sun's rays intercepting the solid curved wall and the plane wall at sunrise and at noon are the same. The energy intercepted by the two walls is equal, since the light apertures are the same. The lower half of Figure 3.9 shows a case where a curved wall will intercept more energy, but only marginally more, for the aperture is enlarged only during the early morning hours.

Figure 3.10 shows the variation in seasonal solar intake for a south facing wall at various tilt angles. Vertical walls receive more ground reflected energy than titled walls, but tilted walls receive more direct and diffuse energy from the sky vault. The two effects combine so that a vertical wall receives only 15 percent less energy than a wall tilted at the optimal angle.

HEAT FLOW

We are comfortable thermally when our bodies are in thermal equilibrium with our environment. Most of the food we consume goes into making waste heat which must be removed at the same rate at which it is produced. Our bodies always are in the process of regulating this heat flow. We are really heat flow meters, not thermometers. This can best be understood by remembering what happens when one sits on a shaded, masonry park bench. When the temperature is in the 70s the bench feels "cold" to the touch, and if possible, one would move to a "warmer" wooden bench. Both benches have been sitting in the same air at 70°F, so they must

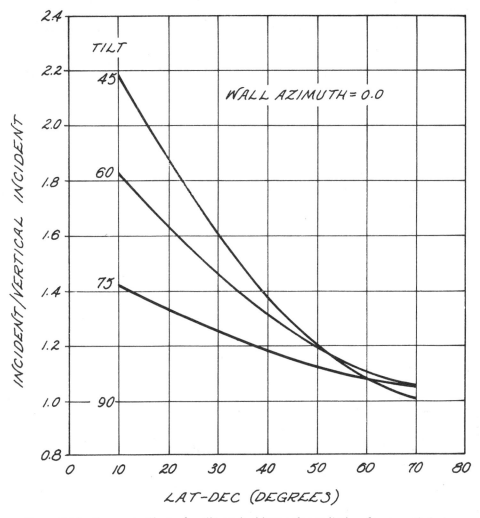

Figure 3.10 Seasonal effect of a tilt on incident solar radiation for a south facing wall at various latitudes (from D. Balcomb, *Passive Solar Design Handbook*, NTIS, Springfield, VA, 1979)

both be the same temperature. The stone bench feels cold because masonry conducts heat 4 to 6 times faster than wood. Our nerves measure the heat flow and tell us when the flow becomes uncomfortable. This form of heat flow is known as *conduction*. Conduction occurs when we are touching an object at a different temperature than our body. Actually, most of our excess body heat leaves us by other heat transfer mechanisms. Convection and radiation keep us comfortable in environments below 80°F. Heat removed through perspiration or evaporation of water in the lungs is not important in this kind of environment when the body is at rest. The following sections show how convection and radiation work and the relative importance of these heat transfer mechanisms.

Convection

Heat is removed from the body by convection when the body is in water or air. Heat is carried away from the body when the warmed air adjacent to the body is replaced by the surrounding fluid. This movement will always occur since warm air is lighter than cold air, causing the locally warmed fluid to rise in the cooler environment. This natural circulation can be seen when particles are suspended in water being heated from below. The particles are carried to the surface by jets of unseen buoyant water, only to fall down the side of the container when the water cools. If neutral density smoke were carefully introduced near our body we could see similar, but less vigorous, movements of the indicator smoke as heat left our skin to the surrounding air. The amount of heat removed by this mechanism is nearly proportional to the temperature difference between the body (or the adjacent clothing) and the surrounding air. When there is no wind or forced circulation to increase the heat transfer, the heat removed, H (in BTU/hr), is approximated by

$$H = A \times h \times (T_{body} - T_{air})$$

where

A = square feet of body surface area

$h = 1$ BTU/hr$°$Fft^2 in windless situations where the heat can flow up

T_{body}, T_{air} = the temperatures in degrees Fahrenheit.

Since the skin temperature is nearly constant at 85°F to 89°F and the area of the body exposed to the air is constant, the above relation says that convective heat flow is influenced only by air temperature. So indirectly, the body measures air temperature as a heat flow. But the body simultaneously loses heat by radiation. What is the body measuring in this case, and how does the radiative heat flow compare with the conductive heat flow?

Radiation

Heat flow by radiation, particularly infrared radiation, is always something of a mystery to most people. Yet in structures heated directly by the sun nearly all the heat in the structure is delivered and distributed by radiation, both day and night. To understand this, visible radiation and infrared radiation will be examined separately.

All light has an energy content spread over wavelengths as shown in the left-hand portion of Figure 3.6. This particular graph shows the distribution for solar energy, but artificial light would show a maximum energy peak displaced towards the longer wavelengths.

TABLE 3.3   Light reflectance of various colors (from the PPG Design-a-Color^{TM} System)

FLOORS

Color	Light Reflectance
Atlantis	9
Really Rust	12
Slate	15
Pepper Corn	13
Slate Brown	14
Tender Taupe	20
Ultramarine Blue	11
Mint Green	22
Crimson Lips	10
Deep Red	9

WALLS

Color	Light Reflectance
Polar Sky	72
Wisteria Blue	53
Rose Morn	76
Mission Beige	75
Old Linen	71
Vanilla Ice	83
Sunny Beige	79
Cream Supreme	81
Sun Yellow	70
Orange-Glow	62
Deep Chrome	50
Ebony Black	5
Gypsum	86

Our body thermal sensors are not sensitive to light or to the near infrared component of solar energy, yet we feel warm in the direct rays of the sun. We feel heat in sunlight because when sunlight strikes an opaque surface, like our skin, the energy is absorbed and produces heat. Sunlight cannot heat air merely by shining through it. Air is transparent (at least over moderate distances of a few thousand feet), and heat from solar energy is produced only at the surfaces of energy absorbing objects. Air gets warm by convection, literally by wafting over warm surfaces.

The amount of heat produced by absorbing sunlight in the skin is much more than the metabolic heat the body is rejecting. Although direct sunlight may feel cozy in a room momentarily, after a while the body will begin to perspire in order to reject the extra heat. So, the sunlight must be placed elsewhere to prevent a thermal overload.

TABLE 3.4 Effective room absorptance *vs* wall color and window geometry for double glazed openings. From: "The Effective Absorbtance of Direct Gain Rooms," J. F. Burkhart, R. E. Jones, Proc. 4th National Passive Solar Conference, Oct. 1979, Kansas City International Solar Energy Society.

Window area/ Total room surface area	*Wall Absorbance*				
	20%	*30%*	*50%*	*70%*	*90%*
0.03	0.888	0.918	0.968	0.985	0.994
0.05	0.823	0.868	0.946	0.975	0.991
0.10	0.688	0.758	0.893	0.949	0.980
0.20	0.495	0.581	0.787	0.893	0.957

Since light is visible, we understand how light can be reflected and even diffused to scatter the sunlight onto other surfaces. The near infrared component, although we cannot see it, bounces around the room like sunlight. Not all of the sunlight striking a surface is absorbed to produce heat. Some is reflected away due to the surface color (Table 3.3 shows the solar absorption of various colors); some light is reflected diffusely (meaning in random directions), depending on the surface texture. Multiple reflections then can occur if the surfaces are light in color. This means that the multiple absorptions will also occur since every color absorbs some light. Even an off-white room, where any one surface reflects 85 percent of the light, will eventually absorb most of the incoming sunlight. Only 12 percent of the energy will escape an off-white room with a window along one wall. Table 3.4 shows the effect of window exposure, room shape, and color on solar absorption. The room will not feel hot if there is something massive behind the absorbing surfaces to soak up the solar energy. We feel comfortable in such a space because the sunlight is directed away from our body and absorbed into the structure. The room will still feel warmer during the sunlit hours than the nighttime hours because of the high level of diffuse sunlight striking the body.

The heat produced at a surface struck by sunlight will divide into three paths. Part of the energy will conduct into the material; part will convect to the air; and part will leave the surface as long-wave infrared radiation. Infrared radiation is more difficult for most of us to understand. Any surface will emit, or send, far-infrared radiation to colder surfaces. This radiation is like light in that it travels through air but, unlike light, it does not cast distinct shadows because of its longer wavelengths. The right-hand curve in Figure 3.6 shows the long-wave infrared energy (centered at a wavelength of about 10μ) emitted by an extraterrestrial surface near room temperature. When sunlight is absorbed at an earthbound surface, the surface temperature increases, which then increases the infrared emission. No net infrared energy would leave this surface if all the surrounding surfaces were the same temperature. As this would never be the case in a natural environment, heat always is transferred by infrared radiation.

The amount of infrared that leaves a body not only is a function of the surface temperature, but also it is related to a surface property known as *emissivity*. Emissivity is a measure of how easily radiation can escape from a surface — also, the emissivity is the same as absorption for a given wavelength of radiation. Shiny metals have low emissivity (absorption) in the far-infrared regions (typically 10 to 15 percent); most building materials (including glass) have high emissivity (absorption) in the far-infrared (typically 90 to 95 percent), regardless of color. This means most materials will emit and absorb infrared radiation equally well for a given surface temperature. Although the amount of infrared radiation (heat) emitted does not vary linearly with surface temperature, the nonlinearity is not noticeable for surfaces exchanging infrared radiation near room temperature (between 100°F and 30°F). The amount of infrared radiation, H (in BTU/hr), exchanged between a warm surface at temperature T_1, and a cooler surface at temperature T_2 is essentially given by

$$H = A \times h' \times (T_1 - T_2)$$

where the emissivity is assumed to be 90% and

A = the projected area, in ft^2, of the smaller surface onto the larger surface

$h' = 1$ BTU/hr°Fft^2

T_1 and T_2 = surface temperatures, in °F

The surface temperatures in a windowless, well insulated room are all essentially the same as the room air temperature. When the room is occupied the warm surface, T_1 in the above relation, is the body of the occupant and T_2 equals T_{air}. When we compare the above relation with the equation given for natural convection, we see that the body heat lost by infrared radiation is equal to the body heat lost by convection. So rather than being an insignificant academic participant, radiation heat loss is just as important in this case as the more acknowledged loss by convection.

Interesting things happen once sunlight enters the room in significant quantities. The surrounding surfaces will rise nearly uniformly in temperature if they are light in color and sunlit diffusely. The air temperature will lag behind the wall temperatures since the air acquires heat from the walls. The temperature difference between the body and the room's surfaces decreases, so the heat loss from the body by radiation decreases. Since the air temperature rises very slowly, the body heat loss by convection remains nearly the same; the net effect is that one feels warmer. It is possible that the surface temperatures can exceed the skin temperature and reverse the heat flow so the body is *gaining* heat by radiation (an obviously uncomfortable situation). The day's absorbed heat will linger into the night if the surfaces have any heat retention capability. The elevated surface temperatures continue to reduce radiative heat loss from the body so its heat loss by convection even can

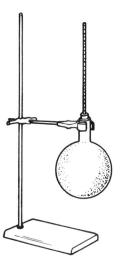

Figure 3.11   Copper ball globe thermometer.

afford to go up without reducing thermal comfort. Thus, air temperatures can be in the low-60s in a radiantly heated room and one can still feel comfortable.

A real room would not have stored heat equally in all surfaces, and certainly the window surface temperature would be cool at night. The effective surface temperature felt at a given point in the room, the *mean radiant temperature* (MRT), is a weighted average of all the surface temperatures given by the following relation:

$$T_{MRT} = \frac{T_1 \times A_1 + T_2 \times A_2 + \ldots T_n A_2}{A_1 + A_2 + \ldots A_n}$$

where

$T_1 \rightarrow T_n$ = the individual surface temperatures and

$A_1 \rightarrow A_n$ = the spherical angles subtended by each surface relative to the point in question

Long-wave radiation heat transfer from the body in an actual room can then be given as

$$H = A \times h' \times (T_{body} - T_{MRT})$$

Infrared heat transfer equals natural convective heat transfer only when T_{MRT} = T_{air}. T_{MRT} can be measured, like T_{air}, but it cannot be measured with an ordinary thermometer; T_{MRT} is measured by a globe thermometer. Figure 3.11 shows a typical globe thermometer which is nothing more than a thin 4-inch diameter copper sphere painted black to absorb infrared and solar radiation. Copper conducts the heat evenly around the sphere. The temperature of the sphere is usually measured electronically by thermistors or thermocouples. We can convert the globe temperature, given an air temperature, into an MRT by using the nomograph shown in Figure 3.12.

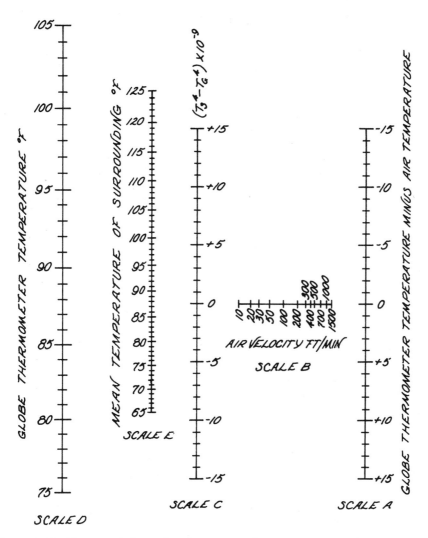

Figure 3.12 Nomograph for estimating mean radiant temperature of surroundings from globe thermometer readings. To use: Intersect scale C with a line from scale A through scale B. Draw a line from this intersection to scale D. The intersection at scale E is the MRT.

Notice that the relation for T_{MRT} says effective radiant heat transfer occurs when a large area is at a moderately elevated temperature or a small area is at a high temperature. Also, the same relation says window surface temperatures cannot get too low at night in order to maintain an elevated T_{MRT}.

The thermal sensation of radiant heat is a pleasant surprise. The heat is even and draft free; the difference in air temperature at a 10 foot high ceiling and the floor is less than 2°F. In the 1950s radiant heating was accomplished by piping hot water at 95°F through concrete ceilings. Many people complained that their legs and feet were cold when they were sitting at tables; the radiant heat could not reach their legs because the table created a partial infrared shadow. This phenomenon of the infrared shadow does not exist in modern buildings heated by solar energy stored in ceilings, because the buildings are insulated two to three times better than the homes built in the 1950s. Better insulation means lower thermal loads, so the ceiling can run at a lower temperature. Lower temperature differences means that re-emitted or bounced infrared becomes more significant. These relatively warm secondary emissions wipe out the infrared shadows as they criss-cross the room. This method of heating is extremely attractive for spaces with cathedral ceilings where excessive temperature stratification can be a problem with convection heaters.

Storage

All materials can store heat. A material acquires heat any time it rises in temperature, and as it falls in temperature, it liberates heat. The amount of heat a given weight of material stores for a given temperature rise is specified by a material property called *specific heat*. This property measures the *sensible heat* (heat we can sense or feel) content of the material.

The specific heat of water is arbitrarily defined as 1 BTU/lb°F, and all other materials' specific heat is measured relative to water's specific heat. The measure for water is actually used to define a *British Thermal Unit* (BTU). A BTU is the amount of heat liberated when one pound of water falls 1°F.

Heat also can be stored as latent (hidden) heat. This happens when a substance changes state, i.e., from a solid to a liquid. The temperature of the material remains constant until the liquification is complete; hence, we cannot sense the heat. Nevertheless, the atomic bonds that made the material solid are broken by the application of heat stored in the broken bonds. A complete accounting of a material's latent and sensible heat, mass, and thermal conductivity is given in the section on Mass in Chapter 6.

Heat Load Calculations

The stored solar heat transferred by radiation and convection will warm a room's occupants during the winter, but this heat will continue to move inexorably toward the cold outdoors. This loss can be minimized so that a day's solar energy intake can last far into the next day.

Heat leaves a building through its weather skin by conduction and by air leaking through cracks in the building. Radiation forms a part of the loss through windows, but this loss is included in the conduction figures given for windows in Chapter 5.

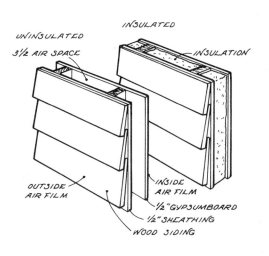

SAMPLE CALCULATIONS OF U-VALUES		
Wall Construction Components	**R-values**	
	Uninsulated	**Insulated**
Outside air film, 15 mph wind	0.17	0.17
Wood bevel siding, lapped	0.81	0.81
½″ Sheathing, regular density	1.32	1.32
3½″ Air space	1.01	—
3½″ Mineral wool batt	—	10.90
½″ Gypsumboard	0.45	0.45
Inside air film	0.68	0.68
TOTALS (R_t)	4.44	14.33
U-values (U = $1/R_t$)	0.23	0.069

Figure 3.13 Typical conductances of wood frame walls (from Anderson, *The Solar Home Book*, Cheshire Books, Harrisville, NH, 1976)

A material's heat conductance is defined as the amount of heat that passes through a 1 foot by 1 foot slab in one hour when a steady 1°F temperature difference exists between the two slab surfaces, given in units of BTU/hr°Fft². Usually the figure is given for a 1-foot-thick section of the material. We determine the conductance for a thinner section by dividing the given conductance by the fraction of a foot that makes up the thinner section. For example, a 1/3-foot section conducts heat three times faster than a 1-foot-thick section.

Most building skins are collections of several layered materials, such as siding, insulation, and gypsum. A combined conductance for 1 square foot of multi-layered building skin can be found by adding the thermal resistances of each layer and inverting the sum. The resistance, R, is the inverse of its conductance, k, or R = 1/k. The higher the material's R value, the higher its insulating value. Appendix 3 shows the R values for various building materials.

The resistance for a section thinner than the listed thicknesses is proportional to the reduction in thickness. For example, Figure 3.13 gives the total resistance, R, and associated combined conductance, U, for an insulated and an uninsulated wood

TABLE 3.5   Average air change rates for various residential construction systems at an average indoor-outdoor temperature difference of $25°F$ and near calm wind conditions.

1. Stick built with no vapor barrier	1.5-2. ac/hr
2. "all electric heating" construction (masonry construction or stick built with filled wall cavities)	0.8-0.9 ac/hr
3. continuous vapor barrier	0.3-0.4 ac/hr

frame wall. To find the heat loss rate for all similarly constructed walls, multiply the U by the total wall square footage. This result is then added to the U values times the areas of each of the other building components, i.e., windows, doors, roof, and the slab on grade. The sum of these products gives the total heat loss rate for the building via conduction. The heat loss rate by air leakage must be added to this.

All buildings leak, no matter how tightly they are built, and this heat leakage increases with higher wind speeds and larger temperature differences between indoors and out. The leakage increases almost linearly with temperature difference, but no correlation is evident yet for wind speed variations. Heat loss by air leakage, known as infiltration, is usually expressed in the same units as the conduction losses. The effect of wind speed is rarely taken into account. The heat loss rate is determined empirically since most attempts to quantify it are too cumbersome for estimation purposes. One way of characterizing the infiltration rate is to quantify the air change rate for various types of structures. Table 3.6 gives average air change rates for various construction types that have at least two walls exposed to the weather. The listed rates occur when there is an approximately $20°F$ temperature difference between inside and outside, and when the wind velocity averages seven miles per hour. Forced ventilation usually is required if only one wall is exposed to the weather, as in apartments. Of course any given structure will vary from these average figures, but the figures do provide useful estimates for design purposes. The figures listed in Table 3.5 have been determined by the author and other researchers using tracer gases to indicate the air exchange. The table is drawn from a limited number of experiments.

Air change rates below 0.4 ac/hr are not recommended because odor accumulation becomes a problem at these rates. Although it is possible to build structures tighter than this, thermal comfort will deteriorate unless fresh air is brought in with fans or closable ventilators. This is sometimes a desirable option, since forced ventilation can be controlled, whereas air seepage cannot. Many times, air-to-air heat exchangers are used in home ventilated with fans to recover some of the heat exhausted through the ducts.

We can use the following relation to find the heat loss rate for each 1°F temperature difference between the inside and outside air, given an estimated air change rate:

Heat loss by infiltration (BTU/hr°F) = ac/hr x volume of residence x 0.018

$$BTU/ft^3°F$$

The constant in the relation is the specific heat for air. For example, assume a 1400-square-foot residence with 8-foot ceilings is built tightly enough to keep the air change rate near 0.5 ac/hr. The heat loss by infiltration becomes

0.5 ac/hr x 1400 ft^2 x 8ft x 0.018 BTU/ft^3°F = 100.8 BTU/hr°F

The total building heat loss rate is found by adding this figure to the conduction loss figure. An example of heat loss calculation for a residence is given in Appendix 4.

The calculated building heat loss rate specifies the heat lost in one hour when there is a 1°F air temperature difference between inside and outside. The weather dictates how many hours a given temperature difference exists throughout the heating season. This accumulation of hours and temperature differences has been condensed to a commonly accepted figure called *degree days*. It is based on the assumption that the thermostat is set to 70°F and the internal gains from lights and appliances provide enough free heat so no auxiliary heat (or solar heat) is required until the outside temperature falls below 65°F. One degree day is accumulated when the outdoor air temperature is 1°F lower than 65°F for 24 hours. If the outdoor air temperature is, on the average, 20°F lower than 65°F, then 20 degree days accumulate for that one day. Weather services publish the sum of a heating season's degree days for several hundred United States locations. Some of these figures are listed in Appendix 2. Your local oil or gas suppliers will also know the degree days for your area. The total heating season load can be estimated by using the building conduction and infiltration heat loss rates in the following relation:

heating season load = (UxA + infilt. loss rate)BTU/hr°Fx24 hr/day x

°F-day/season = BTU/season,

where the last term, °F-day, is the degree day figure supplied by a weather service. For example, a house that loses 225.0 BTU/hr°F by conduction and 100.8 BTU/hr°F by infiltration in a 5629°F-day climate (such as Boston) loses

(225.0 + 100.8) x 24 x 5629 or
49,951,723 BTUs a season

Actually most of today's well insulated buildings do not require auxiliary heat until the outdoor temperature drops well below 65°F, due to better insulation and reduced thermostat settings. So the commonly published degree day figures based on a 65°F balance point do not apply to most residences. Using the normally published figure for predicting a heat load would certainly overestimate the thermal

TABLE 3.6 Average daily residential Internal Gains (for a 4 person family). From: National Bureau of Standards Technical Note No. 789, *Energy Conservation in Buildings.*

ELECTRICAL		
Lights	5.5 kw/day	
Refrigerator	5.0	
television	1.4	
dishwasher	1.0	
clothes washer	0.3	
other	4.3	
	17.1 kw/day x 3400 BTU/kwh	= 59,500 BTU/day
Kitchen range (electric or gas)		= 18,600 BTU/day
4 occupants		= 15,000 BTU/day
		93,100 BTU/day

load and underestimate the solar participation for a well insulated house. Appendix 2 gives degree day figures for major United States cities for balance points down to 50°F. The balance point temperature for a particular building is given by the following relation:

average balance point temperature =

$$\text{thermostat setting} - \frac{\text{average hourly internal gains}}{\text{building hourly heat loss rate}}$$

This relation assumes the building has enough internal mass to smooth out daily variations in internal gains. Table 3.6 shows the internal gains associated with a family of four living in a single family house.

A more refined heat load for the building used in the previous example is calculated below. Assume the thermostat is set at 68°F. The balance point temperature is:

$$68°F - \frac{80{,}000 \text{ BTU/day}/24 \text{ hr/day}}{325.8} = 57.8°F$$

To find the seasonal load for Boston, for example, find the degree day figures closest to the computed balance point in Appendix 2. The appendix gives 4,381 DD for a 60°F set point and 3300 DD for a 55°F set point. Interpolating between these figures gives a weather load of 3905 DD for the 57.8°F set point. The actual seasonal heating load is:

325.8 BTU/hr°F x 24hr/day x 3905 DD = 30,536,791 BTU/yr

Notice the leverage that results in better insulation. First, the seasonal heat load is decreased since the conductance is decreased. Second, the weather load the building experiences also goes down since the balance point decreases. The two reductions combine to give a multiplicative effect that rapidly decreases the building's thermal load.

Another way to characterize a building's heat loss rate is to specify the heat loss per degree day for each square foot of heated floor area. For instance, assume the conduction and heat infiltration loss rate for a house with 1400 square feet of heated floor area sums to 325.8 BTU/hr°F. Then the alternative heat loss quantity becomes

$$\frac{325.8 \text{ BTU/hr}°\text{F x 24 hr/day}}{1400 \text{ ft}^2} = 5.59 \text{ BTU/ft}^2°\text{F day}$$

This alternative figure is used in some state and federal energy codes and later in this book to describe required thermal performance of different residential building types. In the early design stages, one does not know much about a building's configuration except the required heated floor area. Since it is mandatory to meet individual state's energy codes, this prescriptive figure can be used in turn to estimate the building's probable heat loss rate. A table of these figures based on the current HUD minimum property standards is given in Chapter 7 for purposes of estimating heat loss.

DAYLIGHTING

Illuminating spaces with large quantities of natural daylight offers the occupant an ever changing and interesting link to the outside. Moving cloud patterns can be seen; colors change as the day progresses; and the boundary between the outdoors and indoors becomes more inviting. Nowhere is the opportunity to do exciting things with daylighting more pronounced than in structures heated directly by the sun. With daylighting, however, comes the possibility of glare. Glare never has to be a problem, though, if the simple design procedures introduced at the end of this section are followed.

A good daylighting design must work on both sunny and cloudy days. Unfortunately, daylighting rules of thumb have been developed only for the predictable and repeatable condition of uniform clouds. Once the design exhibits satisfactory lighting levels under cloudy conditions, sunny day glare and lighting issues must be studied with physical models.

Cloud filtered daylight reaches a point in a room via three routes, as shown in Figure 3.14. Diffuse light from the sky vault reaches the point via any line that does not intersect an obstruction (shown as, the Sky Component). Additional skylight is reflected to the same point from the ground and nearby structures (shown as, the External Reflected Component). Finally, light from the first two sources reflects off the room's interior surfaces to illuminate the point indirectly (shown as, the Internal Reflected Component).

Light levels fall off exponentially with increasing distance from the window (Figure 3.15) in rooms sidelit with full length windows. Lighting levels in the figure

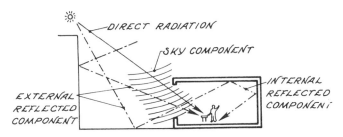

Figure 3.14 Daylight Components (from Course Notes, Architecture 4-26, Harvard Graduate School of Design, 1975)

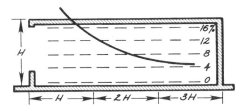

Figure 3.15 Exponential distribution of light (*ibid*) (from Course Notes, Architecture 4-26, Harvard Graduate School of Design, 1975)

are shown as daylighting factors. The daylight factor is expressed as the illumination at a point indoors divided by the illumination received simultaneously outdoors on an unobstructed horizontal surface. Usually, the internal reflected component affects daylighting more than the sky component when the observer is more than several feet from a window. On cloudy days, the sky component is always greater than the external reflected component. Interior surfaces should be light in color. Daylighting factors in dark colored rooms can be 3 to 4 times less than in light colored rooms near the rear of the room. A good rule of thumb for adequate cloudy day illumination in rooms with light colored surfaces, and windows running the length of one wall, is that the depth of the room should not exceed 2 to 2.5 times the height of the window. It is generally agreed the daylight factor for residential spaces should be at least 2 to 3 percent.

The British Research Station (BRS) has designed a protractor, replicated in Figure 3.16, for predicting the cloudy day sky component (SC). The work is based on stimulus response and does not deal with perception response. Because of a scene's perceived visual interest, a low lighting level may not be noticed. Perception is also affected by contrast. High lighting levels may be useless in a room with dark walls. Nevertheless, the BRS method gives a reasonable means of predicting lighting distribution. The protractor is designed for use with architectural plans and sections. Any conveniently sized drawing may be used since daylighting behavior is independent of scale. Figure 3.17a shows how the protractor is used in section for computing the average altitude of the visible sky and the uncorrected sky component. Figure 3.17b shows the use in plan for determining the window length correction factor. The sequence of graphical computation follows.

Select a point in the room, using a section taken through the window. Draw lines from the point to the highest and lowest limits at which the sky can be seen. The lower limit is determined by the sill or the surrounding buildings or vegetation. With the center of the BRS protractor superimposed on the point in question, and the base parallel to the floor, read the values of the sky component where the upper limit line intercepts the protractor edge, and at the lower limit line. Difference the two values as shown in Figure 3.17a. The result is the sky component at the selected point for a room with an infinitely long window (1.85 in this example). A correction for the actual window length is found by using the other protractor half in the plan view. Before leaving the section drawing, note on the inner scale the mean altitude of the visible sky. On the plan of the room, draw lines from the point under consideration to the edges of the visible sky. Place the center of the correction factor side over the point in question with the protractor base parallel to the window. Using the mean altitude of the visible sky found above, estimate an appropriate concentric scale that matches the mean altitude in degrees and read the correction factor for each side of the room where the limit lines intersect the protractor. Add these two values to obtain the total correction factor (.22 + .22 = .44 for this example). To obtain the corrected sky component, multiply the correction factor by the sky component found in the first step (.44 x 1.85 = .81).

The external reflected component is usually taken as 10 percent of the sky component under uniform cloud cover. The internal reflected component for side-lit rooms can be found from the nomograph in Figure 3.18. The average reflection factor is found by first summing the products of the surface areas of the rooms and their individual reflection percentages, and then dividing the sum by the total area. (Reflection for windows is 0.15, or 15 percent). The ratio of window area to total surface area is also computed. The nomogram is used by joining a point on the A scale with a point on the B scale and reading the internal reflected component on scale C. The internal reflected component, external reflected component, and sky component are summed to give the daylight factor as a percentage at the selected point. The effect of other windows is additive, so daylight factors for other exposures at the same point merely are added together.

Valuable electrical energy will be saved any time daylighting can be used in place of artificial lighting. For air conditioned spaces, the question of whether heat from solar energy used for daylighting exceeds heat produced by an equivalent artificial lighting scheme arises. If this were the case, then extra electrical energy for air conditioning would be required to meet the additional solar gain, which would cancel out the savings in electrical lighting energy. Fortunately sunlight has a lumination-to-heat input ratio nearly equal to artifical fluorescent lighting (incandescent

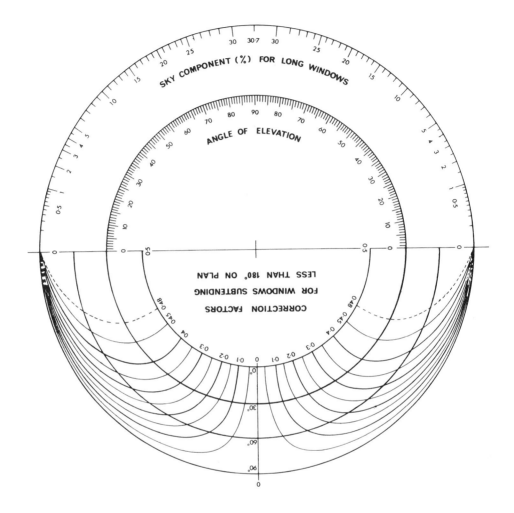

Figure 3.16 The BRS Sky Component Protractor (from British Research Station, London, England)

light produces 70 percent more heat for the same lighting level).* Thus, the heat gain is the same if a room is daylit on a cloudy day or illuminated to the same average lighting level with fluorescents. On a sunny day, the same south facing space would experience much higher lighting levels and higher heat gains near the windows. The excessive clear day lighting could be used to light areas at the back that normally would be too dark on cloudy days. The heat input would still equal the rejected heat from fluorescents if the sunlight were distributed properly. Chap-

---

*A. Rosenfeld and S. Selkowitz, "Beam Daylighting: An Alternative Illumination Technique," *Energy and Building*, 1 Elsevier Sequoia (1977)

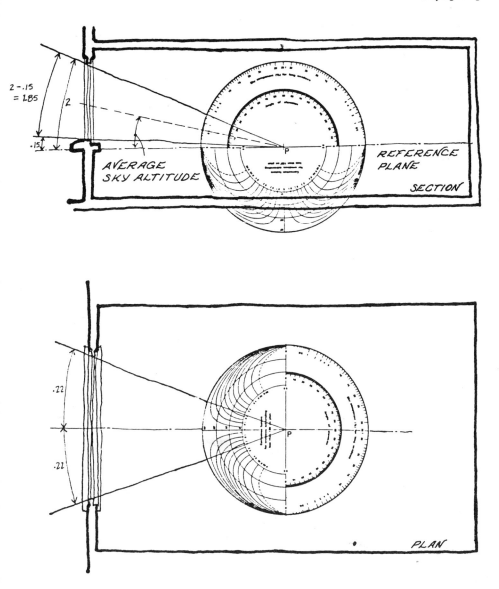

Figure 3.17 Example of the use of BRS Protractor

ter 5 presents some schemes for doing this in south facing spaces so the lights in deep rooms can be turned off on clear days.

The best way to predict daylighting behavior is to build a model and measure the lighting levels with a meter. For glare studies (introduced below), a model is really the only trustworthy method of studying visual comfort. The model should be large enough for the designer to place his or her head (or at least eyes) inside the

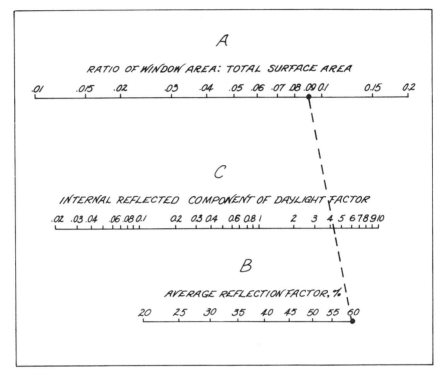

Figure 3.18 Nomograph for determining the Internal Reflected Component

space for a qualitative inspection. Daylighting behavior *does not change* with a change in scale. Daylight levels are affected by finishes and surface reflectance, so the model and its environment should be a realistic simulation of the space. This is difficult to achieve, so in practice the following rules should be met:

1. Window mullion areas and sills should be scaled accurately.

2. Interior surfaces must have the correct reflectances (hue and chroma do not matter).

3. The model must be in the open.

4. Exterior obstructions, such as trees, should be modelled.

5. The model and the light meter must be strictly horizontal so the diffuse sky component exposure is correct (on sunny days, rotate the model in plan to simulate various sun angles).

6. Illumination inside the model and outdoors on a cloudy day should be measured with two meters so simultaneous outdoor and indoor light intensities can be paired to form a daylight factor.

7. Ordinary transparent glass can be modelled by leaving the openings uncovered. All meter readings must be corrected by multiplying the readings by the

window transmission. Translucent glazing can be modelled with vellum of equal diffusing quality, and less transparent glazing must be modelled with a film of equal transparency.

8. Never use a translucent material, such as white cladded Foamcore^R, to model the space.

GLARE

Most of the direct-gain solar heated residences built in this country have suffered unnecessarily from major glare problems. Understanding how glare originates helps us design around the problem. Many glare issues arise on sunny days, but cloudy days can also cause some forms of glare. The various types of glare discussed below are associated with sidelit rooms. The type of glare that occurs when overhead light sources reflect off surfaces and veil the material is not normally encountered in natural daylighting schemes, except when diffusing skylights and clerestories are used.

An unusual, but possible, form of glare is disability glare, which causes indistinct vision in an area around a bright light source. The bright light is scattered sideways inside the eye, casting a haze across the view. This effect is particularly pronounced in the elderly because the internal eye fluid becomes cloudier, resulting in more light scattering. Windows that look on a large sky area can produce this form of glare. Disability glare can be overcome by reducing contrast and raising the interior light levels with additional windows.

Discomfort glare, the more common form of glare encountered in buildings, is caused by a bright light source seen against a darker background. Vision is not impaired in this case. Discomfort glare occurs when areas of sky are seen against dark mullions, dark mouldings, or other dark surfaces adjacent to the window. Meaningless patches of sunlight that fall onto dark areas also cause the same problem. Generally, measured light intensity ratios should be less than 10 to 1. But glare is also a perception effect, not just a stimulus effect. If the bright areas offer visual delight, then high contrast will no longer annoy. Shafts of bright sunlight falling on a planter make a room vibrant. Generally, contrast between room surfaces and the outdoor scene must be minimized. Only clear glass should be used, for translucent materials make the opening too bright. Side windows can be used to get light to the rear of the room and reduce contrast ratios. Generally, windows should have at least one edge next to a corner. This eases the lighting transition from the bright outdoors to the darker indoors by reflecting light from the side wall.

A large vocabulary of antiglare measures exists for natural daylighting design. (See Chapter 7 for more antiglare solutions.) Many elements work together to minimize problems. The design must be verified by studying the lighting and glare behavior with a model; only in this way will the designer have a high degree of confidence in the design.

REFERENCES

1. ASHRAI, *Handbook of Fundamentals*, ASHRAE, New York, 1972.

2. S. Buckley, *Sun Up to Sun Down: Understanding Solar Energy*, McGraw-Hill Inc., New York, 1979.

3. W. Beckman and J. Duffie, *Solar Engineering of Thermal Processes*, John Wiley & Sons, New York, 1980.

4. F. Kreith, *Principles of Heat Transfer*, International Textbook Co., Scranton, 1960.

5. W. Lam, *Perception and Lighting as Form Givers for Architecture*, McGraw-Hill Inc., New York, 1977.

6. V. Olgyay, *Design with Climate*, Princeton University Press, Princeton, 1963.

7. A. Rosenfeld and S. Selkowitz, "Beam Daylighting: An Alternative Illumination Technique," *Energy and Building*, 1 Elsevier Sequoia (1977).

8. *Sunworld*, International Solar Energy Society, vol. 1, no. 3, 1980.

9. D. Turner, *Windows and Environment*, Pilkington, Environmental Advisors Service, Mc Corquidale and Co., Newton-Le-Willows, England, 1971.

Chapter 4

Microclimate

The microclimate is the climate at the site. The site air temperature, wind, and humidity can be affected greatly by local features such as vegetation, topography, and solar exposure. If we learn how to alter the microclimate by manipulating these features, we can reduce heating and cooling loads on the structure, extend the Spring and Fall seasons, create safe pedestrian passages free from buffeting winds and enjoy more pleasant outdoor spaces. As buildings become more highly insulated, they become less susceptible to adverse microclimate effects. But buildings always have windows which remain sensitive to microclimate variations because of their relatively low insulation values. Thus, the microclimate issues become important, even in well insulated structures, when the window area is large, as in passively heated residences.

Microclimate design is not yet a well established discipline. Research on the subject is spotty, although some shining work has been accomplished. This chapter presents the findings of several researchers and the results of some personal design experiences as a starting point in the field. The rewards are satisfying when the microclimate is productively altered; an early spring can lift the spirits and refurbish a weary soul.

VEGETATION AND WIND BREAK

Nature uses vegetation to alter the microclimate for the benefit of the plants. Mature vegetation will moderate temperatures, slow water run-off, reduce wind ero-

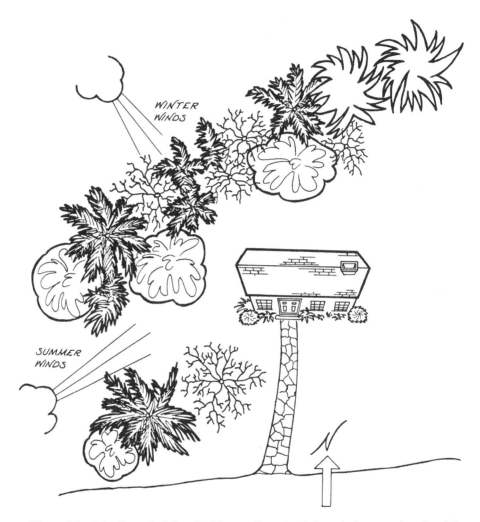

Figure 4.1 Selective wind break. The northwest winter winds are reduced, while the southwest summer winds are funneled into the structure.

sion, and help seedlings get a grip. Learning how these natural forces work can help us alter the microclimate for our benefit, too.

Wind alters our comfort as much as (or more than) air temperature. The relation of the wind to air temperature is publicized in winter newspaper articles as the "wind chill" factor. In the summer we want to maximize the wind velocity to keep cool; during the winter the velocity must be minimized to keep warm and stop large heat losses through the windows. Vegetation in the form of wind breaks and wind channels can help meet both needs. The winter winds usually come from different directions than summer winds. In the northeast United States, the winter winds

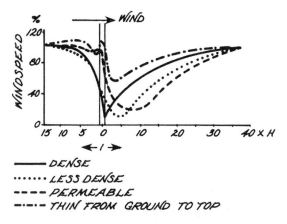

Figure 4.2 Wind reductions with windbreaks of varying density and height H. (from Pantilov, "A Contribution to the Problem of the Effect of Shelterbelts on Wind Velocity on Steep Slopes," Sovetska Agronomiska, Vol. 1, no. 3, 1940).

come from the northwest, and summer winds come from the southwest. Arranging several rows of vegetation as shown in Figure 4.1 can obstruct the winter winds, and also speed the summer winds by funneling them into the structure to cool hot, stuffy areas.

Permeable barriers, such as dense vegetation planted three or five rows deep, create larger wind protection zones than solid barriers at the same height. Figure 4.2 shows the extent of this effect for several barriers. A solid barrier creates relatively large over-pressures on the windward side and similar under-pressures on the lee side of the obstruction. The leeward partial vacuum pulls air down and around the sides causing turbulence and rapid velocity recovery with increasing distance from the barrier. A permeable barrier relieves the pressure differences through the barrier, generating a larger protection zone with almost equal minimum velocities. If the vegetative barrier gets too thick, then the permeability is reduced to that of a solid barrier. The ranges of protection shown in Figure 4.2 are greater than some other researchers have found. Some show protection extending only to 15 times the height of the barrier, rather than 40 times as shown. The extent of the protection is controversial because of the variables present in field experiments. At any rate, most designers would locate structures behind an existing wind break at the point of maximum protection. This occurs at a leeward distance of 2 to 5 times the height of the wind break.

The shelter belt should be densely planted from the ground up as shown in Figures 4.3 and 4.4 to keep wind from slipping underneath the canopies. A square wind break works better than a triangular one (Fig. 4.3). An irregular profile reduces the formation of eddies (Fig. 4.4). The wind speed can be higher than normal near a tree trunk if the air flow at ground level is not blocked by shrubbery.

Figure 4.3 Square windbreaks are more effective than triangular groups of trees (from Carbron, *Shelterbelts and Windbreaks*, Forestry Commission Bulletin 29, Edinburgh, 1957).

Figure 4.4 An irregular profile reduces the formation of turbulences (from Carbron, *Shelterbelts and Windbreaks*, Forestry Commission Bulletin 29, Edinburgh, 1957).

A large percentage of the shelter belt should be composed of evergreens so the vegetation does not become too sparse in the winter. However, a deciduous tree belt in a defoliated state can function as an acceptable wind break if the thickness of the shelter belt is several times its height. If the wind break cannot be formed by prunning existing trees, then a functioning wind break can be created after 3 to 4 years by planting fast growing poplars as nurse trees in conjunction with evergreens and deciduous species native to the area. The poplars will protect the slower growing species while they are becoming established.

Trees can lower the summer air temperature as much as 25°F when the trees grow close enough to form a leaf canopy. The most predominant cooling effect is due to the shading provided by the tree. This not only removes direct solar gain, but also removes much of the reflected and diffuse solar gain if the canopy is large enough. Transpiration occurring in the tree leaves contributes additional cooling. The water evaporating in a mature tree's leaves can remove the same amount of heat as a small room air conditioner if the tree is supplied with all the water it needs. This effect becomes pronounced only if the tree canopy formed by many trees also functions as a wind break, so this cooled air is not blown away.

Even grasses without a tree canopy will lower the summertime air temperature when compared to bare soil or soil covered with paving material. The grass reflects up to 30 percent of the solar energy, reducing the absorption heating effect when compared with darker soils or asphalt. The grass also acts as an insulator, so the remaining heat cannot penetrate to the underlying soil where it would normally be stored and released at night causing excessive nocturnal air temperatures. Transpiration occurring in the blades of grass will remove some of the instantaneous solar heat build up at the grass surface by evaporative cooling if enough water is held in the soil. All these effects add up to lower the air temperature over grassy areas by 5° to 10° when compared with nonvegetated areas in direct sunshine.

The amount of mass in the leaves, branches, and shrubs is not enough to offer any significant thermal storage effect, even when taking into account the high water content of these materials. Nature depends on the previously mentioned effects to locally moderate the environment.

Trees also can warm areas in climates with large diurnal swings, such as in the desert or other low humidity regions where nighttime radiational cooling has a pronounced effect. Clear night skies act as a highly transparent radiation window. The daytime heat stored in the ground, or in structures, then is free to radiate to outer space as infrared energy. This radiation traffic is much lower in high humidity climates where the excessive atmospheric water vapor acts as an opaque barrier to infrared. Large tree canopies can also help retain infrared energy because their opaque leaves block the escape path of ground heat to the sky vault. Nighttime ground temperatures under the tree canopy stay warmer, which results in warmer nighttime air temperatures. This can be seen during early snow falls; the snow under the canopy melts first because the soil is warmer.

All these wonderful things plants do depend on the plants remaining healthy. A good book for determining which species do well in a given region for various soil conditions is Henry Oosting, *The Study of Plant Communities*, W. N. Freeman, 1951.

TOPOGRAPHY

Slopes affect the microclimate in many ways. South facing slopes catch more sun; cold air movement and pooling occur at sites that are part of a local depression; and wind can be affected by local ridges.

A highly inclined south facing surface at mid-latitudes will receive nearly three times the solar radiation a horizontal surface receives during the dead of winter. Even a 10° slope will receive up to 28 percent more sun than a horizontal surface in mid-winter, which is enough to cause spring blooming to occur two weeks earlier. Winter snows melt faster, and the air temperature is noticeably warmer during the day on a tilted, south facing slope. Conversely, north facing slopes run decidedly colder as evidenced by the large population of temperature resistant evergreens found on north slopes. East and west facing slopes maximize solar gain at the ground in the summer when radiation intake should be minimized. An east facing slope is preferred over a west facing slope, since the morning solar heat gain occurs when the air temperatures are still low.

The cold air that forms on windless nights will flow downhill along the line of least resistance. This flow can be 5°F to 10°F cooler than the air at high spots. The flow cannot be dammed effectively since it will overflow the crest in pulsating bursts, but it can be diverted away from structures by vegetation and barriers. The cold air will pool at the end of a run if no outlet is available. Lack of vegetation, or a change in the species in a low spot, points out where cold air pooling takes place. These pools can be drained by running roads through them or by local regrading. Cold air flow does not behave exactly like water running downhill; it does pool at the bottom, but it also dams at the crests as shown in Figure 4.5. Warm air being

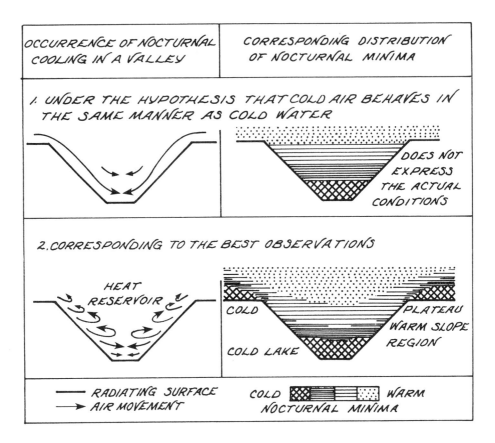

Figure 4.5 Cold air pooling in depressions (from Geiger, *Climate Near the Ground*, Harvard University Press, Cambridge, MA, 1950)

pushed out of the pool causes a reverse vortex of air, as shown also in Figure 4.5, which tends to bank the incoming air at the crest. Thus, it is best to build midway up a slope to avoid the cold and damp at the bottom and the cold at the rim. If the site has nighttime winds, then all these effects are easily overpowered by the stronger breeze.

In underheated climates it is advantageous to locate outdoor activities in naturally occurring (or man-made) sun traps to extend the Spring and Fall seasons. A sun trap uses orientation and thermal capacity to moderate outdoor temperatures. Thermal capacity is used to carry the day's solar heat gain past sunset so the nighttime air stays warm longer. Bare soil performs adequately as a heat sponge if it is damp, but vertical south facing surfaces will intercept more solar energy in the spring and fall at mid-latitudes than slightly inclined or horizontal soil surfaces.

Figure 4.6 shows a well designed sun trap. Rock or masonry is used to form a dark south facing wall. The solar intake can be maximized by using light colored

Figure 4.6   A well designed sun trap.

materials in front of the embankment to reflect the light, but glare could become a problem. A high tree canopy allows the spring and fall sun to come in underneath the canopy while the leaves block the high summer sun. Additional shrubbery is planted to the northwest and west to stop the cold spring breezes that come from this direction in many parts of the eastern United States. Most of the solar heat absorbed in the wall will blow away, leaving less energy for storage if the wind break is not well designed. If the wind is kept away at night, the wall will remain in the mid-70s several hours after sunset and warm the adjacent air. Also, the walls

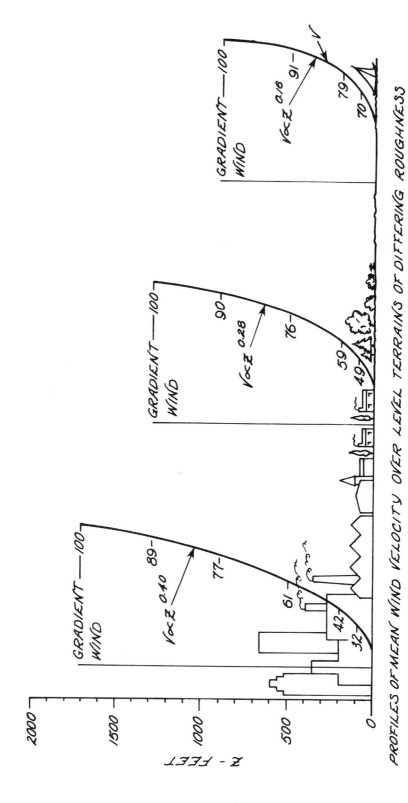

Figure 4.7 Wind velocity gradients for three different regions (from A. G. Davenport, "Relationship of Wind Structure to Wind Loading", Proceedings, 1st International Conference on Wind Effects of Buildings and Structures, National Physical Laboratory, Peddington, Middlesex, U.K., 1963.

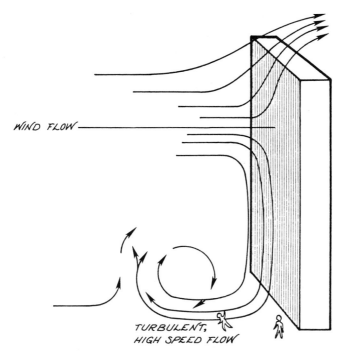

WIND FLOW

TURBULENT,
HIGH SPEED FLOW

Figure 4.8 A reverse wind vortex forms at the windward side of any obstruction.

will radiate heat if the wall area is large enough, for example, greater than 10 feet by 8 feet. These local warming effects will only work within 10 feet of the wall, so activities that occur in the sun trap area must be selected accordingly.

Unfortunately, most of the microclimate effects discussed here work only at a vertical scale that is in keeping with one and two story residences. High-rise structures tower over the local thermal variations nature has designed to protect small scale vegetation. At tower scale, only one microclimate variable remains important — the wind. The wind problem can become so devastating for high-rise construction that wind tunnel studies at the preliminary design stage became necessary to determine if the pedestrian ways are not only comfortable but, in some cases, safe.

The wind speed increases with altitude as shown in Figure 4.7 as a result of less friction from surface features. The wind velocity gradient is shown for three different regions: urban, suburban, and ocean. Buildings and vegetation cut pedestrian level wind speeds to a fraction of the wind velocities aloft when the surrounding structures are of nearly uniform height. A single tower more than 50 percent taller than its neighbors will create high ground wind velocities. The high tower catches the high speed winds aloft and converts them to ground winds in the form of a pulsating reverse vortex on the windward side of the building (shown in Fig. 4.8). This will always happen because pressures created by the wind slowing down when it strikes the face of the building are higher at the top of the building than at the

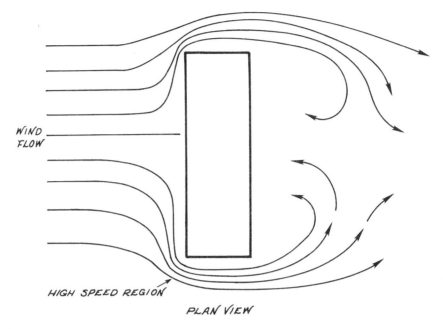

WIND FLOW

HIGH SPEED REGION

PLAN VIEW

Figure 4.9   Wind velocity increases at building corners

ground level. Those high pressures push the wind downward, causing a highly turbulent ground level reverse vortex. Wind speed also increases at the corners of buildings as it compresses to get around the sharp edges (Fig. 4.9).

Very little can be done to stop these effects. Many times neighboring buildings magnify the problem. The usual solution is to locate entrances in the calm areas on the lee side of the building. Of course the wind changes direction, so one side of the building will not always be on the lee side. Local airports have wind data that show wind directions and strengths for a normal year's weather. Usually a predominant direction exists for the winter and summer seasons.

Wind tunnel studies should always be undertaken when one or more tall buildings are placed in a neighborhood of uniform structures. It is almost impossible to predict where trouble spots will occur without modeling the whole neighborhood in a large scale wind tunnel (Table 4.1 gives a partial list of United States wind tunnels that perform architectural services). And sometimes the existing trouble spots in a neighborhood shift to other buildings when a new building goes in. The problem is so widespread that the federal Environmental Protection Agency now requires wind tunnel tests for certain types of new federal buildings.

The microclimate can be colored slightly, or it can be totally altered, when building. The designer must remain aware of microclimate potentials so site use is maximized. More information becomes available each year as people realize how much this subject has been ignored in the past.

TABLE 4.1 Some North American wind tunnels that offer pressure studies with proper wind gradients.

1. Wright Brothers Wind Tunnel
   Massachusetts Institute of Technology
   Cambridge, MA

2. Wind Tunnel
   Colorado State University
   Fort Collins, CO

3. Bolt Beranek and Newman, Inc.
   10 Moulton Street
   Cambridge, MA

4. University of Western Ontario
   London, Ontario
   Canada

REFERENCES

1. A.I.A. Research Corp., *Regional Guidelines for Building Passive Energy Conserving Homes*, U.S. Department of Housing and Urban Development, Washington, D.C., 1978.

2. J. Aronin, *Climate and Architecture*, Reinhold Publishing. New York, 1953.

3. B. Boos, *Energy Conservation in Irban Development Plan*, Swedish Council for Building Research, 1979.

4. J. Carborn, *Shelterbelts and Windbreaks*, Faber and Faber, London, 1965.

5. R. Geiger, *Climate Near the Ground*, Harvard University Press. Cambridge, Mass, 1965.

6. B. Givoni, *Man, Climate, and Architecture*, Applied Science Publishers, Barking Esses, U.K., 1969.

7. V. Loftness, "Natural Forces and the Craft of Buildings, Site Reconnaisance," B.S.A.D. Thesis, Department of Architecture, M.I.T., Cambridge, Mass. 1974.

8. V.Olgyay, *Design with Climate*, Princeton University Press, Princeton, 1963.

9. H. Oosting, *The Study of Plant Communities*, W.B. Freeman, San Francisco, 1956.

10. G. Robinette, *Plants, People and Environmental Quality*, U.S. National Park Service, 1972.

Chapter 5

Windows

Operable windows do an amazing number of things. They admit light and heat; supply fresh air and a view; provide a tantalizing physical and visual connection to the outdoors; insulate interiors from the weather; offer visual privacy; and mirror our world. Windows are an unassailably dramatic building element. Perhaps this is what excites architects and owners alike about direct-gain passive solar heating.

This chapter examines the surprisingly complex subject of windows, from the viewpoint of materials and control. The chapter concludes with a discussion on daylighting methods and devices for minimizing glare.

GLAZING MATERIALS

Glass historically has been the first choice for window glazing because of its architectural beauty, weather durability, and clarity. Glass's exceptional transmission characteristics also make it a prime candidate for a solar collector. But some of today's plastics also have high transmission values.

What determines a glazing material's thermal effectiveness as a solar collector? Glazing thermal properties are best characterized by the ratio of average solar transmission to thermal loss, where the thermal loss is stated as nighttime thermal conductance in $BTU/hr°Fft^2$. The higher this ratio, the more solar energy will be netted for heating.

Dealing with the denominator of this ratio is easy. The thermal conductances of all transparent window films or sheets are the same, except for the selective transmitters. (This new glazing material is discussed later in this section.) A window's thermal conductance is determined by the air film that clings to the glazing material. The thermal resistance of the window material itself is negligible compared to the resistances of the air blanket. In turn, the air film's resistance only varies with the film's thickness and stability. The air film is stabilized when the glazing is protected from the wind by a second layer of glazing. The thickness of the air film is also controlled by the spacing between the glazing layers.

Slightly more than half of a window's thermal losses are due to long-wave infrared radiation traffic. This heat flow path is not greatly affected by material choices except when using the selective transmitters. Radiation loss occurs because glazing materials are either opaque or partially transparent to thermal radiation. In the opaque case, the glazing material absorbs the infrared radiation originating in the room. The absorbed energy warms the glazing and conducts to the outside where it re-radiates to the heavens. The radiation losses are increased slightly if the material is partially transparent to infrared. Many thin plastic films are up to 60 percent transparent to infrared. Radiation emissions are essentially constant among materials; thermal conductance alters with various layers of non-selective glazing and in different wind conditions (shown in Table 5.1).

Glass windows often are characterized as solar radiation traps, since glass is transparent to solar radiation and opaque to thermal radiation. To be sure, solar energy is easily admitted and back radiation losses are retarded by glass and other infrared opaque materials. If the solar gain is greater than the infrared losses, then a net amount of radiation is trapped behind the glass for solar heating. However, it does not follow that the net radiation inside a glass greenhouse is greater than the net radiation outside the greenhouse. Radiation back losses through glass are as high as 70 to 80 percent of the back losses from a neighboring plot of uncovered ground. Furthermore, the solar radiation entering the greenhouse is reduced by the less than perfect transparency of the material. Researchers have found[8] that the net radiation produced by these two effects is lower inside than outside a greenhouse for common commercial grades of glass. The difference in net radiation is not large. If laboratory clear glass were used as a greenhouse cover, the net radiation in the greenhouse would slightly exceed the net radiation outside the greenhouse. Greenhouses really warm up because they act as convection traps; the hot air that forms in the greenhouse cannot blow away.

The numerator of the transmission-to-loss ratio is more difficult to understand. Solar transmission depends on several variables. During the day, the glazing absorbs some of the incident solar energy and elevates in temperature. This lowers the heat loss since the temperature drop from the room to the glazing is reduced. Conceptually, it is easier to view this as an increase in the solar transmittance rather than a variable thermal conductance, as some of the solar energy absorbed in the glass is, in effect, deposited in the room. The sum of the optical solar transmission and the transmission due to the absorption heating is known as the *effective transmission*.

Table 5.1   Thermal conductances of various glazing systems.

U-VALUES OF WINDOWS AND SKYLIGHTS		
Description	*U-values* [1]	
	Winter	*Summer*
Vertical panels:		
Single pane flat glass	1.13	1.06
Insulating glass — double [2]		
3/16" air space	0.69	0.64
1/4" air space	0.65	0.61
1/2" air space	0.58	0.56
Insulating glass — triple [2]		
1/4" air spaces	0.47	0.45
1/2" air spaces	0.36	0.35
Storm windows		
1-4" air space	0.56	0.54
Glass blocks [3]		
6 X 6 X 4" thick	0.60	0.57
8 X 8 X 4" thick	0.56	0.54
same, with cavity divider	0.48	0.46
Single plastic sheet	1.09	1.00
Horizontal panels: [4]		
Single pane flat glass	1.22	0.83
Insulating glass — double [2]		
3/16" air space	0.75	0.49
1/4" air space	0.70	0.46
1/2" air space	0.66	0.44
Glass blocks [3]		
11 X 11 X 3" thick,		
with cavity divider	0.53	0.35
12 X 12 X 4" thick,		
with cavity divider	0.51	0.34
Plastic bubbles [5]		
single-walled	1.15	0.80
double-walled	0.70	0.46

[1] in units of Btu/hr/ft^2/°F
[2] double and triple refer to the number of lights of glass.
[3] nominal dimensions.
[4] U-values for horizontal panels are for heat flow *up* in winter and *down* in summer.

The optical solar transmission of a glazing material is determined by the transparency of the material and the angle of incidence of the solar energy. As the angle of incidence increases, the transmission decreases due to higher reflection losses. The sun's angle of incidence varies during the day, so the solar transmission varies to a great extent. It has been shown that the average angle of incidence between the

Table 5.2 Monthly Average Beam Incidence Angle for a Vertical South Facing Surface at Various Latitudes from Klein, SA. "Calculation of Monthly Average Transmittance-Absorption Product," *Solar Energy, 23*, 547, 1979.

	Latitude			
Month	20°N	30°N	40°N	50°N
January	55	48	41	35
February	62	56	50	43
March	72	65	59	53
April	82	73	67	61
May	88	81	73	67
June	89	83	76	70
July	89	83	76	70
August	85	77	70	63
September	76	68	62	57
October	66	59	53	47
November	57	50	43	37
December	52	46	39	32

sun's rays and a south facing vertical surface occurs at 2:30 P.M. (or 9:30 A.M.).* Table 5.2 shows 2:30 P.M. angles of incidence for each month at several latitudes. The average transmission for a glazing product can be found using this table and the manufacturer's curve for transmission versus angle of incidence. Unfortunately most manufacturers give only solar transmission for an angle of incidence equal to zero (normal transmission). Table 5.3 shows normal transmissions for various single glazing alternatives along with the material's expected mechanical lifetime and the index of refraction. The index of refraction determines the material's solar transmission at various angle of incidence. The average transmission for a single vertical layer of material, Tave, can be determined with the following formulae:

$$T_{ave} = \frac{\frac{1}{2}NT}{\frac{1 - \left(\frac{N-1}{N+1}\right)^2}{1 + \left(\frac{N-1}{N+1}\right)^2}} \times \left[\frac{1 - r_1}{1 + r_1} + \frac{1 - r_2}{1 + r_2}\right]$$

where $r_1 = \frac{\sin^2(L - AI)}{\sin^2(L + AI)}$,

$r_2 = \frac{\tan^2(L - AI)}{\tan^2(L + AI)}$

$L = \sin^{-1}\left(\frac{\sin AI}{N}\right)$

* The average angle of incidence for the diffuse component occurs at an angle of 60°.

TABLE 5.3* Ordinary Single Glazing Materials

Material	Thickness	Initial normal solar transmission %	Mechanical lifetime in years	Index of Refraction	Maximum Use Temperature °F
SHEET					
glass	0.125	88	∞	1.526	400
F.R.P.	0.040	85 to 88	20	1.580	300-350
Acrylics	0.125	89	20	1.491	180-200
Polycarbonates	0.125	87 to 89	12	1.580	250
cellulose acetate butyrate (UVEX)	0.125	89	20	–	150
FILM					
acrylic/polyester	0.011	87.5	20	1.64	270
FEP Teflon	0.002	96	∞	1.34	400
Polyvinyl fluoride	0.004	90	12	1.42	300
Polyethylene	0.004	90	1	–	200
Polyester	0.001	85	10	1.64	300

*Plastics Design Forum, Sept, Oct, 1979

and NT is the manufacturer's normal transmission, N is the index of refraction, and AI is the angle of incidence at 2:30. The average transmission for n layers of material is found by raising T_{ave} to the nth power.

For example, find the transmission of glass at $AI = 60°$ when $NT = .88$ and $N = 1.526$.

$$L = \sin^{-1}\left(\frac{\sin 60}{1.526}\right) = 34.58$$

$$r_1 = \frac{\sin^2 (-25.42)}{\sin^2 (94.58)} = 0.185$$

$$r_2 = \frac{\tan^2 (-25.42)}{\tan^2 (94.58)} = 0.001$$

$$T_{ave} = \frac{0.5(.88)}{\frac{1 - (0.526/2.526)^2}{1 + (0.526/2.526)^2}} \times \left[\frac{1 - 0.185}{1 + 0.185} + \frac{1 - 0.001}{1 + 0.001}\right] = .81$$

A material's effective transmission is always greater than its optical transmission because of its absorption heating effect. Absorption heating only adds 2 to 3 percent to the optical transmission of materials with transmissions higher than 85 percent. However, this effect can become substantial in tinted glasses and selective transmitters. Figure 5.1 shows the amount of absorption heating that occurs in various glasses at different angles of incidence. Not all the energy absorbed in the glass is deposited inside; depending on the wind velocity, some of the heat will transfer to the outside. If the absorbing material is protected from the wind by a second layer of clear glazing, then 50 percent of the absorbed energy will transfer inside. Only 20 to 35 percent of the absorbed heat will conduct into the room if any wind reaches the absorber.

The average effective transmission for a glazing product is determined as follows:

1. Find the percentage of incident energy absorbed in the product.

2. Find the percentage of absorbed energy that is available for room heating by taking 20 to 50 percent of the figure found in Step 1 above, depending on wind conditions.

3. Add the result of Step 2 above to the product's average optical transmission.

A few transmission-to-thermal loss ratios for various material configurations are given in Table 5.4. Notice the ratio does not get substantially better when moving from triple to quadruple glass systems. The ratio is improved when Teflon^{TM} is used for the multiple layers as a result of the Teflon^{TM}'s high solar transmission of 95 percent. Most transmission losses in materials are due to reflection losses. In the future, one can expect to see economical antireflective treatments for most

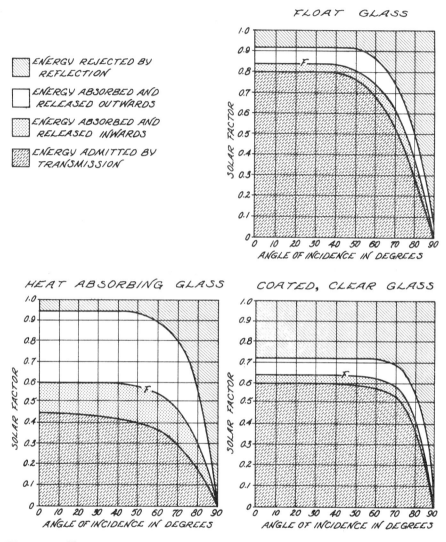

Figure 5.1 Glass transmission and absorbption vs. angle of incidence (from *Windows and Environment*, Pilkington Environmental Advisory Service, 1969)

glazing materials that increase transmission and the glazing thermal ratio accordingly.

The transmission-to-loss ratio must be used guardedly. Any glazing system with the same ratio will keep a building at the same indoor temperatures when the structure is entirely glazed. For a partially glazed building, the glazing that has the higher transmission will outperform the low transmission product, even if their ratios are the same. Overall thermal losses are not due entirely to windows in partially glazed buildings. Enough solar energy must be transmitted to offset the thermal losses

TABLE 5.4 Average solar transmission to loss ratios for various vertical glazing materials.*

1. Single pane D.S. flat glass	$\dfrac{84\%}{1.13 \text{ BTU/hr}^\circ\text{F}}$	$= 74.3$
2. Double glass (½" air space)	$\dfrac{71\%}{0.58 \text{ BTU/hr}^\circ\text{F}}$	$= 121.6$
3. Triple glass (½" air space)	$\dfrac{59\%}{0.36 \text{ BTU/hr}^\circ\text{F}}$	$= 164.6$
4. Quadruple glass (½" air space)	$\dfrac{49\%}{0.28 \text{ BTU/hr}^\circ\text{F}}$	$= 175.0$
5. Selective (ITO) transmitter with D.S. glass spaced ½" away	$\dfrac{65\%}{0.29 \text{ BTU/hr}^\circ\text{F}}$	$= 224$
6. Double FRP (½" air space)	$\dfrac{66\%}{0.56 \text{ BTU/hr}^\circ\text{F}}$	$= 118$
7. Double 2 mil FEP Teflon (½" air space)	$\dfrac{84\%}{0.61 \text{ BTU/hr}^\circ\text{F}}$	$= 138$
8. Quadruple FEP Teflon (½" air space)	$\dfrac{71\%}{0.31 \text{BTU/hr}^\circ\text{F}}$	$= 229$

*Insulation values for glass systems from: ASHRAE, *Handbook of Fundamentals,* 1972.

through the rest of the building, and not just the losses through the windows. Generally, solar transmissions of 60 to 85 percent must be achieved if significant solar heating is expected in partially glazed buildings.

Another way to improve a glazing's thermal ratio is to decrease the heat conductance without greatly affecting the transmission. This really means reducing the heat loss from convection or radiation. Various convection arrest mechanisms are available commercially. One system uses heavy gas hermetically sealed in double glass units to reduce convection losses. Another uses transparent cellular materials sandwiched between glazing sheets. The latter approach, while effective, interferes with view.

Selective transmitters increase the glazing thermal ratio by decreasing the radiation losses without greatly affecting the optical transmission. This happens because the selective transmitter (actually a thin film coated on a glass or plastic base) mirrors long-wave thermal radiation while remaining highly transparent to short

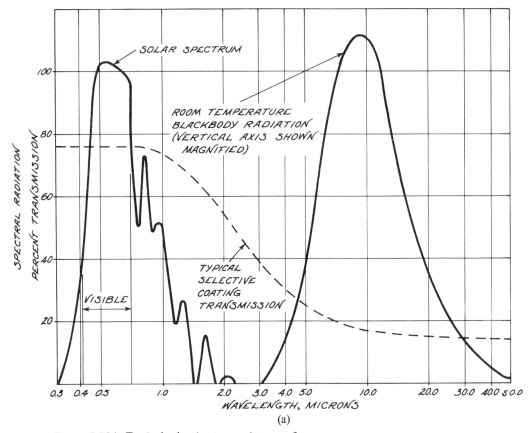

Figure 5.2(a) Typical selective transmitter performance

wave solar radiation. The selective transmitter takes advantage of a fortuitous bifurcation in the solar energy spectrum. Figure 5.2a shows the distribution of solar energy versus wave length. The first bump on the left side of the graph is the energy contained in a ray of sun. Less than one half of it is in the visible spectrum. Most of the energy is contained in the near infrared spectrum. The bump on the right half of the curve shows how this solar energy transforms into the long-wave infrared energy we feel as heat whenever sunlight is absorbed. Notice the clean split between the incoming energy and the re-radiated energy. The selective transmitter capitalizes on this split, as shown by the dashed transmission curve superimposed on the two energy curves. The dashed curve shows how approximately 75 percent of the incoming solar energy is transmitted. Once this energy hits an opaque surface and is transformed into heat, it tries to leave the space as long-wave infrared energy. Approximately 15 percent of this outgoing infrared energy is absorbed by the selective

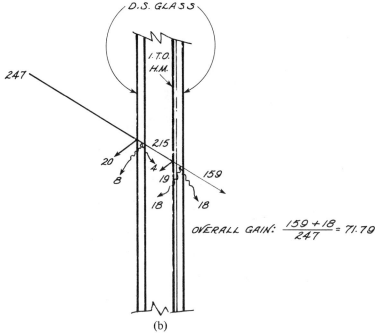

Figure 5.2(b) Winter solar Heat gains for a selective transmitter.

coating; the remaining 85 percent is reflected back into the room. Actually, up to 81 percent of the solar energy is admitted to the interior since some absorption heating takes place in the selective transmitter, Figure 5.2b. Glass selective transmitters can be laboriously fabricated by scribing a grid of lines fine enough to stop long-wave infrared from passing, but which allows short-wave solar energy to pass through the net like a dust particle through an insect screen. Actual selective transmitters are made more economically with materials like indium-tin oxide or copper tin oxide deposited in very thin layers on glass or plastics.

The newer selective transmitters nearly double the thermal resistance of the glass or plastic carrier while only reducing the effective solar transmission to 92 percent of the uncoated carrier. With this kind of gain-to-loss ratio, it becomes possible to solar heat a building on cold, cloudy days using a sealed, double glass unit filled with Argon gas with a selective coating on one of the glazings. The effective solar transmission of this system is 65 to 70 percent with a U-value of 0.28 BTU/hrft^2°F. Most of the building's vertical surfaces would have to be a selective transmitter to supply 100 percent of the heating requirement from the diffuse radiation filtering through the clouds, and the outdoor temperatures would have to be 43°F or higher.

A few simple calculations demonstrate the potential for solar heating in such a climate. We can conservatively assume average cloudy day diffuse radiation falling on a vertical window at 40°N latitude in March is 170 BTU/dayft^2. With an effective transmission of 70 percent, 119 BTU/dayft^2 reaches the interior. A home with an average air temperature of 62°F facing an outdoor air temperature of 40°F would lose the following amount of heat through each square foot of coated glass.

$$0.28 \text{ BTU/hrft}^2\text{°F} \times (62\text{-}40)\text{°F} \times 24\text{hr/day} = 147 \text{ BTU/dayft}^2$$

This leaves a deficit of 28 BTU/dayft^2 for each square foot of selective transmitter. The remaining conduction losses through as much as two thousand square feet of glass, and the infiltration losses caused by that glass, could be balanced by daily internal gains alone (assuming 70,000 BTU/day in internal gains). At an outdoor air temperature of 44°F, the new glass would cancel all its conduction losses.

For higher outdoor temperatures, this means northern exposures are as important as southern exposures for solar heating. Also, it is now possible to achieve 100 percent solar heating in benign winter climates with only 18 hours' worth of thermal storage. Curiously, a building like this is designed to reject clear day solar energy, so overheating is avoided. Thus, whole regions of the world, like Great Britain, Scandinavia, and the United States Pacific Northwest, can now enjoy the advantages of solar energy.

Obviously, the selective transmitter can be used to great advantage in conventional direct-gain structures. The selective transmitter is nearly thermally equivalent to double glass with one inch of nighttime insulation, yet you can always see through it. And, of course, the selective transmitter can be used for energy conservation in all existing windows regardless of orientation.

The selective transmitter can be produced in two forms for economical architectural applications. The coating currently is sold as a factory applied finish on glass. In the near future it will also be available on plastic film, like Mylar^{TM}, which can be applied to existing glass. The glass product is more durable but economically restricted to new construction and the window replacement market. The plastic film will be used most advantageously to upgrade the thermal performance of existing glazing.

The selective transmitter coating in double glazing systems is usually placed on the protected side of the inside layer of glass. The glass surface next to the room runs up to 5°F warmer than if the selective transmitter is on the room side. Warmer glass means higher comfort levels, since the Mean Radiant Temperature of the room is lifted and the formation of cold drafts is minimized. In this case the infrared is absorbed by the ordinary glass surface facing the room. The absorbed heat is conducted to the other side where it meets the selective transmitter. A selective transmitter is also a selective emitter. In other words, the coating retards the emission of infrared energy; the heat cannot leave the glass as radiation so the thermal conductivity of the glass remains low. The coating should not be placed on the opposite glass layer when the window faces south because the absorbtion heating contribution to room heating will be diminished. For other exposures, the coating should be placed on the protected side of the outer layer of glass to maximize thermal resistance.

The impact of this technology can be compared to the impact of hermetically sealed glass on solar heating in 1943. Suddenly, architects like George Keck realized they had a glass that could insulate relative to conventional glazing. This led to the first commercialization of direct-gain solar heating in the 1940s. Today we see a similar doubling of insulating levels in windows, but this time the technology opens up the prospect of solar heating in cloudy climates. Considering the worldwide need for saving energy, this second technical boost will make the direct-gain residence a more common part of the landscape.

FRAME MATERIALS AND GLAZING METHODS

Once a glazing material that gives the desired thermal resistance has been chosen, an economical framing material that does not add significantly to total heat loss of the window assembly must be selected. While aluminum is the most economical framing material, it is also the poorest insulating material. Aluminum framing insulates as well as an equivalent area of glass. Heat loss can be reduced by 30 to 60 percent by adding plastic thermal breaks to the aluminum extrusion. The best thermal break aluminum frame can equal approximately the insulating value of a wood frame, while the emerging urethane and PVC plastic frames can reduce heat flow to 90 to 50 percent of a wooden frame. Table 5.5 compares the nighttime heat loss for a 3 foot by 4 foot sheet of double glass (with and without a selective transmitting coating) with the heat loss for a variety of supporting frames.

TABLE 5.5 Heat conductance for a variety of materials framing a 3'x4' window.

	BTU/hr$^\circ$F
Heat loss from 3'x4' double glazing	6.6
Heat loss from 3'x4' coated double glazing	3.5
Heat loss from framing material	
Aluminum	2-1.75
Aluminum with thermal break	1.3-0.8
Wood or PVC extrusions	0.7-0.6
Urethane	0.6-0.3

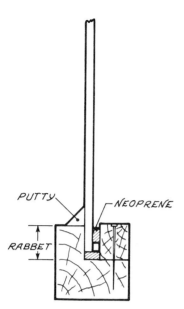

Figure 5.3 Typical large area glazing detail for wooden frames

Notice the heat loss for aluminum frame is up to 30 percent of a 3 foot by 4 foot double glazed window. When using a selective transmitter, the heat loss through a metal frame nearly equals the loss through the coated glass area, effectively cancelling out the advantages of the coating. Of course, larger windows would reduce this imbalance somewhat. Wood frames and good metal frames with thick thermal breaks bring the frame loss under control.

The window material must be mounted properly to the frame or glazed to resist wind loads and water penetration. Mounting is relatively complex and expensive for sheet products. The difference in thermal expansion between the glazing and the frame must be taken into consideration, usually by fabricating a wiping joint which allows relative movement between the sheet and the frame while keeping water out. The usual glazing points and putty seal used to mount glass in sash windows is not adequate for the large glazing areas found in passively heated structures because of large wind loads. Figure 5.3 shows a preferred way of mounting sheet products in wooden frames. An 1/8 inch thick by 1/4 inch wide neoprene tape fastened to one side of the glass perimeter forms a resiliant flat bearing surface to resist wind loading. Several neoprene pads 3 inches to 4 inches long are placed at the bottom and sides of the glass edges to distribute the compressive loads. A positive stop is nailed in place to hold the glass against the rabbeted frame. The whole assembly is waterproofed with a silicone sealant. The integral rubber gaskets used in modern metal extrusions make the whole process simpler and obviate the need for sealants.

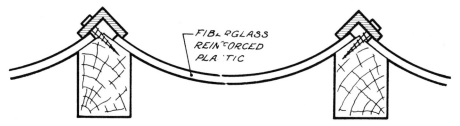

Figure 5.4 A glazing detail for flexible plastic sheet

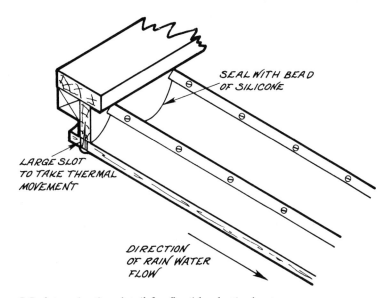

Figure 5.5 A termination detail for flexible plastic sheet

The rabbet dimension (see Fig. 5.3) must be large enough to accept the expansion in sheet products that tend to absorb sunlight, such as tinted glass and selective transmitters. A tinted sheet can reach 110°F in the sunlight so up to 30 percent more thermal expansion than experienced by clear glass can occur. Each glass and plastic sheet manufacturer gives suggested rabbet dimensions for their products for various wind loads and glassed areas. Always add an extra 30 percent to these dimensions when using heat absorbing versions of their products.

Sometimes the rabbet dimension for sheet plastic products becomes excessively large because of thermal expansion that must be accommodated in large spans of plastic. For flexible sheet, such as the FRP products, this expansion can be taken up in the material itself by giving it a curve as shown in Figure 5.4. Expansion across the curve merely changes the radius of the curve. Expansion along the long

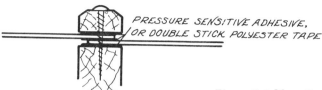

PRESSURE SENSITIVE ADHESIVE,
OR DOUBLE STICK POLYESTER TAPE

Figure 5.6 Mounting films using a simple clamping joint

axis of the cylinder is taken up by the sliding action in the edge mount. The material is terminated as shown in Figure 5.5.

Installing films is relatively easy, as a sliding joint is no longer necessary. The material merely is tightened and clamped as shown in Figure 5.6. Then the material is heat shrunk with an electric space heater and fan (most films will heat shrink to a certain extent). This preloads the film in tension to avoid sagging as the materials expand with elevated temperatures. The film mount must be tested in a mock-up to make sure the material does not rip apart upon heat shrinking.

CONDENSATION

Hermetically sealed double glass units overcome condensation problems by sealing dry air in the cavity. However, many times double or triple glazed units cannot be sealed, perhaps because additional hardware must be placed inside the cavity. Condensation can be overcome by properly venting the cavity to the dry winter air outside. At least six 1/4 inch holes must be drilled through the frame to link the cavity with the outside. Bugs will find their way into the cavity unless screens are placed in the vent holes. The holes admit dry outside air, but are small enough to prevent the build-up of convection currents when the wind blows.

MOVABLE INSULATION

The emerging selective transmitters net nearly as much solar energy in a 6000 degree day climate as most double glass windows with nighttime insulation. Nevertheless, movable window insulation still will be used in certain architectural circumstances that demand unusual window treatments, and in more severe climates. Many varieties of movable window insulation exist, but the principles of construction are the same: (1) room air must not seep between the insulation and the glass; and (2) conduction losses must be significantly lowered by the insulation itself.

This can be done by simply force-fitting an inch of rigid board insulation into the window frame. The insulation must be clad with a fire barrier such as drywall if the insulation is flammable. If the rigid insulation can adhere directly to the window through the use of magnets, as Steve Baer demonstrated, then small perimeters of exposed glass do not add significantly to the heat losses. A minimum thermal nighttime resistance of R-8 can be achieved with these approaches when used with double glass.

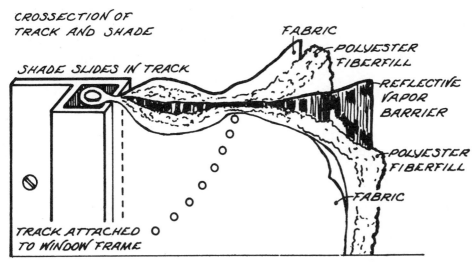

Figure 5.7 Quilted insulation window shade (from Appropriate Technology Corp., Brattleboro, Vermont)

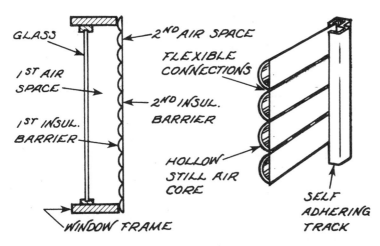

Figure 5.8 Semi-rigid insulating window shade (from Solar Energy Construction Co., Valley Forge, PA.)

More flexible systems that store readily are shown in the following figures. One shade uses a quilted multilayer fabric. Figure 5.7 shows a cross-section of the material and the associated track that provides the air seal. This device provides an R-5.1 thermal resistance when used with double glazing. A semirigid roll-up device, like the old roll-up desk cover, is shown in Figure 5.8. The hinged slats are hollow PCV extrusions. An R of 3.5 could be expected with double glass.

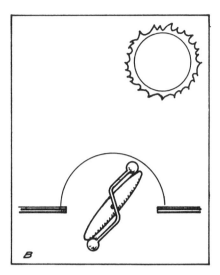

Figure 5.9 Automatic interior insulating shutter (from Zome Works Corp., Albuquerque, NM)

The really effective movable insulations pose an unusual problem. Glass temperature falls to the outdoor air temperature when the insulation is in position at night. Massive amounts of condensation form on the room side of the glass when the insulation is opened suddenly and warm air rushes over the inside glass surface. The problem is overcome if the insulation is removed slowly, or removed after the sun has had a chance to warm the glass. Of course, an automatic control that senses the presence of the sun solves this issue nicely, and it frees the occupant from the need to attend manually to the windows. Steve Baer offers an elegant solution to the control problem with his sky-lid product. Relatively thick insulating louvers that seal when closed are placed in a skylight. The louvers are counterbalanced by interconnected freon filled bottles mounted on each side of a louver. (Fig. 5.9). When the sun heats the bottle on the window side, the freon is driven to the opposite bottle, increasing its weight and causing the louver to open. At night the cycle reverses. Baer and David Harrison also showed the air space between double glazing can be used at night to increase the window's thermal resistance. Their Beadwell[R] system moves Styrofoam[®] beads coated with an antistatic agent into the cavity at night. The beads are fluidized by an air stream so they can be pumped in and out. Both of these products can insulate to an R-9 level.

Ordinary drawn draperies can make double glazing behave like triple glazing if the following steps are taken: (1) use a tight weave, lined drape (to stop air permeation); (2) place weights in the bottom hem so the drape drags on the floor (to seal the room air out); (3) attach the drape's vertical edges to the wall with a demountable strip such as Velcro[®]. The valence can be left unsealed, as the cold air trapped between the drape and the window cannot flow uphill.

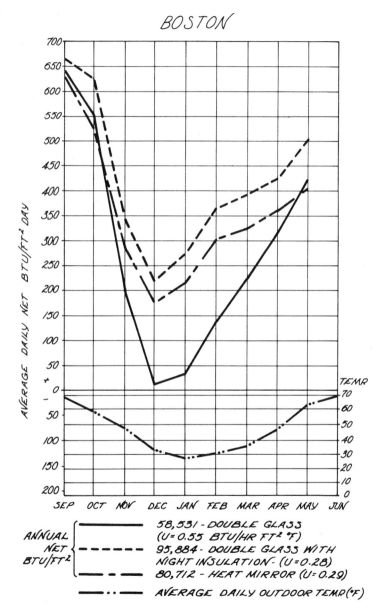

BOSTON

ANNUAL NET BTU/FT²	58,531 - DOUBLE GLASS (U= 0.55 BTU/HR FT² °F)
	95,884 - DOUBLE GLASS WITH NIGHT INSULATION - (U=0.28)
	80,712 - HEAT MIRROR (U=0.29)
	AVERAGE DAILY OUTDOOR TEMP (°F)

Figure 5.10 Average daily net heating energy per square foot of window for three different glazing systems in three different cities.

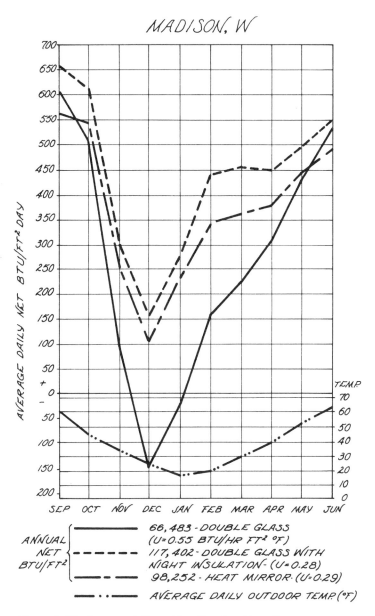

Figure 5.10 Average daily net heating (continued)

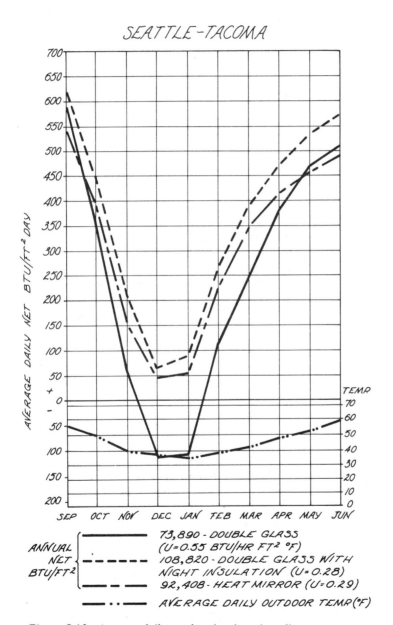

SEATTLE-TACOMA

Figure 5.10   Average daily net hearing (continued)

Ordinary venetian blinds placed between two layers of ordinary glass can almost double the thermal resistance if at least one side of the louvers are reflectorized. Of course, the edges of the slats must nearly touch in the closed position to stop air movement.

The *average* daily heating energy captured by one square foot of south facing window with R-8 nighttime insulation is compared with one square foot of double glazing and one square foot of double glass with a selective coating for three different cities in Figure 5.10. The chart also gives annual net solar intake for each city. The movable insulation is left off the window every day for nine hours. Notice, the ordinary double glazing barely operates with a net heat gain in Boston and is a net loser of heat in Madison, Wisconsin and Seattle, Washington during December and January. Movable insulation or the selective transmitter significantly improves the situation, with movable insulation slightly out-performing the coated glass.

SHADING

Windows should be vertical, both to keep out the rain, and to make them easier to keep clean. Solar intake for vertical windows is almost as great as the intake for apertures tilted at the optimum angle, since average ground reflectances of 20 to 30 percent nearly replace the energy lost by moving the glazing off the optimum angle. Perhaps the most important reason for keeping the windows vertical is that summertime shading is easier, particularly for south facing windows.

Unwanted summer solar gain should be intercepted with shading devices at the outside rather than at the inside of a window, because once the sun's rays pass through the glazing, they are in the building for good. The sun spends very little time in front of a south facing window during the summer. Its south passage is at high altitudes, so window shading with eyebrow-like devices becomes relatively easy. However, space heating loads are not synchronous with the sun's climb in altitude. The sun is nearly at its maximum altitude late in May, but solar heating still can be necessary at this time in northern climates. In September the sun has lowered to half its maximum altitude, yet solar heating is rarely required in this month. Solar heating requirements are significant in March when the sun is at the same mid-latitude. Any fixed overhang device that gives maximum shading in June while permitting the March sun to sneak underneath would admit unwanted sun in September. The most elegant way to get in phase with the seasons is to shade naturally with vegetation. Leaves bud at the right moment in May to arrest the passage of beam sunlight, and they continue to work as shading devices through September and part of October. Trees are not all a bed of roses, though. A bare canopy of branches can still shade up to half of the sun's rays during the winter when maximum intake is required. However, the usual species of trees (oak, ash) will transmit 70 to 80 percent of the wintertime solar energy.[4] One way to overcome the branch shading problem is to place trees so close to the windows that the sun's rays can strike the window by passing underneath the tree canopy between

Figure 5.11 Tree canopy placement to prevent winter shading from the branches

September 21 and March 21, as shown in Figure 5.11. The sun can still reach the window through the branches during April and part of May.

Unfortunately, trees are not always available in the required position and planting take time to mature. Also, some multiple family units are so out of scale with trees that the upper stories tower over the loftiest of trees. Mechanical devices can be used as shades in these cases. They should be movable so adjustments can be made to keep pace with the heating season. Figures 5.12 and 5.13 show some movable external shading devices popular in Europe. These devices are expensive and prone to fouling from ice, but the latter is not generally a problem since a single wintertime setting usually suffices. The devices must be rugged to resist wind loads.

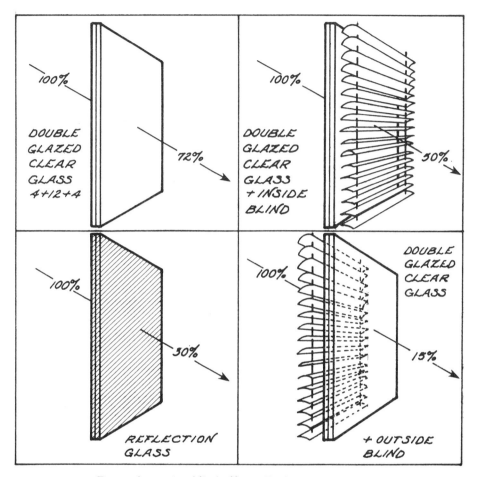

Figure 5.12 External venetian blinds (from: Richard Goder Assoc., Inc., DesPlains, Ill.)

A nice combination of natural and artificial shading is a lattice-work eyebrow covered with deciduous vines. Like the tree canopy that hugs a building, this device's horizontal dimension is short enough to admit the sun underneath the eyebrow in October while the leaves provide shading in September, August, July, and June. Sun can still reach the window through the bare branches in April and May.

A compromise solution is an array of overhead fixed horizontal louvers set at an angle to admit winter sun, while shading the window in the summer. The spaced louvers allow diffuse light to penetrate so natural daylighting levels are maintained inside the room. Summertime heat build-up at the window is avoided, since heat can rise vertically by the windows and through the slats. Fixed, opaque overhangs should be avoided, for they seriously decrease inside natural lighting levels on cloudy days.

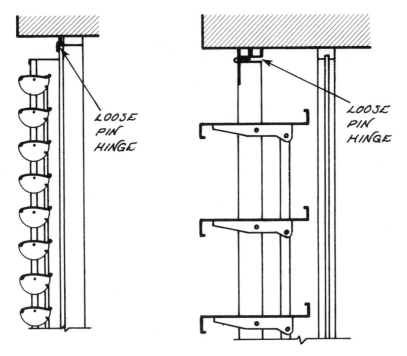

Figure 5.13 External venetian blinds (from Brown Manufacturing Co., Oklahoma City, OK)

Screen devices such as the product shown in Figure 5.14 do an admirable shading job for people who are used to installing insect screens on windows. The external screen is actually a three-dimensional series of mini-louvers that entirely shade the window. Usually the louvers are formed by "punching" an aluminum sheet. The louver dimensions are so fine that the view from inside does not appear striped, but only muted as an ordinary insect screen appears.

A satisfactory shading solution for double glazed windows is upside down louvers with reflectorized upper surfaces between the glazing. Summer sun is reflected back to the outside when the louvers are rotated to the proper angle. The louvers are out of the wind and they stay clean. The view becomes less striped when the slats are narrow (around 1/2 inch). The solution is not ideal since the summer rays do get past one layer of glazing. However, the inner glazing helps to contain the heat build-up that occurs in the air gap.

Any shading device would work ideally if the angle the sun's rays make with the eyebrow, or tree canopy, did not change throughout the day. Of course the angle changes with the movement of the sun, but this change can be minimized by facing the window and its shading device exactly south. This is known as the *profile angle*, the angle between the horizon and the projection of a sun ray in a plane perpendicular to the window (shown in Fig. 5.15). This angle does not vary more

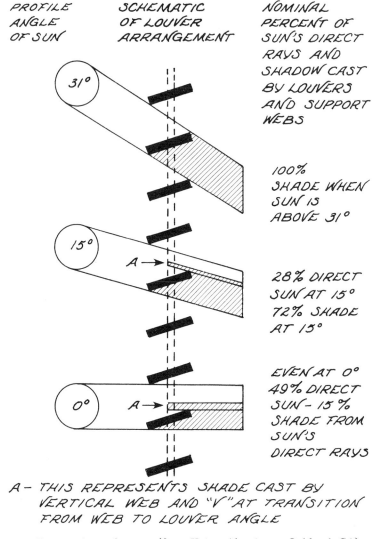

PROFILE
ANGLE
OF SUN

SCHEMATIC
OF LOUVER
ARRANGEMENT

NOMINAL
PERCENT OF
SUN'S DIRECT
RAYS AND
SHADOW CAST
BY LOUVERS
AND SUPPORT
WEBS

31°

100%
SHADE WHEN
SUN IS
ABOVE 31°

15°   A→

28% DIRECT
SUN AT 15°
72% SHADE
AT 15°

0°   A→

EVEN AT 0°
49% DIRECT
SUN — 15%
SHADE FROM
SUN'S
DIRECT RAYS

A — THIS REPRESENTS SHADE CAST BY
VERTICAL WEB AND "V" AT TRANSITION
FROM WEB TO LOUVER ANGLE

Figure 5.14 Louvered metal screen (from Kaiser Aluminum, Oakland, CA)

than five degrees through the day for south facing windows. The profile angle does not vary at all on the Equinox. This can be shown by overlaying the profile angle mask (shown in Fig. 5.16) on the sun paths shown in Figure 3.2. Point the radial line on the overlayed profile mask (labeled "window perpendicular") at true south on the selected sun path diagram. Follow a particular sunpath through a day and note the number of profile angle lines that are crossed. Now rotate the "window perpendicular" line 20° off south and do the same exercise. Notice how much the

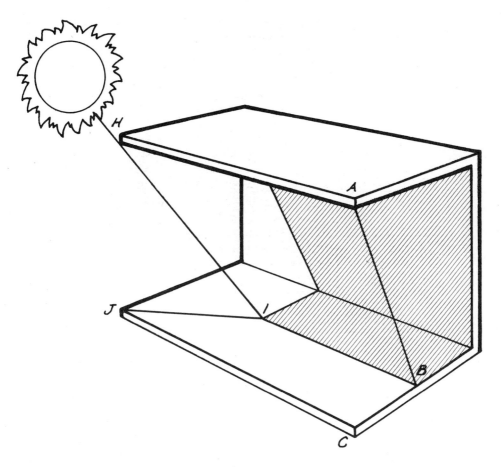

Figure 5.15 Definition of the profile angle (from *The LOF Sun Angle Calculator*, Libbey-Owens-Ford Co., Toledo, Ohio)

profile angle varies for small variations from true south. This shows that it becomes very difficult to control shading throughout the day whenever the window is even slightly off south.

The least ideal shading device is dark colored glazing material. Absorption heating can drive the window temperature up to 110°F which turns the window into a large area radiator. Figure 5.17 shows the slight reduction of heat inflow this approach offers when compared to unshaded glass.

Windows that face east or west also must be shaded in the summer to stop excessive solar gain. Overhanging devices do not work for these orientations, since the sun is low in the sky in the morning and afternoon. Vertical slats that give a northerly view as shown in Figure 5.18 work reasonably well.

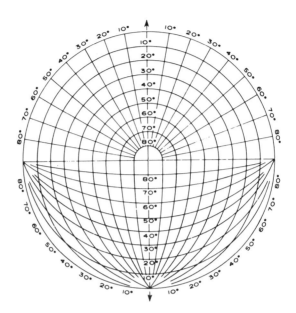

Figure 5.16 Shading mask protractor. The arrow is perpendicular to the window. (from *The Solar Home Book*, Anderson and Riordan, Brick House, Andover, MA)

North facing windows offer the least shading problem. Some summer sun falls on these windows, but the sun is usually so low that even distant trees will shade the window. As noted earlier, one can even accomplish solar heating with north facing windows using the new selective transmittors as glazing materials. The amount of diffuse and reflected solar energy that reaches a north facing window is more than adequate to do a heating job in benign winter climates.

NATURAL VENTILATION

Breezes flow through open windows when the air pressure differs across the openings. When the wind is slowed by a building, a slight overpressure forms on the windward side. A balancing underpressure forms on the leeward side. The underpressures tend to be of lesser magnitudes since the lee side disturbance is distributed over a larger area than the windward side disturbance. The only way a sustained air flow can occur inside a building is to place openings at both the high and low pressure points. In other words, good air movement comes with cross ventilation. Leeward windows should be larger than the windward openings since leeward underpressures are weak. Unfortunately, the wind does not always prevail from a single direction, so opening sizes tend to become uniformly large on all sides of the building.

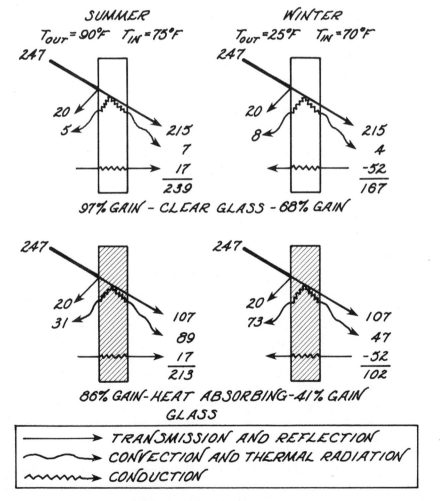

Figure 5.17 Solar heat gains through different types of glass (from *The Solar Home Book*, Anderson and Riordan, Brick House, Andover, MA)

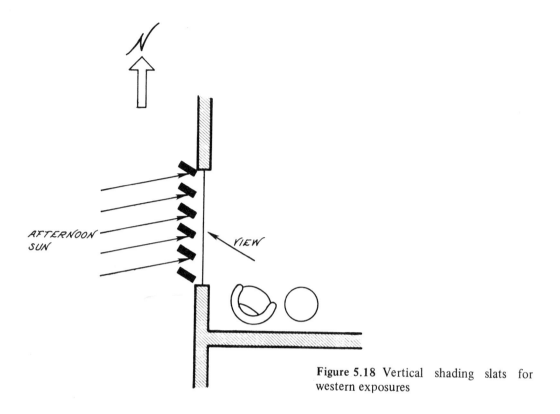

Figure 5.18 Vertical shading slats for western exposures

A more important variable in cross ventilation designs is the vertical placement of the ventilation openings. During the overheated months, any air movement across the body vastly improves thermal comfort. Openings therefore must be designed to maximize the flow of air near the body level.

This is easier said than done, for more times than not air flow can take counter-intuitive bends and cling to the ceiling. Any interior obstruction is likely to throw the flow toward the ceiling, as shown in Figure 5.19. Placing the inlet and outlet windows near the floor height helps, but more stringent steps usually must be taken. Vanes can be used to direct the wind downward, as shown in Figure 5.20, but this positive approach might not be acceptable visually. A variation on this approach is shown in Figure 5.21, where the external shading louvers also help deflect the flow downwards.

Air movement also can be induced by the "stack" or "chimney" effect. Hot air rises, causing cool air to flow in from below to replace it. The larger the distance between the intake and roof top vent, the greater the air flow as given by the following relation where V is the air velocity in feet per minute,

$$V = 9.4\sqrt{h(T_u - T_d)}$$

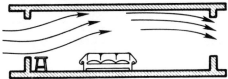

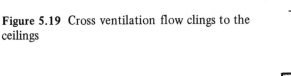

Figure 5.19 Cross ventilation flow clings to the ceilings

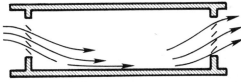

Figure 5.20 Cross ventilation flow directed to the floor with vanes

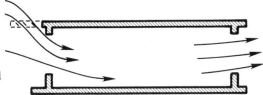

Figure 5.21 External overhanging louvers used to direct flow downward

where

> h = the distance between the intake vent and the exhaust vent, in feet (open upper story windows will short circuit open ground floor windows)
>
> T_u = the average air temperature at the exhaust vent, in °F, and
>
> T_d = the average air temperature at the intake vent, in °F.

For example, if the outdoor temperature is 80°F and the air temperature at the peak of a two story sun space is 100°F, then

$$V = 9.4\sqrt{20 \text{ ft } (100-80)°F)} = 188 \text{ ft per minute.}$$

If the exhaust vent has a cross-sectional area of 10 square feet, then the air flow rate is 188ft/min x 10ft^2, or 1880 cfm. The amount of heat removed is determined by the heat capacity of air, which is 0.018 BTU/ft^3°F. For this example, the heat flow removed in one hour is

$$0.018 \text{ BTU/ft}^3°F \text{ x } 1880 \text{ cfm x } 60 \text{ min/hr x } (100°F-80°F) = 40,608 \text{ BTU/hr}$$

The stack effect is easily overpowered when the wind comes up.

Ventilation and natural daylighting should not be studied independently. Once a lighting model is built, it is a simple proposition to add some scale furniture, some cigarette smoke to the interior of the model, and a fan some distance from the window openings. Turn on the fan and watch the smoke dissipate. If the floor cleared first you are lucky, for natural ventilation flows are always weaving about where least expected.

DAYLIGHTING

One role for windows is to daylight without glare, especially for structures heated directly by the sun. Interior daylighting on cloudy days usually should exceed a daylight factor of 2 to 3 percent to insure visual comfort. Window placement, interior reflectances, and outdoor reflectivity can all affect the lighting levels in a room.

Figure 5.22 shows the effect of changing the placement of the same size window opening under a uniform cloudy sky. High windows allow much better light penetration than low windows. As the window is moved into the ceiling, lighting uniformity increases. High light colored ceilings also help distribute the light.

When a second window is placed on the opposite wall, overall lighting levels are vastly increased, as shown in Figure 5.23. Notice for this example that daylighting from one side gives only adequate light levels for a room depth up to 2.5 times the window height.

Reflectivity of outside and inside surfaces can affect the room daylighting levels as shown in Figures 5.24 and 5.25. For a room sidelit from one side only, an opaque overhang will greatly reduce lighting levels (Fig. 5.26). In effect, an opaque overhang moves the window away from the back wall by a distance equal to the overhang width. One way of overcoming this serious problem is to use external fixed louvers to block summer beam radiation without blocking the entire sky component.

On clear days the extra sunlight striking south facing spaces can be distributed deeper into the room to save on artificial lighting cost. A light shelf (Fig. 5.27) can be used to bring direct light deep into the room while minimizing contrast. The shelf allows the lower glass to be set back for seasonal heat gain control without losing lighting levels. The view is uncluttered and the shelf provides a natural architectural break to define different functions and materials.

GLARE CONTROL

Most glare problems in direct-gain structures result from discomfort glare caused by large windows looking towards the bright sky. Besides using additional windows and light interior colors to lift the lighting levels in the room, several classical solutions exist for minimizing discomfort glare.

Figure 5.22 Window placement effects lighting distribution (from Architecture 4.26 class notes, March 1975, Graduate School of Design, Harvard University)

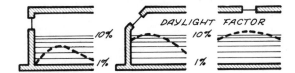

Figure 5.23 The effect of bilateral daylighting compared with unilateral daylighting (from Architecture 4.26 class notes, March 1975, Graduate School of Design, Harvard University)

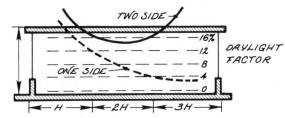

Figure 5.24 The reflectivity of outside surfaces can effect internal natural daylighting (from Architecture 4.26 class notes, March 1975, Graduate School of Design, Harvard University)

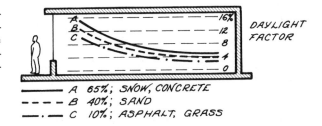

Figure 5.25 The effect of varying the reflectivity of various room surfaces (from Architecture 4.26 class notes, March 1975, Graduate School of Design, Harvard University)

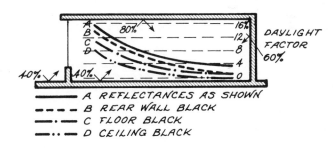

Figure 5.26 The effect of varying the length of an opaque overhang (from Architecture 4.26 class notes, March 1975, Graduate School of Design, Harvard University)

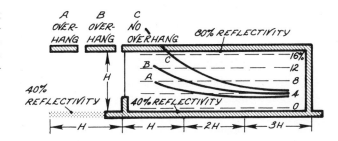

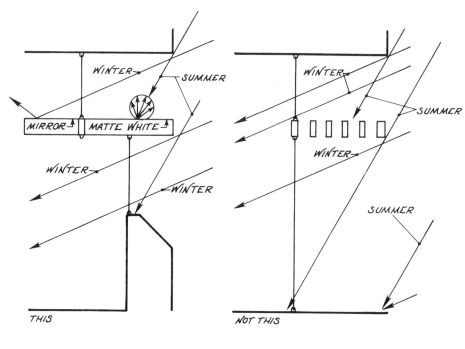

LIGHT SHELF

- REFLECTS SUN AND SKYLIGHT TO CEILING
- LIGHT DEEPER INTO SPACE
- REDUCES CONTRAST
- ALLOWS SETBACK OF GLASS FOR SEASONAL
    GAIN CONTROL
- SHADES LOWER ZONE WHILE MAXIMIZING
    USE OF GROUND REFLECTED LIGHT
    NEAR GLASS
- UNCLUTTERED VIEW
- NATURAL ARCHITECTURAL BREAK TO
    DIVIDE DIFFERENT FUNCTIONS AND
    CONTROL MATERIALS
- OPTIMIZED IF SUN ANGLE (ELEVATION) IS
    CONSTANT (I.E., TVA SOLAR COURT CONCEPT)

Figure 5.27 Proper light shelf design (from Office Communications, William Lam and Assoc., Cambridge, MA)

The splayed reveal (Fig. 5.28) has been used successfully through the ages to ease the transition from the bright outdoors to the darker indoors. Daylight strikes the light colored, angled side walls of the window, reducing the contrast around the window opening. The mullions should be white to reduce contrast at the window.

Figure 5.28 The splayed window reveal

On sunny days, glare problems usually worsen. Large pools of sunlight falling on the floor can cause discomfort glare from high lighting contrast between the sun patch and the surround. One way to avoid this is to make the scene interesting. Distributing plants throughout the floor area is a classical way of creating visual interest. Another way to avoid glare (and the attendant furniture fading problem) is to reflect sunlight overhead at the windows with mirrored louvers, as demonstrated in the MIT Solar 5 building. Since the normal cone of vision does not include the ceiling, the bright areas of sunlight on the ceiling are not as noticeable as sun patches on the floor. The louvered reflectors (Fig. 5.29) must reflect light specularly rather than diffusely so the louvers do not appear as bright sources of light.

Most spaces heated directly by the sun operate better if sunlight enters the room diffusely, rather than specularly, so solar energy is distributed uniformly over the room mass. The ideal diffuser would meet the following requirements:

1. View to the outside cannot be impaired.
2. The diffuser cannot become a bright source of light.
3. Light must be broken up and distributed uniformly.
4. Solar gain must be maintained.
5. Ventilation must be possible.

Of course, no diffuser meets all the listed requirements. In fact, a good diffuser for solar applications has not yet been designed. Patterned glass causes glare because the faceted structure of the glass breaks down the sun disk into thousands of bright pin points of light. Ground glass, or similar translucent products, suffer from one of three problems, depending upon the level of translucency. Nearly transparent glazings, such as the FRP products, enlarge the sun image, making it difficult to avoid looking into the sun. If the diffusion is increased, such as in ground glass, the sun disk spreads out over the whole glass area and the window becomes an intolerably bright light source. If the translucency is lowered to reduce the brightness, most of the solar gain is sacrificed. Low transmission diffusers are formed by

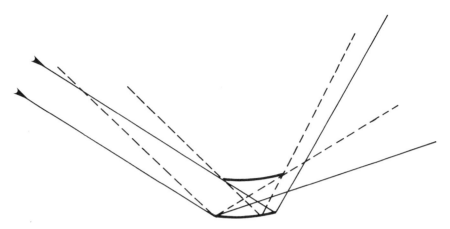

Figure 5.29 Reflectorized louver sun ray diagrams for Nov. 21 through Jan. 21 at 42° latitude

draping canvas over the windows, using lightweight drapes, or stuffing angel hair (a diaphenous glass fiber) between two layers of FRP. Two designs that come close to the ideal diffuser are discussed below.

Upside down mirrored louvers can act as a diffuser when used with a light colored ceiling. The sunlight is not diffused at the window, but merely rerouted towards the ceiling. The ceiling becomes the diffuser by reflecting light in all directions from the white matte surface. Daylighting improves on sunny days because the sunlight reaches the back walls. Outside views are maintained, but the scene appears striped because of the horizontal louvers at the windows. Using narrow louvers minimizes this problem. Solar gain is reduced slightly because of the 10 to 15 percent light absorption that occurs at the mirrored slats, but most of this absorbed heat is usable since the louvers are either inside the room or inside double glazing.

The lighting behavior of the blinds depends on the solar profile angle, just as the shading behavior of an overhang depends on the same angle. A light shelf or louver assembly works best when facing exactly south, since the solar profile angle does not vary more than 5° in a day for this orientation. South facing louvers give the best lighting distribution, as they can be adjusted to compensate for the seasonal variation in profile angle. Normally, the louvers would be adjusted every two weeks to maximize lighting distribution.

Sunlight can be brought in overhead, through clerestories or monitors. The light can be broken up by light colored fixed louvers or an egg crate diffuser (similar to those used for fluorescent fixtures) mounted horizontally in the light well formed by the vertical opening. The diffusers become a bright source of light when the sunlight reflects off the matte finished slats, but the brightness is not very noticeable since it is overhead. This solution definitely interferes with view, but solar gain is not reduced appreciably.

Whatever is used to minimize glare must be studied with a lighting model. Cookbook solutions cannot be applied without first experiencing how the solution looks. Physical models are an inexpensive means of reliably testing for visual comfort.

REFERENCES

1. W. Beckman and J. Duffie, *Solar Engineering of Thermal Processes*, John Wiley & Sons, New York, 1980.

2. J. Holton, "Daylighting of Buildings — A Compendium and Study of its Introduction and Control," NBSIR 76-108, National Bureau of Standards, Washington, D.C., 1976.

3. R. Hopkinson, J. Longmore and P. Petherbridge, *Daylighting*, Heinemann, London, 1966.

4. T. Holzberlein, "Don't Let the Trees Make a Monkey of You," proceedings, 4th Annual Passive Conference, October 1979, International Solar Energy Society.

5. A. Meinel and M. Meinel, *Applied Solar Energy*, Addison-Wesley, Reading, Mass., 1976.

6. V. Olgyay, *Solar Control and Shading Devices*, Princeton University Press, Princeton, 1957.

7. W. Shurcliff, *Thermal Shutters & Shades*, Brick House, Andover, Mass., 1980.

8. K. Ya Kondrat' Yev, *Radiative Heat Exchange in the Atmosphere*, Pergamon Press, Oxford (1965).

Chapter **6**

Complementary Building Elements

Solar collection could not take place without windows in a direct-gain structure, yet glazing is only one of the elements necessary for successful solar heating. Like any other solar collecting system, the building must have a thermal storage element (the building mass), a distribution system (the architectural plan), a thermal barrier to the weather (the building insulation), and a back-up heating system. Each of these elements complements the other and each contributes to thermal comfort in important ways.

MASS

Solar energy flows into a well insulated, direct-gain building four to eight times faster than it is used. This excess heat must be stored for short term use without allowing the indoor air temperature to skyrocket. This is usually done with massive interior building elements that rapidly soak up the solar energy during the day. The same mass releases the heat slowly as needed at night. The mass, in the form of masonry, containerized water, or phase-change material, must be placed carefully in relation to the windows to accomplish this regulatory function.

Placement, Material and Color Choice

Significant solar heating happens when windows are large enough to admit more solar energy than a space needs during the day. Heat absorbing mass must be placed where it can absorb solar energy much faster than it releases it, to prevent over-heating. If a window must be opened to release uncomfortable heat build-up, then the glass area is too large relative to the interior mass. This condition would be acceptable in climates where clear days are unusual, but, for climates where 40 to 80 percent of the days are clear, overheating means wasted energy.

The fastest way to pump heat into thermal storage is to flood it with sunshine; the slowest way is to transfer heat by natural convection. The storage mass must be placed in such a way that it is in sunshine during the day and in position to convect and radiate its heat at night. A room cannot be heated only by natural convection using the low operating temperatures thermal mass usually acquires. The mass must be in the room and have a large exposed area, so it can also heat by long-wave infrared radiation.

Merely placing the mass in direct sunlight does not always work, for the choice of materials and color must be in keeping with the sun's behavior. Thick masonry can store a lot of heat if the energy is applied over a long period so it can conduct into the core. The sun is not up long enough to pump heat into masonry sections greater than 5 inches. Adequate storage capacity can only be achieved with thin, large-area masonry slabs. Typically, the masonry area must be at least five to seven times the area of the window to expose enough of the mass to solar radiation. Table 7.5 in Chapter 7 shows the effective heat content of various masonry materials. Notice very little additional participation is achieved by increasing the masonry thickness beyond 5 to 6 inches. Sunlight has to be diffused in order to strike a mass area that is many times the window area. Several methods for accomplishing this are suggested in Chapter 5. The heat absorbing capacity of the room becomes inde-pendent of color once this much area is used. Seventy percent of the transmitted solar radiation is absorbed in an all-white room when one of the long walls is half glass and facing south.[4] White paint is not a perfect reflector; it absorbs 10 percent of the solar radiation that strikes it. A solar ray entering such a room will undergo many multiple reflections and absorptions before it reaches the window again. The room will absorb more than 80 percent of the entering solar energy if the window wall is less than 50 percent glazed (the room absorption goes above 90 percent when an off-white is used). Light colors are preferred since natural daylighting is enhanced in brightly colored rooms. When the mass area gets this large, it usually means not only the floor, but also the walls, or the ceiling, are masonry. Over-heating never will be an issue in spaces like this if a proper light diffuser is used. But not every building type or budget can afford this much distributed mass. What is one to do when only limited area is available for thermal mass, particularly in carpeted rooms?

Only two choices present themselves when the area available for exposed mass is limited: containerized water storage, or phase-change storage. Water storage works because large thicknesses of water (greater than 4 inches) always participate thermally, since natural convection mixes the water. Phase-change material works because the energy storage capacity is large, even in sections thin enough for good heat transfer (less than one inch). In either case, sunlight is applied to a mass area that is one to three times the window area. This relatively small target must be

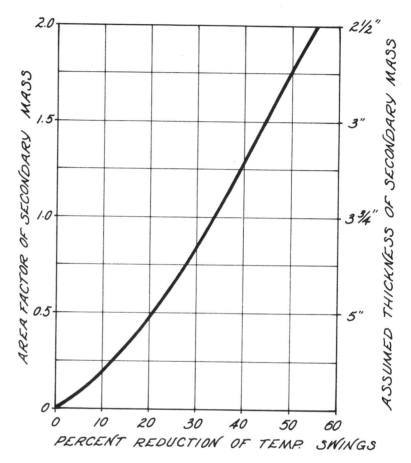

Figure 6.1 Effect of secondary mass on room air temperature swings (from *Passive Solar Heating Design*, Ralph Lebens Applied Science Publishers, London, 1979).

painted a dark color since it is the only mass available for storing solar energy. Dark does not mean black. Usually any color that absorbs up to 75 percent of incident solar energy will do (dark blues, greens, and earth colors).

A third type of mass, known as *secondary mass*, can be used, although it is not as effective as the first two approaches. Any mass radiates infrared energy to other room surfaces once its surface temperature rises. Lightweight materials (i.e., drywall, wood panelling) that intercept this radiation will warm up quickly and contribute to room overheating during the day. Heavier surfaces (i.e., concrete slabs) will absorb most of this reradiated energy for nighttime release. Figure 6.1 shows the effect of a masonry secondary mass when used opposite a dark masonry mass exposed to solar energy. Notice changes in room air temperature are reduced by 30 percent when the secondary mass area approaches the area of the mass in sunlight.

Table 6.1   Mass configurations to avoid overheating in buildings with large solar heating fractions (greater than 50%)

Masonry	*Water or Phase-Change Material*
Only used where sunlight is diffused over mass areas at least 5 to 7 times greater than the window area (4" of concrete will do). Any color will do.	Used where the storage area can only be one to three times the area of the window (5 inches of water will do, or less than 1 inch of phase-change material. The absorbing surfaces must be dark.

A series of rules can be extracted from this discussion on mass sizing and placement.

The table above shows the mass area to use with a given window area to avoid overheating in spaces with large amounts of glass. Rules of thumb for window sizing are given for various underheated climates in Chapter 7. The graphical design methods given in the same chapter can be used to predict the temperature extremes a space will experience for a given mass-to-glass ratio under various weather conditions.

Walls and floors are not the only good locations for thermal mass. The ceiling is also a good candidate. Sunlight can be placed on the ceiling from below with reflectorized louvers or light shelves, or from above with vertical clerestories in the attic space. Although warm air rises and tends to stratify, heat transfer from the ceiling to the room is better than generally thought. The flow of heat by radiation is independent of orientation, but heat flow from convection is reduced when heat flows downward. Nevertheless, the convective heat flow is higher than a fully stratified condition would give because the air currents induced by air infiltration and the convection currents from appliances break up the stratifying layers of air. The combined ceiling to room heat transfer rate for convection and radiation can be as high as 1.6 BTU/hrft^2°F. Nighttime measurements in the MIT Solar 5 building show differences less than 2°F in air temperature between the floor and the 10 foot thermal storage ceiling.

Masonry

The thermal storage effectiveness of masonry varies widely among materials. The amount of heat penetrating the mass and subsequently stored is a function of the mass's density (p), thermal conductivity (k), specific heat (c), and the mass thickness (x). The relationship between these properties can be seen in the nondimensional graph shown in Figure 6.2. The graph shows the progression of a heat wave through a mass where the right side is insulated and the left side is exposed to a sudden step change in temperature. The mass starts out at the temperature indicated by the horizontal line. The line labelled 1 is the temperature distribution through the mass after a time period T, the line labelled 2 shows the temperature after two time periods have expired, and so on. Notice it takes five time periods for

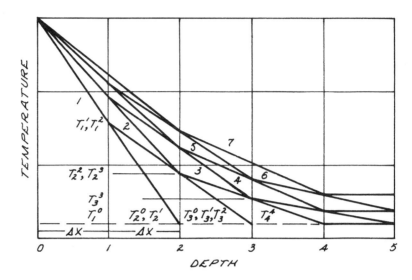

Figure 6.2 Dimensionless temperature profiles in a homogeneous wall with insulation on the right-hand face, when the temperature of the left-hand face is suddenly raised three units. Each curve is labeled with number of expired time periods. (from *Principles of Heat Transfer*, Frank Kreith, International Textbook Co., Scranton, PA, 1958).

a change in temperature on the left side to reach the right side. The length of the time period is related to the properties of the material by the equation

$$T = \frac{x^2 cp}{2k}$$

where x = W/5, and W equals the width of the masonry slab, in feet. Table 6.2 shows the thermal properties for masonry materials and some other building products. Notice every material except wood has a specific heat (c) equal to approximately 0.2 BTU/lb°F. Thus, the controlling parameters are conductivity (k), and density (p). A short time period, T, means more of the material participates in a given time frame. This time period, T, for 6 inches of pine is

$$\frac{(\frac{0.5 \text{ ft}}{5})^2 (0.67 \text{ BTU/lb°F}) \ 31 \text{ lb/ft}^3}{2(0.06 \text{ BTU/hrft°F})} = 1.73 \text{ hrs}$$

The time period for 6 inches of concrete is

$$\frac{(\frac{0.5 \text{ ft}}{5})^2 (0.20 \text{ BTU/lb°F}) \ 144 \text{ lb/ft}^2}{2(0.54 \text{ BTU/hrft°F})} = 0.27 \text{ hrs}$$

Thus, a given temperature pulse will penetrate 6 inches of concrete 6.5 times faster

TABLE 6.2 Thermal properties of various building materials from: *Principles of Heat Transfer*, Frank Kreith, International Textbook Co. Scranton, 1958.

Material	Average Temperature (F)	Conductance k (Btu/hr ft F)	Specific Heat c (Btu/lb$_m$F)	Density p (lb$_m$/cu ft)
Insulating Materials				
Asbestos	32	0.087	0.25	36
	392	0.12	—	36
Cork	86	0.025	0.04	10
Cotton, fabric	200	0.046		
Diatomaceous earth, powdered	100	0.030	0.21	14
	300	0.036	—	
	600	0.046	—	26
Molded pipe covering	400	0.051	—	
	1600	0.088	—	
Glass wool				
Fine	20	0.022	—	
	100	0.031	—	1.5
	200	0.043	—	
Packed	20	0.016	—	
	100	0.022	—	6.0
	200	0.029	—	
Hair felt	100	0.027	—	8.2
Kaolin insulating brick	932	0.15	—	27
	2102	0.26	—	
Kaolin insulating firebrick	392	0.05	—	19
	1400	0.11	—	
85% magnesia	32	0.032	—	17
	200	0.037	—	17
Rock wool	20	0.017	—	8
	200	0.030	—	
Rubber	32	0.087	0.48	75
Building Materials				
Brick				
Fire-clay	392	0.58	0.20	144
	1832	0.95		
Masonry	70	0.38	0.20	106
Zirconia	392	0.84	—	304
	1832	1.13	—	
Chrome brick	392	0.82	—	246
	1832	0.96		

(Table 6.2 continued on next page)

TABLE 6.2 *(Continued)*

Material	Average Temperature (F)	Conductance k (Btu/hr ft F)	Specific Heat c (Btu/lb$_m$F)	Density p (lb$_m$/cu ft)
Concrete				
Stone	~70	0.54	0.20	144
10% moisture	~70	0.70	–	140
Glass, window	~70	~0.45	0.2	170
Limestone, dry	70	0.40	0.22	105
Sand				
Dry	68	0.20	–	95
10% H$_2$O	68	0.60	–	100
Soil				
Dry	70	~0.20	0.44	–
Wet	70	~1.5	–	–
Wood				
Oak ⊥ to grain	70	0.12	0.57	51
‖ to grain	70	0.20	0.57	51
Pine ⊥ to grain	70	0.06	0.67	31
‖ to grain	70	0.14	0.67	31
Ice	32	1.28	0.46	57

than 6 inches of wood. Notice it takes 5 time periods x 0.27 (or 1-1/3) hours for the heat wave to reach the other side of a 6 inch concrete slab (for a concrete slab of double thickness, the time period would be 4 times as long, or 5-1/3 hours).

The amount of heat stored in the material is given by the area under any given temperature profile times cpLH (where L and H are the length and height of the slab of width W). If both the wood and concrete slab go through five time periods, so their temperature profiles are the same, then the heat contained in the concrete will be proportional to a cp of (0.2) x (144 lbs/ft^2) = 28.8 BTU/ft$^{3\circ}$F, and the heat contained in the wood will be proportional (0.67 BTU/lb°F) x (31 lbs/ft$^{2\circ}$F) = 20.8 BTU/ft$^{3\circ}$F. The concrete can hold 40 percent more heat, and it acquires the heat 6.5 times faster. Thus, concrete is effectively 1.4 x 6.5, or 9.1, times better than wood in acquiring and storing heat. Some masonry materials are even better than concrete. Magnesium brick has a conductivity (k) of 2.20 BTU/hrft°F and a p of 120 lbs/ft^3 (c still is 0.2 BTU/ft°F). The time period for this material is six times greater than ordinary concretes and, although its heat content is 69 percent of concrete, the effective participation of the special brick is four times better than concrete. Adobe, with a heat content equal to 88 percent of concrete and a penetration time 64 percent slower than concrete, is one of the worst masonry materials for storing heat.

Material choices make a very large difference in thermal storage effectiveness. We can see that the time it takes to penetrate thick masonry sections is relatively long. Using thin sections over large areas illuminated with diffuse solar energy can overcome this limitation.

Phase-Change Material

Phase-change material can soak up direct solar radiation fast enough to prevent space overheating when only a limited area is available for thermal storage. The material is lighter in weight and consumes less volume than the water storage alternative. Several varieties of phase-change material are now on the market.

Any material that changes state (phase) from a solid to a liquid (or, for that matter, from a liquid to gas) absorbs great quantities of heat in the process. The same heat is liberated as the material solidifies. Where ordinary materials such as masonry must rise in temperature to absorb heat, a phase-change material can absorb heat at nearly constant temperatures. Any of this material placed in a room absorbs solar energy without getting hot if the phase-change temperature is near room temperature. This means the room cannot overheat, since the only way room air can turn hot is by coming in contact with hot surfaces. Many materials can perform this way; organics, and salt hydrates are examples of phase-change materials that are on (or near) the market.

Some materials melt congruently; that is, all the material turns to a liquid. Others melt incongruently, where some solid material still remains in the melt. These last materials are prone to separation difficulties when the solid is a different density than the liquid. The separation can lead to reduced lifetime of the material. Packaging techniques overcome these problems, while still keeping the cost down, by packaging the material in sections thin enough (usually less than 3/8 inch thick) to allow crystallization by diffusion and by adding thickeners.

Typical storage densities range from 40 to 80 BTUs per pound (the materials usually weigh 90 to 110 pounds per cubic foot). Most phase-change materials must be packaged in thin sections (less than one inch) to promote heat transfer, since most of these materials do not conduct heat very well. This means 200 to 500 BTUs/ft^2 can be placed in radiation contact with a room. This heat capacity is larger than the daily solar intake on a horizontal surface behind most glazing systems. These materials can be formulated to change state at one of many temperature choices, typically between 65°F and 90°F. Usually 73°F to 75°F phase-change temperatures are used in solar heating applications. This temperature is low enough to control overheating, and high enough to provide radiant heating at night.

One very effective, inexpensive way of placing a phase-change material in radiation contact with a room is to place it in the ceiling. The material is bagged in plastic coated foil pouches measuring 3/4 inch thick by 2 feet by 1 foot. The bags are placed on top of a plaster ceiling. Any board product that weighs at least 90 lbs/ft^3, such as cement asbestos board, can be used instead of plaster (Fig. 6.3). This high density ceiling should conduct heat at least twice as well as ordinary gypsum board. The material must be attached to the joists with drywall screws spaced every 8 to 10 inches since the bag weighs 5 lbs/ft^2. The bags can receive solar radiation from above (through an attic space), or from below as in the MIT Solar 5

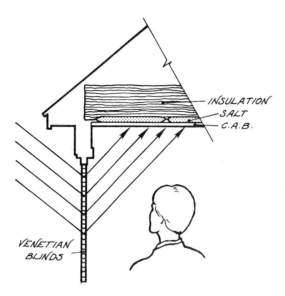

Figure 6.3 Use of bagged phase change material in the ceiling

house. They can also store various forms of auxiliary heat (see the section on auxiliary heat later in this chapter).

It is difficult to charge most phase-change materials with sunlight when the material is packaged in containers thicker than one inch. These larger containers are really designed to acquire heat via forced convection and should not be considered to be radiant heat sinks.

The area of sunlit phase-change material required for a given window size is between one and three times the window area, depending on the phase-change storage capacity and the lighting scheme. Adjustable louvers like the ones demonstrated in the MIT Solar 5 building will light a ceiling area equal to two times the louver area at any instant. The same design methods introduced in Chapter 7 for predicting room temperature fluctuations can be used to size the phase-change area necessary to prevent overheating by using a simple assumption. The design method assumes the heat storage material absorbs heat sensibly; that is, the material must rise in temperature to absorb heat. Actually, any phase-change material does absorb heat over a limited temperature range, usually over a 5° to 10°F range. The design method can be adopted for phase-change materials simply by conservatively assuming the entire storage capacity of the material is developed over an 8°F range. Divide the BTUs stored per square foot by 8°F to get the effective volumetric heat capacity of the material for use with the design method introduced in Chapter 7.

Many phase-change materials will appear on the market in as many different packages. They will soon be as much a part of a builder's material vocabulary as the words "concrete" and "block."

Water

Using containerized water for thermal storage can sometimes be an attractive alternative to phase-change material when sunlight cannot be diffused to distributed masonry. If the direct rays of the sun strike the water containers from the side or from below, then natural convection will mix the water so all the water participates as thermal storage. The higher specific heat and mixing potential of water means four times the heat can be stored over an equal volume of masonry.

Enough water must be placed in the wall or ceiling containers to prevent overheating of the adjacent space. Between three and five gallons* of water per square foot of south facing, vertical double glazing are required to limit the room air temperature to a 13°F swing (the water will go through an 18°F swing). The 3 gal/ft^2 of glass figure is used in 6000 degree day climates with moderate amounts of sunshine, as in New England; the 5 gal/ft^2 is used in 6000 degree day climates with brilliant sunshine, as in New Mexico. If a water wall is used, assume it is not directly behind the southern glazing where thermal back losses are high. The water wall should be placed deep in the room where it is exposed to the entire thermal load. This can be accomplished by sunlighting the water wall with overhead monitor skylights.

Water containerization is a difficult job that easily can lead to unsightly spaces. The water wall presents a heavy load over a narrow line that usually must be reinforced to take the weight. Various containers have been used. Sealed steel 55 gallon drums, and steel culverts with plates welded on the ends, have been installed directly in the heated space and painted dark colors. Corrosion will not be a problem if the containers are filled with water so no air can reach the inside walls. For large containers, some air inside acting as an accumulator is desirable, so the container does not stress when the water expands with the application of heat. In these cases, a coat of high quality epoxy paint will save the interior from rust. If the top seal is leaky, a thin layer of mineral oil floated on the surface of the water will retard evaporation. Flexible plastic liners should be avoided since they can rip open at unsupported corners. Glass reinforced polyester sheet is sometimes bent into a cylinder and sealed at the sides and bottom. Some commercial versions of this have sprung pinhole leaks which, although not catastrophic, are annoying. Usually pans are placed under the tubes to collect the dribbles until a repair can be made. Stackable plastic and metal containers that measure approximately one foot high are also available. The faces are plain and when stacked form a textured wall. A high heat conducting overcoat material must be used if any of these containers are veneered to enhance their appearance. No air gaps between the veneer and the containers can be tolerated, because they act as insulators. Even two inches of concrete veneer will seriously detract from the water wall's performance. Thin reinforced plaster can be considered. Containers for ceilings have not been de-

---

*One cubic foot of water = 7.48 gallons = 62.4lbs.

veloped yet, but heat sealed bags of plastic or sealed plastic milk bottles would work well. High density board products can be used to support containers, but the boards must be reinforced with screws every five inches to take the weight. All containers in these kinds of spaces (or the spaces themselves) must be rodent proof, or squirrels, rats, and other creatures will gnaw into the void during the winter to keep warm and drink the water. In all cases, an algicide (either copper sulphate or chlorine) must be added to stop growths.

Rock Bed Storage

Overheating never need be a problem when heating a space directly with the sun. The design methods introduced in the next chapter can be used to build a space that acquires the majority of its space heating needs from the sun without getting too hot. Nevertheless, in certain cases overheating is unavoidable, such as in greenhouses, where the requirement for very large glass areas overrides the need for thermal comfort. It is tempting to pull the 90°F air off the greenhouse peak with a fan and deposit it in a rock bed for nighttime withdrawal. In some climates mildew will form in the rock bed, rendering it useless. If the climate is dry, the approach will work only if the rock bed is in radiant contact with the space to be heated at night. Typically, this direct thermal coupling can be achieved by building a horizontal rock bed directly under a four inch concrete floor that is not entirely insulated with rugs. The rock bed container becomes the floor surface. One should not attempt to discharge the rock bed using forced convection; rather, depend on large area radiant discharge and natural convection at the floor surface to do the job. The average temperature of a rock bed rarely exceeds 76°F when charged with air at 90°F. Air temperatures at the exit will rarely exceed 75°F when heat is removed by forced convection in the opposite direction of the charging flow. Air at this low temperature feels unpleasantly cool due to the elevated velocities necessary to remove the heat. But a large area floor surface at 76°F does transfer heat to the room comfortably, since the heat exchange mechanism is mostly radiant.

The amount of heat a rock bed can store is proportional to its volume. The maximum heat capacity of a rock bed is 20 BTU/ft³°F, assuming 42 percent of the bed is void due to the rock packing. Not all the rock bed volume participates equally in storing heat, however. Temperatures fall off exponentially along the direction of heat flow, as in the concrete wall case.

Generally one can assume the equivalent uniform temperature elevation in the rock bed after several hours of charging is one-third to one-half the difference between the inlet and outlet air temperature. For large rock beds, the outlet temperature is the daily average room temperature. The inlet temperature from a greenhouse peak can be 80°F to 90°F for six hours a day. For a typical air temperature difference of 15°F between inlet and outlet, a rock bed will store $\frac{20 \text{ BTU/ft}^3°\text{F} \times 15°\text{F}}{3}$, or 100 BTU/ft³. The amount of heat available for deposit in the rock bed is generally one-third to one-half of the net solar energy deposited in

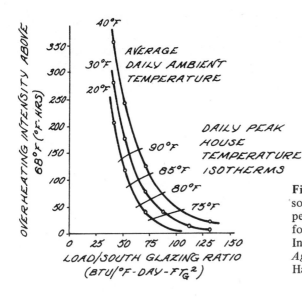

Figure 6.4 Overheating intensity vs. load/ south glazing ratio with daily peak temperature isotherms in three winter climates for a conventional light mass house, TEA, Inc., Harrisville, January, 1979 (from *Solar Age*, December 1979, Solar Vision Inc., Harrisville, NH).

the green house.[3] Dividing this figure by the volumetric heat capacity of the rock bed (100 BTU/ft³) determines the size of the bed. The amount of air circulated by the fan during the charging cycle is usually limited by the duct size used to bring the air down from the greenhouse peak. Air velocities in the ducts should not exceed 800 feet/min if silent operation is required. The majority of the pressure drop due to friction is generated in the ducts and not the rock bed when operating near this limit. The interested reader can find the fan horsepower necessary to power air through a given duct diameter in *ASHRAE Fundamentals*. Generally, operations with duct velocities under 800 feet/min will not call for fan horsepower greater than 1/2 horsepower.

What To Do When Mass Is Not Affordable

Any added construction cost in today's competitive home building market can spell no sale for a builder. In other words, many homeowners cannot afford to add mass to a residence, no matter what the form of the material. The only way to directly solar heat a lightweight structure like the so-called platform frame building is to limit the size of south facing windows so overheating does not occur on clear days. A very nice method for sizing windows in a case like this has been formulated by the folks at Total Environmental Action in New Hampshire. Figure 6.4 shows their graph for determining a south glazing area.

The figure is used by selecting a daily ambient temperature curve closest to the conditions for the given site. Table 6.3 shows the remaining weather conditions assumed for each of the three curves. March is a good month to use for average outdoor temperatures because the March average temperature is close to the heating season average outdoor temperature. Next select a tolerable peak indoor air temper-

TABLE 6.3   Assumed Weather Conditions for TEA overheating curves

Three typical average winter days were defined by three average daily ambient temperatures, their daily swings, and clear day insolation through double glazing as noted:

TYPICAL WEATHER

Winter Daily Average Ambient Temperature	*Average Temperature Swing*	*Clear Day Noon Insolation Through Double Glazing $BTU/hr/ft_g^2$*
20°F	±8°F	231
30°F	±8°F	233
40°F	±8°F	232

ature and find the corresponding intersecting temperature curve. The intersection is followed vertically downward to select a number from the horizontal axis, labelled *load/south glazing ratio*. For example, a peak indoor temperature of 80°F and an average outdoor air temperature of 30°F gives a *load/south glazing ratio* of 76 BTU/ft²°F. To find the corresponding south glass area, divide this number into the building heat loss rate given in units of BTU/°Fday. Table 7.2 in Chapter 7 shows recommended daily building heat loss rates per square foot of heated area for various climates. Continuing the example, the loss rate in the Boston climate is 7.1 BTU/°Fdayft². This converts to a total heat loss rate of 11,360 BTU/°Fday if house is 1600 square feet. Dividing 11,360 BTU/°Fday by 76 BTU°Fft² (from the design curve) gives a maximum south glass area of 150 square feet. A larger area of glass would cause the indoor area temperature in the wood frame, "massless" house to exceed 80°F. These curves assume no internal gains from lights or appliances occur during a sunny day and the thermostat is set at 68°F. The overheating intensity index shown on the vertical scale is the number of hours times the degrees above the 68°F thermostat setting occuring on a sunny day. These curves quickly can tell the designer how to avoid a hot-box situation while still collecting a reasonable amount of solar heat. Up to 30 percent of a well insulated house's heating load can be supplied by the sun when south windows are sized by this method.

INSULATION

The emerging energy conservation building codes call for levels of thermal insulation in new construction that were unheard of only a few years ago in all but pioneering solar buildings. New super-insulation products are appearing to meet this demand. These products should be used only when their added insulation is in keeping with the total thermal performance of the building. It does not make sense to have R-30 walls when the air infiltration rate is one air change per hour, or when the window area exceeds 35 percent of the floor area. A perspective on the relative thermal importance of each building component must be maintained. If the window performance is improved with nighttime thermal insulation or with selective transmitters, then the R-value of the wall can increase.

Buildings easily can be built tightly enough to keep air infiltration between 0.4 and 0.5 air changes per hour in the winter. Odor build-up becomes a problem below this rate. It is possible to build structures with rates of 0.1 air change per hour using building systems common in Scandinavia; however, forced ventilation is required to bring in fresh air. This approach will make eminent sense when counterflow air heat exchangers (and the associated duct work) are designed to resist ice formation, and become inexpensive enough to pay for themselves in five years. Then, the outgoing warm, moist room air can be coaxed into giving up its heat to the incoming cold fresh air. The lower ventilation heat loss would justify higher wall and ceiling R values. This, in turn, makes it possible to reduce the window area to virtually nothing and heat the residence solely on the internal gains from light and appliances. This defensive approach to energy conservation works, but it also removes the joy of natural daylighting, and severs the connection to the outdoors. However, new building product technologies, like the selective transmitters, will also make it possible to conserve as much energy by opening the building to the outdoors.

The emerging state energy conservation building codes will dictate the appropriate levels of insulation for the near future. Insulation techniques that meet these standards vary with location in the building. Below-grade insulation materials are not dealing with the same problems as the more familiar wall and ceiling insulators.

Crawl Spaces, Walls and Ceilings

Most wall and ceiling insulation is permeable to water vapor. In certain situations, water can condense in the material and turn the insulation into a worthless, soggy mass. The surrounding wooden structure would then succumb to rot. This was never a problem with older buildings. The old sidings were not particularly air tight, and loose fill insulation was used, if at all. Any water build-up would simply evaporate. If a building is sheathed with a relatively low permeable material, such as rigid board insulation, then any water condensing in the wall cannot readily vent away and rot begins. This normally is overcome by using a vapor barrier of 6-mil polyethylene on the inside wall to prevent water vapor from entering the wall in the first place. (In the winter, the water content in room air is always higher than outside since water is added internally by people, washing machines, combustion processes, and cooking.) The seams in the vapor barrier overlap and are tight, particularly at electrical boxes that pierce the inner wall. The basic rule in an underheated climate is: always use the lowest permeable material on the inside wall, with the highest permeable material on the outside so water can leave the wall. Table 6.4 gives a list of permeation rates for common building products. The most conservative construction practice is to omit the plumbing in weather walls so vapor barrier penetrations are minimized. The only openings left for water vapor are at the edges of electrical boxes, doors, and windows. Leaks at these edges can be minimized by

TABLE 6.4 Permeance and Permeability of Materials to Water Vapor[a] (From ASHRAE, Handbook of Fundamentals, 1972)

Material	Permeance (Perm)	Resistance (Rep)	Permeability (Perm-in.)	Resistance/in. (Rep/in.)
Materials used in construction:				
Concrete (1:2:4 mix)			3.2	0.31
Brick masonry (4-in. thick)	0.8[f]	1.3		
Concrete block (8-in., cored, limestone aggregate)	2.4[f]	0.4		
Tile masonry, glazed (4-in. thick)	0.12[f]	8.3		
Asbestos cement board (0.2-in. thick)	0.54[d]	1.8		
Plaster on metal lath (0 75 in.)	15[f]	0.067		
Plaster on wood lath	11[e]	0.091		
Plaster on plain gypsum lath (with studs)	20[f]	0.050		
Gypsum wall board (0.375 in., plain)	50[f]	0.020		
Gypsum sheathing (0.5 in., asphalt impreg.)			20[d]	0.050
Structural insulating board (sheathing qual.)			20-50[f]	0.050-0.020
Structural insulating board (interior, uncoated, 0.5 in.)	50-90[f]	0.020-0.011		
Hardboard (0.125 in., standard)	11[f]	0.091		
Hardboard (0.125 in., tempered)	5[f]	0.2		
Built-up roofing (hot mopped)	0.0			
Wood, sugar pine			0.4-5.4[f,b]	2.5-019
Plywood (douglas fir, exterior glue, 0.25 in. thick)	0.7[f]	1.4		
Plywood (douglas fir, interior glue, 0.25 in. thick)	1.9[f]	0.53		
Acrylic, glass fiber reinforced sheet, 56 mil	0.12[d]	8.3		
Polyester, glass fiber reinforced sheet, 48 mil	0.05[d]	20		

Thermal insulations:				
Air (still)			120[f]	0.0083
Cellular glass			0.0[d]	α
Corkboard			2.1-2.6[d] 9.5[e]	0.48-0.38,0.11
Mineral wool (unprotected)			116[e]	0.0086
Expanded polyurethane (R-11 blown) board stock			0.4-1.6[d]	2.5-0.62
Expanded polystyrene—extruded			1.2[d]	0.83
Expanded polystyrene—bead			2.0-5.8[d]	0.50-0.17
Unicellular synthetic flexible rubber foam			0.02-0.15[d]	50-6.7
Plastic and metal foils and films[c]				
Aluminum foil (1 mil)	0.0[d]			
Aluminum foil (0.35 mil)	0.05[d]	20		
Polyethylene (2 mil)	0.16[d]	6.3		3100
Polyethylene (4 mil)	0.08[d]	12.5		3100
Polyethylene (6 mil)	0.06[d]	17		3100
Polyethylene (8 mil)	0.04[d]	25		3100
Polyethylene (10 mil)	0.03[d]	33		3100
Polyester (1 mil)	0.7[d]	1.4		
Cellulose acetate (125 mil)	0.4[d]	2.5		
Polyvinylchloride, unplasticized (2 mil)	0.68[d]	1.5		
Polyvinylchloride plasticized (4 mil)	0.8-1.4[d]	1.3-0.72		

Table 6.4 Permeance and Permeability of Materials to Water Vapor[a] (continued)

Material	Permeance (Perms)			Resistance [i] (Rep)		
	Dry-Cup	Wet-Cup	Other	Dry-Cup	Wet-Cup	Other
Building paper, felts, roofing papers[g]						
Duplex sheet, asphalt laminated, aluminum foil one side (43)[h]	0.002	0.176		500	5.8	
Saturated and coated roll roofing (326)[h]	0.05	0.24		20	4.2	
Kraft paper and asphalt laminated, reinforced 30-120-30 (34)[h]	0.03	1.8		3.3	0.55	
Blanket thermal insulation back up paper, asphalt coated (31)[h]	0.04	0.6-4.2		2.5	1.7-0.24	
Asphalt-saturated and coated vapor barrier paper (43)[h]	0.2-0.3	0.6		5.0-3.3	1.7	
Asphalt-saturated but not coated sheathing paper (22)[h]	3.3	20.2		0.3	0.05	
15-lb asphalt felt (70)[h]	1.0	5.6		1.0	0.18	
15-lb tar felt (70)[h]	4.0	18.2		0.25	0.055	
Single-kraft, double (16)[h]	31	42		0.032	0.024	
Liquid-applied coating materials						
Paint – 2 coats						
Asphalt paint on plywood	0.3-0.5					
Aluminum varnish on wood		0.4			2.5	
Enamels on smooth plaster			0.5-1.5	3.3-2.0		2.0-0.66
Primers and sealers on interior insulation board			0.9-2.1			1.1-0.48
Various primers plus 1 coat flat oil paint on plaster			1.6-3.0			0.63-0.33
Flat paint on interior insulation board			4			0.2
Water emulsion on interior insulation board			30-85			0.03-0.012

Paint — 3 coats

Exterior paint, white lead and oil on wood siding	0.3-1.0	3.3-1.0
Exterior paint, white lead-zinc oxide and oil on wood	0.9	1.1
Styrene-butadiene latex coating, 2 oz/sq ft	5.5	0.18
Polyvinyl acetate latex coating, 4 oz/sq ft	5.5	0.18
Chloro-sulfonated polyethylene mastic, 3.5 oz/sq ft	1.7	0.59
7.0 oz/sq ft	0.06	16
Asphalt cut-back mastic, 1/16 in., dry	0.14	7.2
3/16 in., dry	0.0	–
Hot melt asphalt, 2 oz/sq ft	0.5	2
3.5 oz/sq ft	0.1	10

---

[a]Table 1 gives the water vapor transmission rates of some representative materials. The data are provided to permit comparisons of materials; but in the selection of vapor barrier materials, exact values for permeance or permeability should be obtained from the manufacturer of the materials under consideration or secured as a result of laboratory tests. A range of values shown in the table indicated variations among mean values for materials that are similar but of different density, orientation, lot or source. The values are intended for design guidance and should not be used as design or specification data. The compilation is from a number of sources; values from dry-cup and wet-cup methods were usually obtained from investigations using ASTM E96 and C355; values shown under *others* were obtained from investigations using such techniques as *two-temperature, special cell,* and *air-velocity*. Values included were obtained from Ref 8, 10, 12, 13 and other sources.

[b]Depending on construction and direction of vapor flow.

[c]Usually installed as vapor barriers, although sometimes used as exterior finish and elsewhere near cold side where special considerations are then required for warm side barrier effectiveness.

[d]Dry-cup method.

[e]Wet-cup method.

[f]Other than dry- or wet-cup method.

[g]Low permeance sheets used as vapor barriers. High permeance used elsewhere in construction.

[h]Basic weight in lb per 500 ft^2.

[i]Resistance and resistance/in. values have been calculated as the reciprocal of the permeance and permeability values, respectively.

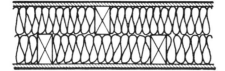

Figure 6.5 Staggered stud construction to reduce thermal bridging

running the vapor barrier right over the rough opening and attaching window and door mouldings over the barrier. Only when the window finish carpentry is complete should the vapor barrier be cut away to expose the window. Some builders go one step further by venting the sheathing. Staggered 2 inch by 1/2 inch battens are nailed over the last layer of insulation, with the weather sheathing nailed over this. Vents to the outside are provided at the top and bottom of the wall so outdoor air can slowly move over the outer layer of insulation to dry it. Attic spaces above the ceiling insulation should always be vented to the outside to remove water that inevitably leaks through the shingles and to keep the house cool in the summer.

Thermal bridging by stud work and joists can sometimes short circuit the thermal insulation between the structure. Although wood does not cause too much of a problem (it does make 6 inch thick fiberglass batt behave like 5.5 inch), steel studding can be a thermal disaster. Six inches of fiber glass will only act like 1 to 2 inches of insulation when wind gauge steel studs are used on 16 inch centers. To stop such extreme thermal bridging, one inch wood battens are run at right angles to the stud work on both faces to hold the sheathing material off the steel. This greatly reduces the contact area over the faces of the studs, which then reduces the heat flow through this area. Using staggered studs as shown in Figure 6.5 is a better solution; or, the entire outer wall can be sheathed with rigid insulation.

Slab on Grade and Basements

Basement walls should be insulated on the exterior with 2 inches of rigid insulation. Closed cell Styrofoam SM™ can be used because it resists water absorption and attack by grubs and other living things. The insulation must extend at least 5 feet below grade. The soil will stabilize at room temperature below this level. Vapor barriers still must be used on the room side of the wall. The board insulation must be clad to resist ultra violet attack and abrasion when it extends above grade. Reinforced stucco or other outdoor plasters will do the job.

A basement floor, or a slab on grade, will need a 1-inch layer of insulation board under the slab if the water table is within 10 feet. Otherwise the damp soil will rapidly draw the slab's heat away. Polyethylene sheet should be placed between the board insulation and the slab to stop the passage of water.

A slab on grade perimeter should always be insulated to lower heat losses and to prevent frost heaving. Normally, 2 inch thick insulation covers the outside of the footing down to the frost line. A more economical placement which also prevents frost heaving is shown in Figure 6.6. Here board insulation extends downward 1.5 feet, then turns 90° to run horizontally for 4 feet. The lengths of the heat flow

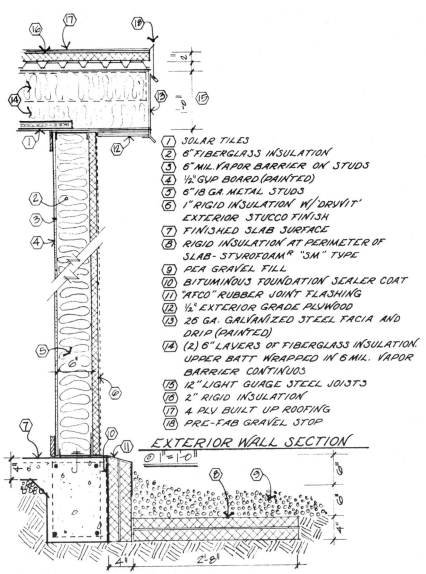

1. SOLAR TILES
2. 6" FIBERGLASS INSULATION
3. 6" MIL. VAPOR BARRIER ON STUDS
4. 1/2" GYP BOARD (PAINTED)
5. 6" 18 GA. METAL STUDS
6. 1" RIGID INSULATION W/ 'DRYVIT' EXTERIOR STUCCO FINISH
7. FINISHED SLAB SURFACE
8. RIGID INSULATION AT PERIMETER OF SLAB - STYROFOAM^R "SM" TYPE
9. PEA GRAVEL FILL
10. BITUMINOUS FOUNDATION SEALER COAT
11. "AFCO" RUBBER JOINT FLASHING
12. 1/2" EXTERIOR GRADE PLYWOOD
13. 26 GA. GALVANIZED STEEL FACIA AND DRIP (PAINTED)
14. (2) 6" LAYERS OF FIBERGLASS INSULATION. UPPER BATT WRAPPED IN 6 MIL. VAPOR BARRIER CONTINUOS
15. 12" LIGHT GUAGE STEEL JOISTS
16. 2" RIGID INSULATION
17. 4 PLY BUILT UP ROOFING
18. PRE-FAB GRAVEL STOP

EXTERIOR WALL SECTION

@ 1" = 1'-0"

Figure 6.6 A perimeter insulation detail (from *MIT Solar Building 5: The Second year's Performance*, T. Johnson *et al.,* MIT Department of Architecture, Cambridge, MA 1979).

paths are the same as in conventional placements, but excavation costs are lowered since the footings only go down 1.5 feet. The horizontal insulation is back filled with soil to protect it from ultra violet exposure. This method of reducing the heat flow from a slab has been used successfully in Scandinavia for more than ten years. This method of insulation is also recommended for basement walls subjected to freezing temperatures. Merely placing internal vertical insulation adjacent to the wall causes the soil outside this wall to freeze and expand and causes the wall to rupture.

FLOOR PLANS AND ORGANIZATION

Passive solar heating is not appropriate for every residence. A typical 800 square foot city apartment in the Northeast United States, with a corridor on one side, a weather wall on the other side, and more apartments on the remaining sides uses less than 100 gallons of oil per year for heating. Improving the insulation in the wall would lower the consumption to 75 gallons per year. The heating bill is low because there is very little wall area through which to lose heat, and the internal gains from people and appliances are relatively high. Solar heating becomes appropriate when there are at least two surfaces exposed to the weather. Townhouses, row houses, and garden apartments have even higher heating loads. What type of spatial arrangements lend themselves to passive solar heating of these building types?

Direct-gain passive heating really is radiant heating where infrared rays bounce throughout a space. Open plan organization promotes this infrared traffic. Living, dining, and perhaps the kitchen become one large space that shares a southern exposure. Low walls or furniture can help define the space. The same open plan organization promotes natural ventilation when openings can be placed in opposite weather walls. Daylighting also is improved by opening the spaces. Each residential building type has organizational issues of its own.

Apartments

Apartments are characterized by a single level, or floor, and by a lack of access to a roof for solar heating and daylighting. Desirable flow-through organization (an organization that permits cross-ventilation) can be accomplished by repetitious vertical circulation (stair wells) or by the skip-stop organization (See Fig. 6.7). Living and dining areas can share the southern exposure. Storage mass can be added economically in this limited south facing area by using phase-change material. The bedrooms usually end up on the north side, but they can be partially heated with diffuse solar energy when using the new selective transmitting glasses. This approach requires a north wall that is nearly all coated glass, which would cause a visual privacy problem if the bedrooms are occupied during the day. Drapes could be used during the night for privacy. This approach only works well when the average daily outdoor temperatures are above the freezing mark. East and west windows must be avoided to prevent summertime overheating from the low altitude morning and afternoon sun.

Townhouses

This building type is similar to a single family detached residence with its second floor and roof access. The difference is the party walls in a townhouse lower the

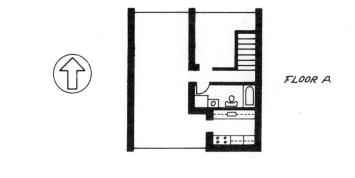

FLOOR A

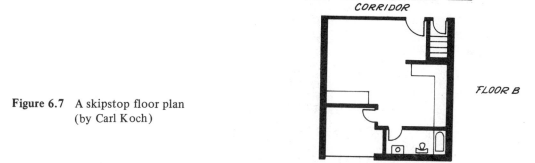

CORRIDOR

FLOOR B

Figure 6.7 A skipstop floor plan
(by Carl Koch)

heating load. Many times, these party walls are built with masonry to act as fire barriers. This presents the opportunity to use these walls for thermal mass providing a good light diffuser can be designed for the south facing windows.

Planning in a townhouse becomes simpler. The living and dining areas can share the southern exposure. The kitchen can go on the north wall of the first floor to buffer the thermal load with the surplus heat gains from the stove and refrigerator (Fig. 6.8). The bedrooms and private areas on the top floor can gather sunlight from the south or from monitor skylights.

Single Family Detached

The only real differences between solar heating this building type and townhouses are: (1) there are more weather walls; (2) unheated spaces like closets, corridors, storage, and the like can be placed on the nonsouth walls to buffer the heat loss; (3) the glazed areas required to heat the single family detached are large due to the increased heat loss; and (4) the plan tends to elongate along the east-west axis to maximize southern exposure since land-use density is relaxed.

Direct-gain solar heating brings the benefits of the outdoors inside. Natural daylighting and cross-ventilation are part of the approach. Good architectural organization will produce spaces that offer exquisite thermal and visual comfort all year round.

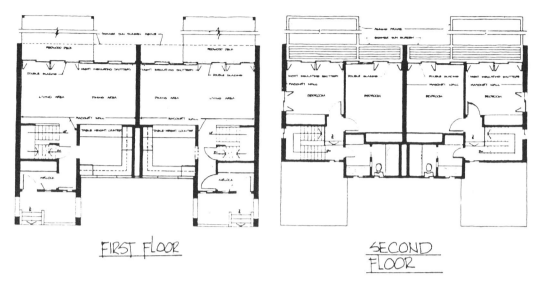

FIRST FLOOR   SECOND FLOOR

Figure 6.8 A direct gain townhouse organization by Team Works, Cambridge, MA. (from *The First Passive Solar Home Awards,* U.S. Dept. of Housing and Urban Development, Jan., 1979).

AUXILIARY HEAT

The new selective transmitters make it possible to achieve 100 percent solar heating, even in cloudy climates, if the temperature does not go below 40°F and the occupants can accept large areas of the coated glass (See Chapter 5). Otherwise, an auxiliary heating system will be required. Most designers unfortunately leave the choice of an auxiliary heating system to the end. This is often a mistake, because a wrong choice can elevate electrical peak loads on a strained power grid or drive up the first cost of the project. Correctly coupling the auxiliary heating system with the direct gain heating concept can result in (1) an overall system cost of auxiliary heat plus solar that is less than or equal to a conventional heating system, and (2) a thermally plesant space that utilizes the storage capabilities of the direct-gain system to regulate the auxiliary heating system. Three examples introduced below show how this can be done; the first deals with wood auxiliary heating. Others deal with more conservative approaches that attract mortgage money: off-peak electrical resistance heating and water-to-air heat pumps.

Wood

Wood stoves are now a common sight in passively heated homes, probably because the people who are interested in solar heating are more prepared to fend for themselves than are most people. Unfortunately, the occupants usually find the house is either too hot (so they buy fans to blow the heat around), or it is too cold because the fire has died down, or the heat distribution is too weak. The problem lies in the wood stove. Most wood heaters heat by radiation, using a small surface area at a high temperature to distribute heat. A single radiant source will not heat rooms out of the line of sight with the stove. Little goes into convective heat that could be potentially distributed by natural processes to other rooms. To make matters worse, the excess heat from the stove is not stored well.

There are some wood heaters that overcome these problems, and also behave as central heaters without using ducts. Most of the wood heat can be converted to convective heat by using an integral heat exchanger. Wood stoves of this type are known as circulators. Hot air leaves the top of the heat exchanger at 100°F-110°F where it rises to the ceiling, forming a hot air pillow about 1-1/2 feet in depth that spreads over the entire ceiling. This undulating mass of 100°F air will actually wend its way through transoms and flood the ceilings of adjacent rooms, and the rooms adjacent to the adjacent rooms. Each ceiling gets warm and heats the space *radiantly*, which is another way of saying the air temperature at the floor and at head height are an even 73°F. The same ceiling will store the wood heat if the ceiling is masonry, or plaster (or a high density board like cement-asbestos) covered with phase-change material. The thermal storage regulates the room temperatures while the wood heater is on, and continues to heat the room long after the fire has gone out. It is possible to heat a two story space with a single wood convection heater, as shown in Figure 6.9. Some of the heat is piped to second floor by the only duct in the system. The return loop from the second floor is down the stairwell. The warm ceiling air on the first floor is prevented from flowing up the stairs (any flow up the stairs would keep the first floor hot air pillow from spreading further horizontally) by ringing the stair well at the first floor level with a one foot deep baffle. Thus, one wood stove can do it all. It is not difficult to keep the incremental cost of the passive solar system and circulator wood stove below the cost of a conventional auxiliary heating system. This means the solar heated house with auxiliary heat has a payback period of zero years, so savings are accrued immediately.

Off-Peak Electricity

Most lending organizations do not accept wood heat as the sole auxiliary heating system. A more conventional heating system which uses electricity priced at off-peak rates can be designed to lower operating and first costs. More and more fossil fueled utilities are offering electricity at one-half to three-fourths the normal rates during the hours when their generating capacity is underutilized as an incentive to lower the growing peak demand on their systems. These off-peak periods usually run for 10 to 12 hours at night and during the entire weekend. Electricity at these prices becomes cheaper than oil in many parts of the country. Unfortunately, some utilities are not discounting their high fuel adjustment charges during off-peak hours which lessens the economic attractiveness of the concept. Nearly all the utilities levy a penalty charge for day-time use.

Of course, heat storage must be provided so the residence will stay warm during the day when the electricity is too expensive to use. Domestic hot water can

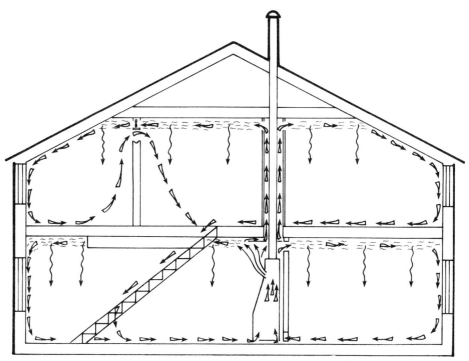

Figure 6.9 Central heating using a circulating wood stove (from Combitherm, Stockholm, Sweden).

be stored by using a larger tank size (usually 50 percent larger) and by adding more insulation to the tank. The electrical space heating energy can be stored in the ceiling where radiant heating can go to work.

One way of doing this is demonstrated in a small one story residence located in Mattapoisett, Massachusetts (Fig. 6.10). This figure shows a cross-section of the ceiling where heat delivery, storage, and distribution take place. The same principle used for storing solar energy with bagged phase-change material is used here. Fire coded dry-wall is used as the ceiling. Three-quarter-inch thick bags of Glauber salts are laid between the joists on top of the 1/2-inch thick sheetrock. The phase-change material is formulated to melt at 88°F.

Ribbons of electrical resistance material embedded in plastic sheet are laid on top of the bags. Response times are shortened if the resistance heaters are layed between the drywall and the bags. Finally, 11 inches of fiber glass insulation is laid on top of the heating pads to keep heat from escaping to the attic. The electric heating mats connect to individual room thermostats. During the night the bags get charged when the thermostats call for heat, while some heat conducts through the dry-wall to heat the room. The thermostats turn off the electrical heating mats when the bags are charged. During the day, the stored heat conducts through the dry-wall to radiantly heat the room.

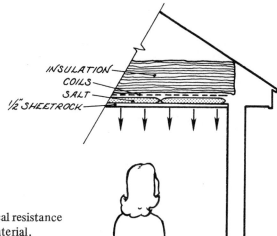

INSULATION
COILS
SALT
½" SHEETROCK

Figure 6.10 Off-peak electrical resistance
heating using phase change material.

A few precautions must be followed to avoid overheating, particularly during a
sunny day. Solar energy is placed in the ceiling in the Mattapoisett house with in-
verted, reflectorized louvers similar to those used in the MIT Solar 5 house. The
phase-change pouches used to store the solar energy are formulated to melt at
73°F so solar energy can be stored without overheating the room (as discussed
earlier in the Mass section of this chapter). No electrical heatng mats are placed on
the 73°F bags so these bags are never charged at night and are always ready to
absorb the next day's solar energy. Mats are only placed at the rear of the rooms on
pouches formulated to melt at 88°F. The higher temperature bags reduce the electrical mat area which reduces costs. A design procedure is given below for sizing
such a system.

The approach is to chose an electrical mat area and a solar heated ceiling area
so the house does not overheat on a sunny day when it is 40°F to 45°F outside
(some venting can occur when it gets in the mid-50s, since not much heat will be
lost to this relatively warm outdoor air). When the outside air temperature drops,
the load increases, and the inside air temperature will drop on cloudy days though
the ceiling temperature remains constant. The reduced air temperature will not be
noticed for most winter loads since the radiantly heated ceiling compensates. It
will be necessary to supplement the stored electrical heat when the room air
temperature goes below 62°F on extremely cold days. This can be accomplished
with a small electric baseboard convector. Typically, less than 5 percent of the total
electrical heating energy load will be used during the peak hours in this system. The
real purpose of the secondary electric baseboard units is to provide momentary,
instant heat when sudden temperature drops occur, since a massive radiantly heated
system is slow to respond to large changes in thermal load.

The design procedure follows:

1. Determine the heat loss coefficient (UA in BTU/hr°F) for the room.

2. Select enough 73°F pouches of Glauber salts according to the design method presented in Chapter 7 to keep the indoor air temperature swing on a clear day less than ±6°F.

3. Choose the maximum indoor air temperature one could tolerate for a day when it is 40°F outside.

4. Subtract the temperature rise due to solar heating (6°F) from this temperature to arrive at the room temperature that will be maintained by the off-peak electrical heating system. Call this temperature T_r.

5. Using the following relation, given UA from above, and setting T_o equal to 40°F, solve for A_{88} (the area of pouches at 88°F necessary to heat the room).

$$1.00 \text{ BTU/hr}°\text{Fft}^2 \ (88-T_r)°\text{F x } A_{88} = (T_r-T_o)°\text{F x UA BTU/hr}°\text{F*}$$

where

$$A_{88} = \frac{(T_r-T_o) \text{ X UA}}{1.00(88-T_r)}$$

6. Select the watts/ft² rating for the A_{88} area of electrical heating pads using the following relation, where Q is the latent heat capacity of phase-change material in BTU/ft², T_d is the coldest average outdoor temperature expected, and H is the number of hours the off-peak rate is available:

$$\text{watts/ft}^2 = \frac{Q + \dfrac{\text{UA}(62°\text{F}-T_d) \text{ x H}}{A_{88}}}{\text{H x 3.413 BTU/watthr}}$$

To see how the space behaves for colder daytime temperatures, use various outdoor temperatures for T_o in the relation given in Step 5 above, where A_{88} is the area previously given in Step 5.

For example, assume: (1) the space to be heated is an open plan area which has a heat loss coefficient (UA) of 381 BTU/hr°F; and (2) the design method in Chapter 7 shows the indoor air temperature will not go higher than 6°F above the average indoor air temperature on a sunny day.

Then the remaining steps are:

3. Choose 76°F as the maximum sunny day indoor air temperature

4. T_r becomes 76°-6° = 70°F

5. $A_{88} = \dfrac{(70°-40°\text{F}) \text{ x } 381 \text{ BTU/hr}°\text{F}}{1.00 \text{ BTU/hr}°\text{Fft}^2 \ (88°-70°\text{F})} = 635\text{ft}^2$

---

*This relation says the heat flow from the ceiling to the room equals the heat flow from the room to the outside. The heat transfer coefficient through ordinary ½ inch dry-wall and the air film at the ceiling (including the radiation component) is 1.00 BTU/hr°Fft². This heat flows according to the area of the pouches and temperature difference between the 88°F pouches and the room. The left-hand side of the equation gives the total heat leaving the ceiling. The right-hand side gives the total heat leaving the space to the outdoors.

6. Assuming $Q = 273$ BTU/ft^2, $T_d = 6°F$, $H = 12$ hrs, then,

$$\text{watts/ft}^2 = \frac{273 \text{ BTU/ft}^2 + \dfrac{381 \text{ BTU/hr°F}(62°-6°)}{635\text{ft}^2} \times 12\text{hrs}}{12 \text{ hrs} \times 3.413 \text{ BTU/watthr}} = 16.5 \text{ watts/ft}^2$$

To find the room air temperature for other daytime outdoor temperatures, solve relation 5 for T_r:

$$T_r = \frac{88 \times A_{88} + UA \times T_o}{1.00 \times A_{88} + UA}$$

When $T_o = 30°F$,

$T_r = 66°F$.

When $T_o = 20°F$,

$T_r = 63°F$. (The radiant ceiling would compensate for this low room air temperature.)

The thermostat would regulate the space at the thermostat setting during the night when the off-peak rates are in effect, regardless of the outdoor temperatures.

The cost of this system, plus the direct-gain add-on costs of the louvers, phase-change pouches, and the extra window area equalled the cost of a standard gas hot air furnace system and the utility connection for the Mattapoisett house. The house was insulated slightly above the new standards specified by the Massachusetts Building Code.

Ground Water Heat Pump

The water-to-air heat pump provides another form of inexpensive auxiliary heat at sites that have a flowing high water table. A heat pump removes the heat from a low temperature source and places it in a high temperature surround. A household refrigerator is an example of an air-to-air heat pump. Heat is removed from the refrigerator compartment (it seeps in through the insulation) and is dumped into the kitchen by the high temperature heat exchange coils at the back of the refrigerator. Air-to-air heat pumps are common heating systems for homes. Using the refrigerator analogy, one can think of the refrigerator compartment being open to the great outdoors, and the refrigerator heat exchange coils being the heat source for the entire house. The efficiency of an electrically powered heat pump drops rapidly with dropping outdoor temperatures. Ice will form on the heat pump's outside heat exchanger coils when the air nears the freezing mark. This ice is periodically removed by applying heat which is better off inside the building.

A water-to-air heat pump brightens the efficiency picture considerably. Here the outside heat exchanger coils are placed in ground water (water brought to the surface from a stream, a well, or a nearby aquifer). The deep ground water temperature rarely falls below 45°F in winter, so the efficiency of a water-to-air heat pump does not deteriorate as much as that of an air-to-air heat pump, and freezing is never a problem. Water transfers heat better than air so less expensive heat exchangers are needed. All these advantages make a water-to-air heat pump twice as efficient, on the average, as an air-to-air heat pump, and high efficiency means lower electricity consumption. In some cases the consumption is so low that the operating costs are comparable to off-peak electricity costs. Actual off-peak electricity can be used to run the heat pump if the heat can be stored. One way to store the heat is to use a water-to-water heat pump to move the heat into a large insulated tank which feeds a water coil in a forced hot air heating system.

The disadvantage of the approach is that large capacity water-to-air heat pumps are not common and the first costs of the system are up to 25 percent more than a conventional heating system plus the costs for water access. Some of this additional cost can be offset against the savings in oil tank or gas connection costs and possible chimney construction costs. Also, further savings accrue for projects requiring cooling since a heat pump can be run in reverse as an air conditioner. Ground water can be a problem, though, for at least 120 gallons per hour of 45°F ground water must be brought to the heat exchanger coils for each 10,000 BTU/hr of heating capacity. Unfortunately, most sites do not have this much water available. Nevertheless, one should always determine the ground water potential of the site, for the operational savings can be high.

Other Alternatives

When building a single home, only individual heating systems can be considered. However, centralized heating becomes attractive for some medium density residential projects when using heat pumps or liquid (or gas) fuel systems. A single heating plant can be used to supply two or three low-rise buildings via highly insulated underground pipes. The first costs of the system are decreased and heating efficiencies are increased because the heating plant does not cycle on and off as much as individual heaters cycle. This approach is a particularly attractive means of reducing the high first cost of a water-to-air heat pump system. Other advantages are reduced fuel storage cost for oil systems and reduced maintenance costs due to the scaling effect.

REFERENCES

1. B. Anderson and M. Riordan, *The Solar Home Book*, Cheshire Books, Harrisville, N.H., 1977.
2. ASHRAE, *Handbook of Fundamentals*, ASHRAE, New York, 1972.

3. J. Balcomb, "Designing Fan-Forced Rockbeds," *Solar Age*, Vol. 4, No. 11, Nov., 1979.

4. T. Burkhart and R. Jones, "The Effective Absorption of Direct Gain Rooms," proceedings, 4th National Passive Solar Conference, October 1979, International Solar Energy Society.

5. M. Harris, *Heating with Wood*, Citadel Press, Secausus, 1980.

6. F. Kreith, *Principles of Heat Transfer*, International Textbook Co., Scranton, 1958.

7. ___, *First Passive Solar Home Awards*, Franklin Research Center, Philadelphia, D.O.E., 1979.

8. E. Mazria, *The Passive Solar Energy Book*, Rodale Press, Emmaus, Penn., 1979.

Chapter 7

A Graphical Thermal Comfort Design Method

Heating a space directly with the sun is conceptually the simplest form of passive solar heating. Every additional square foot of south facing double glazing reduces the annual auxiliary heating bill in most underheated climates. Overheating can become an issue, however, when significant amounts of glazing are used. The heat build-up in a south facing room is a complex process that depends on the sun's dynamics and the thermal storage response times. The design methods commonly used for predicting heating behavior in buildings are not adequate for such a dynamic situation. This chapter introduces an applicable, simple design procedure for avoiding overheating and for maximizing visual and thermal comfort in buildings with large south facing window areas. The chapter concludes with an accurate procedure for predicting the attendant annual energy savings.

DESIGN ISSUES IN DIRECT-GAIN DESIGN

The designer of a direct-gain building is concerned with many issues of secondary importance in a conventional design.

Direct-gain building are characterized by larger than normal areas of glazing on the south side. Windows perform many functions simultaneously; they provide view, ventilation, insulation, light, heat, and physical access. Chapter 5 shows how each of these functions can be improved.

Direct-gain buildings may include massive materials for heat storage such as masonry, water, or phase-change materials. This mass reduces interior temperature fluctuations for increased comfort control, and must be correctly placed and finished. Chapter 6 details the steps in designing mass storage systems.

Direct-gain buildings respond to solar availability and microclimates. The path of the sun, the lay of the land, the building shape, and the wind all affect how well a building will thermally fend for itself. Chapters 3 and 4 introduce ways of altering the microclimate for the benefit of the site's occupants.

Direct-gain residences work well when room layouts are determined by solar influences. How a building is laid out and insulated determines how well solar energy is utilized. Chapter 6 discusses the concerns for correct planning.

A design method should productively knit these issues together. One way to proceed is shown below. This method is primarily concerned with controlling thermal comfort, but the procedure also includes the steps for rigorously predicting the yearly auxiliary heating requirements and the resulting energy savings. One must design first for comfort, however, for energy savings will never accrue if comfort is sacrificed.

The amount of south facing glass added to a building can conveniently be considered in two increments. The first increment is limited to the glass area that can be added to a conventional house without causing overheating. Though a stud frame house is built largely of lightweight materials, it is not massless. Large areas of medium weight materials such as sheetrock and wood provide some thermal capacity. The acceptable south facing glass area depends on the building's location and heat loss coefficient. In the northeast, the southern glass area will vary from 8 to 15 percent of the floor area, assuming the building is well insulated (R-19 walls, R-38 ceilings, double glazed windows and low infiltration rates). Typically, a 30 percent solar heating fraction is the upper limit for the first glass area increment. Chapter 6 gives the procedure for determining this limit.

The second glass area increment is limited only by the amount of thermal storage that can be placed in radiant contact with the living spaces. This approach requires careful design when thermal comfort is under consideration. The remainder of this chapter is concerned with this more complex case.

METHOD FOR PRELIMINARY DESIGN OF DIRECT-GAIN BUILDINGS WITH LARGE AREAS OF SOUTH FACING WINDOWS.

It is relatively simple to achieve a moderate amount of solar heating in conventional buildings, but to achieve larger amounts of solar heating requires more sophisticated design. In the early stages of design, building geometrics are not known; sometimes only the square footage is available. Yet, one must determine how the building will behave thermally at this stage so subsequent choices can be based on soundly predicted performances. The following method deals expressly with preliminary design issues.

TABLE 7.1   South glass areas that limit overheating, assuming optimal use of heat storage mass and insulation.

Housing Type	South glazing area/heated floor area Climate	
	Less Than 4000 DD	4500-8000 DD
1. Single family detached	0.15-0.17	0.22-0.25
2. Single family attached	0.11-0.13	0.17-0.19
3. Low rise residential	0.09-0.11	0.14-0.16

The first step in the design process is to **formulate a spatial organization concept** that addresses the occupants' living needs. This concept deals with the usual elements of architectural design such as living patterns, privacy, form, and site.

Choose a natural daylighting concept. Daylighting on sunny days is accomplished by either admitting the sun as beam light, or as diffuse light, or by a combination of these. The daylighting concept in turn dictates the thermal storage system. Beam daylighting relatively small areas requires the use of a high heat capacity mass at the target areas, such as water or phase-change material. Diffuse daylighting requires the use of relatively thin, spatially distributed masonry as discussed in Chapter 6. Either choice carries the potential of creating a high glare interior. Chapter 3 introduces some principles for controlling glare.

Choose a south facing window area in keeping with the architectural program. Most of the time, the architectural program limits the amount of south facing glazing. If these limits are not operating, the following rules of thumb illustrated in Table 7.1 can be used to choose the area of southern glazing necessary to meet more than 70 percent of the residence's heating requirement with solar energy.

Determine the building heat loss rate. One must know how fast a building loses heat in order to predict the wintertime interior temperature excursions due to solar gains. At the preliminary stages of design, the wall and roof area and the insulation system are not usually known. What is known is the square footage of heated floor area. One way of estimating the heat loss rate is to use the fairly stringent federal (or state) energy codes for predicting insulation levels. These codes give maximum heat loss rates for a given square footage of heated floor area. The table below is based on the HUD Minimum Property Standards (3607-3, 5-607-3). These standards will inevitably be regarded as too lax and the reader should use up-to-date state codes as they are enacted. The table gives the heat loss rates for residences with total double glazed window areas equal to 8 to 10 percent of the heated floor area. If Step 3 calls for additional glazing areas, then the following figure must be added to heat loss rates given in Table 7.2 to get the total heat loss for the building:

Heat loss correction term = average window heat loss coefficient $(BTU/hr^\circ Fft^2)$ x

$$90\% \text{ x } 24 \text{ hr/day x } \frac{\text{Additional south glass area}}{\text{heated floor area}}$$

TABLE 7.2   Recommended Insulation Levels for Various Climates

Housing Type	Heat Loss Rates (BTU/ft² Degree Days)*		
	less than 4500 DD	4500-8000 DD	greater than 8000 DD
Single family detached (1600 ft² area)	7.3	7.1	5.4
Single family attached (1370 ft² area)	6.6	6.2	4.8
Multiple family low rise (17,000 ft² area)	8.8	6.7	5.1

*Booz, Allen and Associates

(The 90% figure is used to compensate for the normally insulated wall that is replaced by windows)

The hourly heat loss for a building can be found by multiplying the appropriate figure in Table 7.2 by the building's square footage and dividing by 24 hrs/day. For example, a 1000 square foot single family detached building in a 5600 DD climate gives

$$\frac{7.1 \text{ BTU/ft}^2 \text{DD} \times 1000 \text{ ft}^2}{24 \text{ hrs/day}} = 295.8 \text{ BTU/hr}^\circ\text{F}$$

If the building has an extra 100 square feet of glass, then the heat loss correction term is: $0.55 \text{ BTU/hr}^\circ\text{Fft}^2 \times 90\% \times 24 \times \frac{100}{1000} = 1.19 \text{ BTU/ft}^2 \text{ DD}$, and the corrected heat loss coefficient is:

$$(7.1 + 1.19) \times 1000/24 = 345.4 \text{ BTU/hr}^\circ\text{F}$$

Choose a mass concept. Given a natural daylighting concept, choose the accompanying thermal storage system. Either one of two mass concepts is possible, depending on the lighting concept: distributed, low energy density mass; or concentrated, high energy density mass. If the distributed mass approach is used, choose a masonry material and a color (usually off-white), and estimate its probable thickness and area. If the concentrated mass approach is used, choose a color that has a light absorbtion of at least 75 percent, and a heat storage capacity for each square foot of material exposed to the sun.

Test for visual comfort in each open plan zone bordering the southern windows. Lighting levels are difficult to determine during preliminary design because room geometrics are still unknown. At this stage, principles of daylighting and glare control (Chapter 3) will help estimate performance. At later stages, a lighting model will be used to fully test for visual comfort.

Test for thermal comfort. Thermal comfort is lost when a room gets too hot or too cold. The building's auxiliary heating system will kick on to keep the room from getting too cold in the winter, but the room may also become too warm on sunny days. What is too warm for one person may be just right for another. The designer must choose an appropriate room temperature that represents the comfortable upper limit for the client. Given this, it is possible to predict if this limit is exceeded. The following method for determining interior temperature excursions is based on a design note produced in 1981 by the North East Solar Energy Center, Boston, Massachusetts.

The interior air temperatures of a direct-gain building depend on the cycles of the sun, the outdoor temperature, and the physical characteristics of the building. Sophisticated numerical methods that can accurately assess air temperatures at any time of the day using thermal networks have been developed. Generally, these methods are too cumbersome and time consuming for the designer and are more suited for fine tuning a building or testing innovative ideas.

Philip Niles of California Polytechnic State University, San Luis Obispo, has developed the graphic method that is presented here. This method has several advantages. First, it can be used in a matter of minutes. Second, it is sensitive to changes in individual parameters. Thus, the building's sensitivity to changes in mass thickness, mass configuration, glazing area, and heat loss can readily be assessed. This flexibility permits the graphs to be applied to a wide range of building types. Appendix 1 includes the TI59 calculator codes for even faster assessment.

The assumptions implicit in the graphs include a one-zone heated space, south facing vertical glazing, no auxiliary heating system, no night insulation, no intermittent ventilation, and an isothermal storage mass.

Obviously, this is a large set of assumptions, and many buildings will not fit them all. However, given the design aid nature of the graphs, they can be very useful in predicting overheating. Since they assume no auxiliary heating, they are most useful for buildings which are largely solar heated on a clear day. If auxiliary heating proves necessary, the outdoor air temperature can be raised artificially to approximate the effect of auxiliary heating in the modeled zone. The average outdoor air temperature used in the model should be raised until the average indoor temperature is in the comfort zone. The effect of internal heat gains also can be included in the model by raising the average outdoor air temperature by the following amount:

$$\frac{\text{(Daily heat gains in BTU)}}{24 \text{ hrs/day}(UA_{blg})}$$

The single thermal zone restriction is not always difficult. An entire residence can be modeled as one zone when most of the spaces are open plan. The method cannot be used for rooms that are out of radiation contact with south facing glass. Small, individual south facing rooms must be modeled as separate zones. The hourly heat loss rate used to model a zone must not include losses experienced by separate zones.

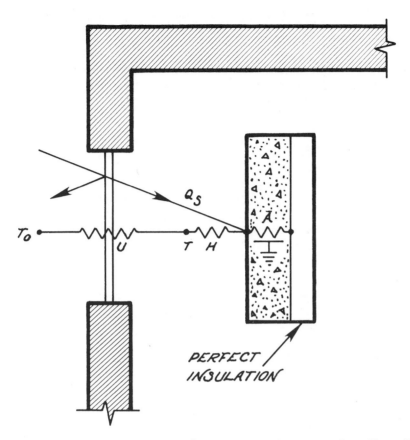

Figure 7.1 Radiatively coupled case (from "Graphs for Direct Gain House Performance Production", Phillip W. B. Niles, *Passive Systems '78'*, ISES, Jan. 1979).

The graphs give room air temperature swings for mass that is either convectively or radiatively coupled. The difference in the two cases is shown schematically in Figures 7.1 and 7.2. In the case of convective coupling, the sun is assumed to strike a perfect insulator where the energy is then convected to the room air. Therefore, any heat stored by the thermal mass would be absorbed by the air. This is what would happen if all the incoming sunlight were to strike dark rugs, furniture, and other lightweight surfaces. For radiative coupling, the sun is assumed to strike the surface of the thermal storage mass. Actual situations will be somewhere between these two cases, so it is up to the designer to decide which one predominates. In most cases, it will be clear that radiative coupling is desirable, if not essential.

A building will overheat on clear days when the outdoor temperature is warm, but temperatures can be lowered merely by opening the windows. The same space

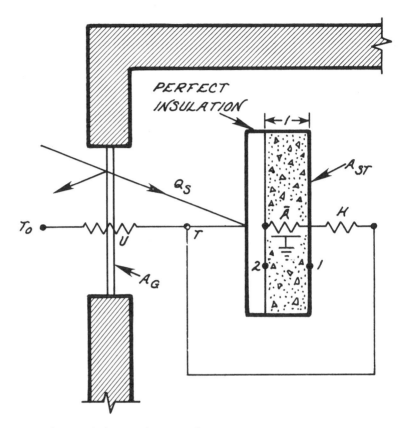

Figure 7.2 Convectively coupled case (from "Graphs for Direct Gain House Performance Production", Phillip W. B. Niles, *Passive Systems '78'*, ISES, Jan. 1979).

could overheat on a cold clear day, but venting becomes undesirable in the winter because it wastes energy. It is impractical to test for overheating on every clear day of every month; so it becomes necessary to choose weather data to represent typical days in the heating season. A clear day in March works well. In March, the average monthly outdoor temperature usually equals the average for the entire heating season and the sun is at its average altitudes for the heating season. The interior temperature excursions for March are only slightly higher than for January or, for that matter, for all the other heating months except September and October.

Given representative weather data, the first steps in the method are concerned with boiling down the data to useable form:

Step 1. Calculate the average hourly clear day solar heat gain (Q_s).

The daylong clear day solar heat gain must be determined and then divided by 24 to yield the average hourly value. In the absence of measured data, the ASHRAE

TABLE 7.3 Daylong Solar Heat Gain Factors for Vertical, South-Facing, D.S. Glass for the 21st Day of Each Month, Btu/ft^2 da.

Latitude	38	40	42	44	46	48
January	1680	1626	1570	1514	1458	1402
February	1622	1642	1638	1634	1630	1626
March	1336	1388	1425	1461	1498	1534
April	927	976	993	1009	1026	1042
May	662	716	779	841	904	966
June	585	630	691	751	812	872
July	652	704	765	826	887	948
August	887	948	1005	1061	1118	1174
September	1295	1344	1377	1409	1442	1474
October	1563	1582	1576	1570	1564	1558
November	1618	1596	1540	1484	1428	1372
December	1589	1550	1481	1411	1342	1272

NOTE: These figures were obtained by linear interpolation of tables published in the ASHRAE Handbook of Fundamentals. They assume 20 percent ground reflectance and an atmospheric clearness of 1. To account for lower atmospheric clearness in urban locations, reduce these figures by 10 to 15 percent. Snow would increase the ground reflectance and thus increase these values by 10 to 15 percent.

solar heat gain factors may be used. In this case, compute the average hourly incoming insolation from the following formula:

$$Q_s = \frac{\text{Daylong solar heat gain factor x shading coefficient}}{24 \text{ hours}} = \frac{\text{DSHGA x SC}}{24}$$

The daylong solar heat gain factors (Table 7.3) represent the solar heat admitted over a clear day, through one layer of vertical, south facing, clear, double strength window glass. The values include both transmitted energy and inward flowing absorbed energy.

It has been determined that there is an essentially constant ratio between the solar heat gain for any type of glazing and the solar heat gain for clear, double strength window glass. This ratio is known as the *shading coefficient*. Relevant values are listed in Table 7.4.

Step 2. Determine the equilibrium temperature (A_g, T_e).

This step can be used to calculate the equilibrium temperature resulting from a known amount of south facing glass. The equilibrium temperature equals the average daily room air temperature and is not related to a thermostat setting. Note carefully that a south glass area and equilibrium temperature consistent with this step must be used in all following steps.

TABLE 7.4 Transmission Coefficients (shading coefficients)

Glass Thickness and Type	Shading Coefficient
Single	
1/8"	1.00
1/4"	.94
Double	
1/8"	.83
1/4"	.76
Triple	
1/8"	.69
3/16"	.66
1/4"	.63
Selective Transmitter double with 1/8" glass on the outside, coated 1/8" glass on the inside)	.74

NOTE: Normal transmission values for single and double glazing were taken from the ASHRAE *Handbook of Fundamentals* and discounted for varying angles of incidence. Values for triple glazing were taken from Lilly, Owens, Ford Technical Literature. Values for the selective transmitter were measured from 1980 samples of AIRCO TEMESCAL coated glass.

For the particular case of double glass glazing, the value may be determined graphically from Figure 7.3. For other glazing systems, use the following formulas:

$$T_e = T_{out} + \frac{A_g \times Q_s}{UA_{total}}$$

where:

$$T_e = \text{equilibrium temperature } (^\circ F)$$
$$A_g = \text{south glass area } (ft^2)$$
$$Q_s = \text{clear day solar heat gain } (BTU/hrft^2)$$
$$T_{out} = \text{average daily outdoor temperature } (^\circ F)$$
$$UA_{total} = \text{total house losses } (BTU/hr^\circ F)$$

Step 3: Calculate the outdoor air temperature amplitude (ITI).

The outdoor temperature amplitude is defined as one-half the outdoor daily temperature swing and is computed from the following formula:

$$ITI = \frac{T_{max} - T_{min}}{2}$$

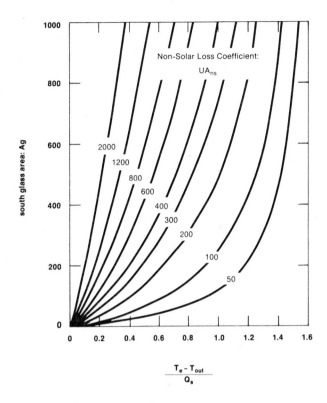

Figure 7.3 South glass area vs. equilibrium temperature for double glazing (from "A Simple Direct Gain Passive House Performance Prediction Model", Phillip W. B. Niles, *Passive Solar: State of the Art*, Proc. of the 2nd National Passive Solar Conference, Philadelpia, PA ISES, March 1978).

where:

$\qquad$ ITI $\ =$ outdoor temperature amplitude (one half daily temperature swing) ($^\circ$F)

$\qquad$ T_{max} $=$ normal daily maximum temperature, ($^\circ$F), from local weather data

$\qquad$ T_{min} $=$ normal daily minimum temperature, ($^\circ$F), from local weather data

Step 4: Find the zero mass amplitude (IZI).

The zero mass amplitude is a required intermediate value. It is a fictitious "worst case" value defined as one-half the temperature swing that would result if the building contained *no* thermal mass. It is determined from Figure 7.4, using the difference between the average indoor and outdoor air temperatures ($T_e - T_{out}$) and the value from Step 3 as indices.

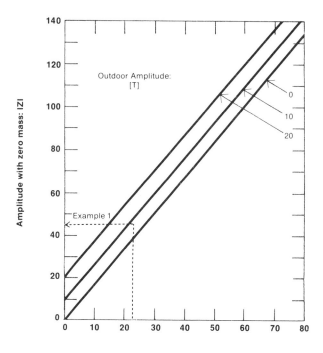

Figure 7.4 Temperature amplitude with zero mass (from "A Simple Direct Gain Passive House Performance Prediction Model", Phillip W. B. Niles, *Passive Solar: State of the Art*, Proc. of the 2nd National Passive Solar Conference, Philadelpia, PA ISES, March 1978).

Step 5:   Look up the effective storage mass heat capacity (MC_{sto}).

The graphs used to compute temperature swings assume that the storage mass behaves isothermally, i.e., that heat will be distributed evenly and instantly through the entire mass. Though this is a fair assumption for water, it is not accurate for masonry thicknesses over 3 inches. Since masonry has a relatively low conductivity, the outer portion of the mass will store more heat than the inner portions. To compensate for this phenomenon and to model storage surface temperatures accurately, an effective heat capacity lower than the volumetric heat capacity is used.

This effective heat capacity is the isothermal "equivalent" of various storage materials, and is used to compensate for the temperature gradients that will form in most thermal storage materials. It represents the heat capacity of a thermal storage material in direct sunlight over a daily cycle. Thus, it is the "diurnal heat capacity" for radiant coupling. Values of effective storage mass heat capacity for various masonry materials (and pine wood) are listed in Table 7.5.

The effective heat capacity is greatly reduced for convective coupling. The capacity value for a material greater than 3 inches in thickness is approximately

TABLE 7.5 Effective Diurnal Heat Capacity for sunlit mass (Btu/Fft^2 of surface area)

Properties Used	Concrete	Lime-stone Rock	Brick	Pine	Dry Sand	Adobe	Sheet Rock
density (lb/Ft^3)	143	153	112	31	95	120	50
specific heat (BTU/lb F)	0.21	0.22	0.22	0.67	0.19	0.20	.20
thermal conductivity (Btu/hrft°F)	1.00	0.54	0.40	0.097	0.19	0.332	.09
Thickness							
1"	2.50	2.80	2.05	1.71	1.51	2.00	0.84
2"	4.99	5.52	4.04	2.96	2.90	3.92	1.60
3"	7.37	7.81	5.73	3.14	3.86	5.44	2.04
4"	9.47	9.17	6.74	2.93	4.14	6.20	2.11
6"	11.94	9.30	6.86	2.76	3.82	6.05	1.92
8"	12.14	8.63	6.36	2.77	3.62	5.62	1.84
12"	10.99	8.29	6.10	2.77	3.61	5.49	1.85
16"	10.65	8.33	6.13	2.77	3.62	5.52	1.85

equal to the effective heat capacity of 3 inch material radiantly coupled to the room. The effective heat capacities are equal in either coupling case for thicknesses of less than 3 inches.

This method is not restricted to a one side insulated storage mass when water is the thermal storage medium. It can also model freestanding water barrels, tubes, and tanks. As stated earlier, water storage is assumed to behave isothermally since convective currents evenly distribute the heat through the mass. Thus, by properly forming the heat storage capacity per exposed surface area, two-sided storage can be modeled.

If freestanding water containers are used, they may be imagined as spread out and flattened into the one-sided insulated storage mass. The surface area of the storage (A_s) will be the total area of the containers exposed to room air. This will be the area through which the storage transfers heat to the room. The storage mass heat capacity (MC_{sto}) will be the volumetric heat capacity per surface area of heat transfer. This heat capacity does not have to be reduced to an effective heat capacity since thermal gradients will not occur in the water storage. For freestanding water storage:

$$MC_{sto} = \frac{62.4 \ (BTU/ft^3°F) \times \text{Total volume of water } (ft^3)}{\text{Surface area of storage containers exposed to room air } ft^2}$$

Strictly speaking, this method cannot model phase-change materials. However, a rule of thumb that has proven accurate for the tiles used in the MIT Solar 5 test building has been to assume a heat capacity of 22 BTU/ft^2°F. This was determined

TABLE 7.6   Surface Film Conductances (h)

Orientation	$h \; (BTU/hrft^{2\,\circ}F)$
vertical wall	0.8
horizontal floor	1.0
horizontal ceiling	0.6

by dividing the heat storage capacity of the Glauber salt material (220 BTU/ft²) by the actual temperature change experienced by the phase-change material when struck by the sun (10°F).

Step 6:   Determine the storage surface film conductance (h).

This factor represents the convective heat transfer coefficient from the storage mass surface to the room air. Room air is heated directly by convection between the surface of the mass and the air. Also it is heated indirectly when radiation from the mass surface strikes the room walls. The walls then heat the air by convection. This radiant heating effect is included in the design curve.

The exact value of the convective heat transfer coefficient depends on the geometrical relationships in a room. Table 7.6 lists these values for various surface orientations. The figures account for the mixing induced by infiltrating air, and assume the surfaces are always warmer than the room air as would occur in the radiant coupling. For the convectively coupled case, the figures for the floor and ceiling are interchanged.

Step 7:   Find the convective temperature swings (ICI).

To determine the temperature swings in the case of convective coupling, first find the ratio of the convectively coupled case to the zero mass indoor temperature amplitude (ICI/IZI) from Figure 7.5, using the following value to select the appropriate curve on the graph,

$$\frac{(T_e - T_{out}) h \, A_{sto}}{Q_s A_g}$$

and the value of MC_{sto}/h to select a figure on the horizontal axis. A_{sto} is the mass area illuminated by the sun. When the sun is diffused, A_{sto} is the entire exposed area of mass. When the sun sweeps the mass with beam energy, A_{sto} is approximately 80 percent of the swept area.

Calculate the maximum and minimum air temperatures for the convective case from the following formulas using the value for (ICI/IZI) from Graph 7.5:

$$ICI = IZI \; x \; (ICI/IZI)$$

$$\text{Maximum interior air temperature} = T_e + ICI$$

$$\text{Minimum interior air temperature} = T_e - ICI$$

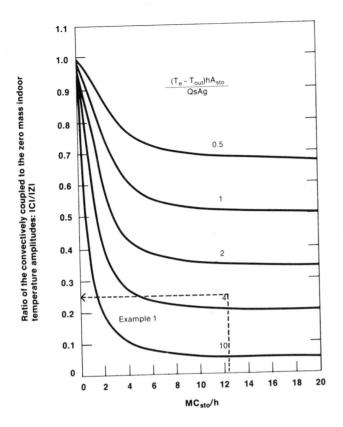

Figure 7.5 Convectively coupled temperature amplitudes.

where:

ICI = one-half temperature swing (amplitude) in convectively coupled case (°F)

IZI = one-half temperature swing (amplitude) with zero mass (°F) — From step 4.

T_e = Equilibrium temperature (°F)

Step 8: Find the radiative temperature swings (IRI).

To determine the temperature swings in the radiative case, first find the ratio of the radiantly coupled to the convectively coupled indoor temperature amplitudes (IRI/ICI) from Figure 7.6. Use the value for $(T_e-T_{out})/$ITI to select the appropriate curve on the graph. Then calculate the maximum and minimum temperatures for the radiative case from the following formulas:

$$IRI = ICI \times (IRI/ICI)$$

$$\text{Maximum interior air temperature} = T_e + IRI$$

$$\text{Minimum interior air temperature} = T_e - IRI$$

where:

IRI = one-half temperature swing (amplitude) with radiatively coupled mass ($^\circ$F)

ICI = one-half temperature swing (amplitude) in convectively couple case ($^\circ$F)

Example: A 10,000 ft^2 loft with 2200 ft^2 of coated south glass is located in Boston (latitude = 42°N) where the average March outdoor temperature, T_{out} = 38.1°F. The average March minimum and maximum temperatures (T_{min}, T_{max}) = 31.5°F and 44.6°F, respectively.

The warehouse is formed with 8 inch concrete walls and floor slab which have a combined area of 13,000 square feet. The solar collection is to take place through double glazed, selectively transmitting monitor skylights which can be expected to diffuse the sunlight over the entire storage area. The special glass has a U value of 0.27 BTU/hr$^\circ$Fft^2. The building heat loss rate, UA_{ns}, exclusive of the south glass losses, has been calculated to be 3500 BTU/hr$^\circ$F.

Step 1: Calculate the average hourly solar gain.

$$Q_s = \frac{DSHGF \times SC}{24} = \frac{1425 \times 0.74}{24} = 44 \text{ BTU/ft}^2 \text{ hr}$$

Step 2: Determine the equilibrium temperature.

$$T_e = T_{out} + \frac{A_g \times Q_s}{U_{ns} + U_{glass} \times A_g}$$

$$T_e = 38.1 + \frac{2200 \times 44}{3500 + 2200 \times 0.27} = 61.7^\circ F$$

Step 3: Calculate the outdoor air temperature amplitude.

$$ITI = \frac{44.6 - 31.5}{2} = 6.55^\circ F$$

Step 4: Find the zero mass amplitude.

From Figure 7.4,

$$IZI = 44^\circ F$$

Step 5: Look up the storage heat capacity.

From Table 7.5,

$$MC_{sto} = 12.14 \text{ BTU/ft}^2 {}^\circ F \text{ of surface area}$$

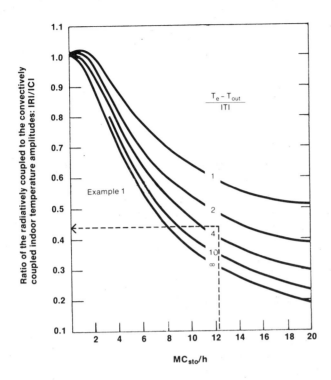

Figure 7.6 Radiatively coupled temperature amplitudes (from "A Simple Direct Gain Passive House Performance Prediction Model", Phillip W. B. Niles, *Passive Solar: State of the Art*, Proc. of the 2nd National Passive Solar Conference, Philadelpia, PA ISES, March 1978).

Step 6: Determine the storage surface film conductance.

Since most of the storage mass is in the floor, we will assume a surface fim conductance,

$$h = 1.0 \text{ BTU/hrft}^2$$

Step 7: Find the convective temperature swings.

$$MC_{sto}/h = 12.14/1.00 = 12.14$$

$$\frac{(T_e - T_{out})A_{sto}h}{Q_s A_g} = \frac{(61.7 - 38.1) \times 13,000 \times 1.00}{44 \times 2200} = 3.2$$

From graph 7.5,

$$ICI/IZI = 0.25$$

$$ICI = IZI \times (ICI/IZI) = 44 \times .25 = 11°F$$

TABLE 7.7 Nomenclature

Term	Definition	Units
A_g	South glass area	ft^2
A_{sto}	Surface area of thermal storage mass	ft^2
ICI	One-half temperature swing with convectively coupled mass	F
DSHGF	Daylong solar heat gain factor	Btu/ft^2 da
h	Storage surface film conductance	$Btu/hrft^2$ F
MC_{sto}	Effective storage mass heat capacity per thickness specified	Btu/ft^2 F
Q_s	Daylong clear day solar heat gain (divided by 24)	$Btu/hrft^2$
IRI	One-half temperature swing with radiatively coupled mass	F
SC	Shading coefficient	None
ITI	One-half of outdoor temperature swing	F
T_e	Average daily room air temperature (equilibrium temperature)	F
T_{out}	Average daily outdoor temperature	F
T_{max}	Normal daily maximum temperature (exterior)	F
T_{min}	Normal daily minimum temperature (exterior)	F
U_g	South glass loss coefficient	$Btu/hrft^2$ F
UA_{ns}	Non-solar loss coefficient $UA_{total} - UA_g$	Btu/hr F
UA_{total}	Total loss coefficient (including south facing glass)	Btu/hr F
IZI	One-half temperature swing with zero mass	F

Therefore, if the mass is convectively coupled to the sunlight:

Maximum interior air temperature = $T_e + ICI = 61.7 + 11 = 72.7°F$

Minimum interior air temperature = $T_e - ICI = 61.7 - 11 = 50.7°F$

Step 8: Find the radiative temperature swings

$$\frac{T_e - T_{out}}{ITI} = \frac{61.7 - 38.1}{6.55} = 3.6$$

From Figure 7.6,

    IRI/ICI = 0.42

    IRI = ICI x (IRI/ICI) = 11 x .42 = 4.6°F

Therefore, if the mass is radiatively coupled to the sunlight:

    Maximum interior air temperature = T_e + IRI = 61.7 + 4.6 = 66.3°F

    Minimum interior air temprature = T_e - IRI = 61.7 - 4.6 = 57°F

ANNUAL ENERGY SAVINGS

Once suitable comfort levels have been established by sizing the windows and thermal storage, one can determine the amount of energy the design saves. The amount of heating fuel saved over conventional nonsolar residences is a function of (1) the annual building thermal load, (2) the annual solar intake, and (3) the building load for a conventional structure of comparable design, but without the added solar windows. The auxiliary energy used in a passively heated residence is equal to the building load minus the solar intake. The amount of energy saved equals the auxiliary energy required to heat a comparable nonsolar building minus the auxiliary energy required to heat the solar building. Sometimes the thermal load for a solar building on cloudy days is larger than a conventional building's load due to the extra window area. So although the sun may supply a large percentage of the solar building's thermal load, the auxiliary heating bill could be only slightly less than the bill for a similar structure without solar windows.

    The thermal load a residence experiences during a heating season is determined by the climate, insulation levels of the structure, and internal heat gains from people, lights, and appliances. The rejected heat from people and appliances is regarded as "free" heat, since this heat is inescapably generated whenever light or mechanical movement is produced. It would be possible to heat a building entirely with this "free" heat if the insulation levels were high enough, and hardly any outside air leaked into the residence. Of course, no building can be insulated this tightly because of the high cost involved; also, breathing would be difficult in such a space. Nevertheless, today's well insulated buildings can go farther with their free heat than the older, poorly insulated buildings. A well insulated building has, in effect, a shorter heating season since the thermostat turns on the heat much later in the fall and for a shorter time in the spring. The thermostat calls for auxiliary heat when the outdoor temperature goes below a certain point. This temperature is known as the *building balance point temperature*, as given by the following relation:

$$\text{Balance point temperature} = \text{thermostat setting} - \frac{\text{daily average hourly internal gains}}{\text{building heat loss rate}}$$

This relation shows that the better the building is insulated, the lower the building's heat conductance, which lowers the balance point temperature. Table 3.6 shows average hourly internal gains for various residential building types. The building will not require heat when the outdoor temperature is above the balance point temperature. The amount of auxiliary heat required for a day when the outdoor temperature goes below this point is proportional to the balance point temperature minus the average daily outdoor temperature. The seasonal auxiliary heating load for the structure is proportional to the sum of similar temperature differences for each day that the outdoor temperature is below the balance point. This sum is known as the *degree days figure* by virtue of the units used to measure this number. Appendix 2 shows monthly and annual degree days as a function of the balance point temperature for major United States cities. Linear interpolation will suffice to find the degree days for a balance point that lies between the given figures. Many references give degree day figures for various cities, but usually only for a single balance point temperature of 65°F. If no balance point temperature is given, then a 65°F balance point temperature is assumed.

The building thermal load for a month, or a year, is found by multiplying the appropriate degree day figure by the building heat loss rate for a 24-hour period. This heat loss rate is a function of the building insulation levels and the air leakage rate of the building. Chapter 3 shows how ths figure is computed when the building configuration is known. However, during preliminary design, the building configuration usually is not available. A figure based on the projected square footage can be estimated from code requirements as shown in the previous design method for estimating indoor temperature swings. The steps in computing the seasonal building load are summarized at the end of the chapter.

The solar intake from south facing windows goes toward meeting the building's thermal load and reducing the auxiliary heating bill. Average solar radiation data is used for computing solar intake and enough thermal storage is assumed present so the interior air temperature does not rise more than 4°F to 6°F above the average daily room air temperature. Appendix 2 gives the incident solar radiation on a horizontal and a vertical south facing surface for an average day in each month of the year for major United States cities. Not all of this listed energy passed through the windows, of course, for there are transmission losses and occasional shading losses. (See the tables at the end of this chapter.)

Normally, the auxiliary heating usage is determined by comparing each month's solar intake with the month's thermal load. For months when the solar intake exceeds the load, the auxiliary energy use is zero, which implies that venting must have taken place to dissipate the surplus solar energy. Each month's auxiliary demand is summed to find the annual heating requirement. This month-by-month analysis can be tedious and certainly becomes too time consuming for quick estimates desired at the preliminary design stage. A quick estimate of annual auxiliary use in buildings with south facing windows can be reached by analyzing just the March weather data. The building load fraction supplied by solar energy in March will be within +0% or -15% of the annual building load fraction supplied by the sun. The method always gives an optimistic solar heating fraction, because the average March solar intake is slightly higher than most of the other winter months, but the average outdoor temperature for March nearly equals the average outdoor temperature for the heating season. This rule of thumb is valid for regions of the United States that undergo reasonably smooth changes in average solar exposure and outdoor air temperatures. It is not valid when the building balance point is below $60°F$ and for regions with heavy winter cloud cover or other unusual weather patterns such as temperature inversions. For unusual areas, a month-by-month analysis is warranted. Once the March percentage of building load supplied by the sun is determined, then the annual solar intake can be found by taking the same percentage of the annual thermal load. Then find the annual auxiliary heating load by subtracting the annual solar intake from the annual thermal load. The remainder of this chapter lists the steps of both the shorthand and longhand methods for determining annual auxiliary energy demand and annual energy savings.

Shorthand Method (only for buildings with south facing vertical glass)

Step 1: Compute the building *balance point temperature*, **in °F, using the following formula:**

$$\text{Balance Point Temperature} = \text{average indoor thermostat setting} - \frac{\text{daily average hourly internal gains}}{UA_{total}}$$

Step 2: Compute the *modified building load* **(BTU/month) for March using the following formula:**

$$\text{Modified building load} = UA_{total} \times 24 \text{ hrs/day} \times \text{March degree days}$$

where the degree days are found in Appendix 2 for the closest listed city and for the balance point computed in Step 1.

Step 3: Compute the *solar intake* **using the following formula:**

Solar intake = (average March daily vertical radiation, BTU/ft² day)

x (transmittance factor)

x (shading factor)

x (reflector enhancement factor)

x (number of days in month)

x (south glazing area, ft²)

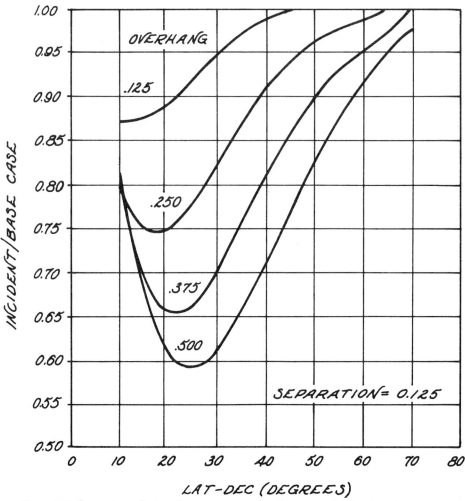

Figure 7.7 Correction factor for an opaque overhang vs. declination for various overhangs to window height ratios with overhang height of 112.5 percent of the window height (from *Passive Solar Design Handbook*, J. Douglas Balcomb, *et al.*, DOE/CS-0127/2, NTIS Springfield, VA 1980).

The various factors contained in the above equation are explained below:

Average daily vertical radiation: This factor is defined as the average daily radiation incident on a square foot of south facing, vertical surface in March. See Appendix 2.

Transmittance factor: This factor is designed to correct for the transmission of various glazing systems. The figures account for varying angles of incidence.

For normal 1/8 inch glass use.:

> single glazing: 0.825
> double glazing: 0.68
> triple glazing: 0.56

For a selective transmitter coated on 1/8 inch glass used with another lite of ordinary 1/8 inch glass, use 0.62.

Shading factor: This factor can be used to reduce the solar input for shading due to overhangs, mullions, trees, buildings, and so on. Use the factors shown in Figure 7.7 when windows are shaded with an opaque overhang. When no shading occurs, use a value of 1.

Reflection enhancement factor: This factor is used to enhance the solar input for reflection from specular surfaces, as shown in Figure 7.8. When no reflector is present use a value of 1.

Step 4: Compute the March *solar heating fraction* using the following relation:

$$\text{SHF}_{\text{March}} = \frac{\text{Solar intake}}{\text{Modified building load}}$$

Overheating takes place if this value is greater than 1. The design method for limiting temperature swings introduced at the beginning of this chapter must be used to properly size the windows and thermal storage mass.

Step 5: Compute the *annual auxiliary energy* used from the following formula:

Annual Auxiliary Energy Use = annual degree day for the balance point given in Step 1 x UA_{total} x 24 hrs/day x $(1 - \text{SHF}_{\text{March}})$

This relation assumes March's SHF equals the annual SHF. The percentage of auxiliary used is then proportional to 1–SHF.

Step 6: Compute the *annual energy savings:*

A. Compute a normal UA total for a similarly insulated building with an ordinary amount of glazing (a glass area equal to 8 to 10 percent of the floor area).

B. Compute the *balance point temperature* for the normal building.

C. Compute the *annual auxiliary energy* use for the ordinary building using the following formula: normal annual auxiliary energy use = annual degree days for the balance point given in Step 6B x normal UA_{total} x 24 hrs/day.

D. Determine the *annual* energy saving using the relation: Annual energy savings = normal annual auxiliary energy use – annual auxiliary energy use (from Step 5).

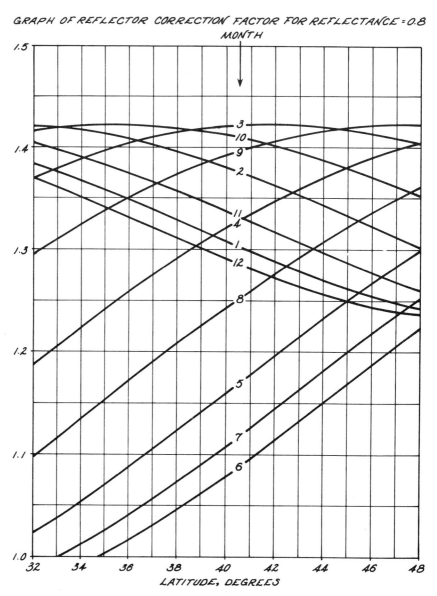

Figure 7.8 Correction factor for reflectance (from "Monthly Auxiliary Heating Profile," Douglas Balcomb, in *Passive Solar Workshop Passive Solar Associates*, 1978).

Step 7: Compute the annual *fuel consumption savings*

 A. If the auxiliary heating unit is an oil burner, divide the annual energy savings by *98,000 BTU/gal* to find the gallons of oil saved (assumes 70 percent burner and distribution efficiency).

 B. If the auxiliary heating unit is a gas burner, divide the annual energy savings by 75,000 BTU/CCF to find hundreds of cubic feet saved (assumes 75 percent burner and distribution efficiency).

 C. If the auxiliary heating is electrical resistance heating, divide the annual energy savings by 3412 BTU/kwh to find kwh saved.

Longhand Method (use for locations with unusual weather patterns)

 A. Complete Steps 1 through 3 of the shorthand method for each month of the heating season.

 B. Compute the *monthly auxiliary energy* use using the following relation:

  Monthly auxiliary energy use = monthly modified building load –
                monthly solar intake

  If the result is negative, set the monthly auxiliary energy use to zero.

 C. Sum each monthly auxiliary energy use to find the *annual auxiliary energy* used.

 D. Find the energy savings using Steps 6 and 7.

The two methods are exemplified below by continuing the example used for the temperature swing design method introduced at the beginning of this chapter. Assume the internal gains from people, lights, and appliances are 300,000 BTU/day and the average indoor air temperature is 62°F.

Example:

Shorthand Method

Step 1: Balance point

$$BP = 62°F - \frac{\dfrac{300{,}000 \text{ BTU/day}}{24}}{3500 \text{ BTU/hr}°F + 2200 \text{ ft}^2 \times 0.27 \text{ BTU/hr}°Fft^2} = 59°F$$

Step 2: Modified building load (MBL)

The total UA = 3500 BTU/hr°F + 2200ft^2 x 0.27 BTU/hr°Fft^2 = 4094 BTU/hr°F

 The interpolated March degree day from Appendix 2: 648 DD

 MBL = 4094 BTU/hr°F x 24 hr/day x 648 DD = 63.67 x 10^6 BTU

Step 3:   March solar intake

$$\text{Solar intake} = 1127 \text{ BTU/ft}^2\text{day} \times 0.62 \times 1 \times 31 \text{ day/mo} \times 2200 \text{ ft}^2$$
$$= 47.65 \times 10^6 \text{ BTU/mo}$$

Step 4:   March solar heating fraction

$$\text{SHF}_{March} = 47.65 \div 63.67 = 75\%$$

Step 5:   Annual auxiliary energy

The interpolated annual degree days from Appendix 2 for a $59°$F balance point:
4165 DD

$$\text{Annual auxiliary energy} = 4165 \text{ DD} \times 4094 \text{ BTU/hr}°\text{F} \times 24 \text{ hr/day} (1\text{-}75\%)$$
$$= 102.31 \times 10^6 \text{ BTU/yr}$$

Step 6:   Compute the annual energy savings

A. Assume the non-solar building has a UA_{total} of 3700 BTU/hr°F

B. B.P. $= 62 - \dfrac{\dfrac{300{,}000}{24}}{3700} = 58.7°\text{F}$

C. Annual auxiliary = 4100 DD $\times$ 3700 BTU/hr°F $\times$ 24 hr/day = 370.97 $\times$ 10^6 BTU/yr

D. Annual energy savings = (370.97 - 102.31) $\times$ 10^6 BTU/yr = 268.66 $\times$ 10^6 BTU/yr

Step 7:   Fuel consumption savings

$$\frac{268.66 \times 10^6 \text{ BTU/yr}}{98{,}000 \text{ BTU/gal}} = 2740 \text{ gallons/yr.}$$

Longhand Method

| | | $\times 10^6$ *BTU* | | |
Month	*Load*	*Solar In*	*Solar Used*	*Auxiliary Energy*
October	14.25	50.40	14.25	0
November	40.78	35.76	35.76	5.02
December	79.19	33.32	33.32	45.87
January	90.79	37.13	37.13	53.66
February	78.70	40.18	40.18	38.52
March	63.67	47.65	47.65	16.02
April	31.06	42.15	31.06	0
May	8.35	39.92	8.35	0
	406.79			159.09

From **Step 6**: Annual Energy Savings (370.97-159.09) x 10^6BTU/yr = 211.88 x 10^6BTU/yr

REFERENCES

B. Anderson and D. Balcomb, et al., *Passive Solar Design Handbook, Volumes 1 & 2,* U.S. Department of Energy, Washington, D.C., DOE/CS-0127/2, Dist. Cat. UC-59, 1980.

P. Niles, "A Simple Direct Gain Passive House Performance Prediction Model," Proceedings, Second National Passive Solar Conference, International Solar Energy Society, 1978.

_, *Engineering Weather Date.* U.S. Department of the Air Force, The Army, and the Navy, AFM 88-29, 1978.

P. Niles, and K Haggar, *Passive Solar Handbook,* California Energy Commission, Sacramento, 1980.

Chapter **8**

The Future

Building a passively heated residence is not difficult. The design can look traditional or progressive. Glass areas can be tastefully designed to increase thermal comfort and decrease glare. Nevertheless, the designer must responsibly advise the homeowner that some things are different in a direct gain solar residence. "Going passive" always holds some surprises for the home or apartment owner. The rush to save energy can easily end up costing too much or adversely affecting comfort.

PERFORMANCE BARRIERS TO SOLAR ARCHTECTURE

Most homeowners are surprised to learn they must tolerate air temperature fluctuations when heating passively. Although the sunny day temperature amplitide can be as low as $\pm 3°F$ in buildings with adequate mass, most temperature fluctuations are more than twice this amount. Of course, air temperatures fluctuate in conventionally heated homes, since thermostats can only control the temperature to ± 1.5 or $2°F$; this fluctuation is not sensed by most people, although three times this amount is easily felt.

The large amount of glass used in direct-gain buildings can produce intolerable glare unless the space is carefully designed. Most homeowners sense this problem during the design stages and tend to limit the glass area for fear of creating a visually uncomfortable space, or a space that lacks privacy. Concern for fabrics that may fade rapidly in sunny spaces also creates pressure to reduce window sizes.

Cost can easily get out of hand when using conventional masonry materials for storing heat. Massive heat storage walls have to be supported solidly; joints must be made carefully between masonry and wood elements to account for different shrinkage rates, and capable masons must be located.

Movable insulation systems for windows are the most difficult direct-gain item to select. Personal aesthetic and cost restrictions rule out most alternatives. All these extra costs sometimes can add up to more than the costs for an active solar heating system.

Other barriers not related to performance, but to policy, do exist. Tax breaks for passively heated structures are not yet defined. Solar access rights cannot legally be secured; and many banks still do not mortgage solar homes. Once the homeowner is advised of the risks involved in building a passively heated house, a responsible design can emerge that answers the homeowner's requirements.

THE MATERIALS REVOLUTION

This book shows how to apply new building materials designed for passive solar space heating. These new materials often come to the market with limited track records, and the ultimate lifetime of a new offering is not really known. Yet, past failures make companies more conservative with new products. A good case in point is coated glass.

When window glass was first tinted several decades ago, quick market introduction led to some embarrassing failures. Many of the coatings corroded into blotchy messes. The industry was given a bad name that took years to eradicate. This history explains why the selective transmitting glass had been slow to come to market. The industry does not want to repeat history with this new product. Yet users are demanding the product now. What reaches the market are heavily tested coatings. But a risk of discoloration 15 to 20 years from now is there, though the probability of failure is small.

Window product advances will accelerate as consumer confidence increases. Selectively transmitting windows will become available in a variety of different products specifically tailored to different applications and different regions of the country. There will be products on glass and plastic, for heating or cooling, in different colors or crystal clear. Window manufacturers all over the country will offer the product in their existing and new lines once the public understands that an invisible coating can nearly double the insulating value of a window. Less window will do more solar heating, which means glare problems will be reduced and movable insulation can be abandoned in most climates.

The high costs of thermal storage will be reduced greatly as more phase-change alternatives make their way to market. The public may be slow to trust the materials at first, but acceptance is inevitable as the material finds its way into more and more building elements. The future will bring constant temperature heat storage material encapsulated in blocks, floor tiles, and even ceiling and wallboards. Temperature fluctuations will not exceed the fluctuations caused by an ordinary thermostat when the more refined heat storage materials emerge. Nature offers innu merable compounds that store heat latently; it remains for the chemical engineers to discover these alternatives.

These material advances are most important to the homeowner; for homes will not have to be designed defensively to conserve valuable energy. Superinsulated residences with small windows do save energy, but they also cut the user from his environment. The materials revolution will give the designer the freedom once again to open up to the outdoors, to bring it in, and to create exquisitely comfortable spaces that also save energy.

Appendix 1

TI-59 Programmable Calculator Codes

Title INTERIOR AIR TEMPERATURE SWING

Programmer Stephen Hale   **Date** Jan. 1979

Partioning (Op 17) Std.   **Library Module** Any   **Printer** No   **Cards** 1, 2

PROGRAM DESCRIPTION

Given a data base, the program calculates the 24 hour average and min-max indoor air temperature for a single zone heated directly by the sun when the storage mass is either dominated by radiative or convective coupling. Internal gains and night-time window insulation are not modeled. Only south facing windows can be modeled.

This program follows the analytic method given by: Philip Niles, "A Simple Direct Gain Passive House Performance Prediction Model," Proceedings of the 2nd National Passive Solar Conference, International Solar Energy Society, March 1978.

USER INSTRUCTIONS

STEP	PROCEDURE	ENTER	PRESS	DISPLAY
1	Read card sides 1, 2	0		1,2
2	Enter Ave. 24 hr. outdoor air temp.	Temp ($^\circ$F)	STO 02	Temp.
3	Enter zone UA minus window UA	BTUH/$^\circ$F	STO 03	Conductance
4	Enter total daily insolation transmitted by a sq. ft. of window/24	BTUH/ft^2	STO 04	Insolation
5	Enter window conductance	BTUH/$^\circ$Fft^2	STO 05	Unit Conduct.
6	Enter outdoor daily air temp. swing/2	$^\circ$F	STO 06	Temp.
7	Enter storage surface area/ window ft^2	Ratio	STO 07	Ratio
8	Storage surface convective conductance use: 1.0 BTUH/$^\circ$Fft^2 for heat flow up. 0.6 BTUH/$^\circ$Fft^2 for heat flow down	BTUH/$^\circ$Fft^2	STO 08	Unit Conduct.
9	Enter 24	24	STO 09	24
10	Enter equivalent storage heat capacity per ft^2 of exposed area	BTU/$^\circ$Fft^2	STO 10	Heat Cap.
11	Enter window area	ft^2	STO 11	Area
12	Run Program		E	Average Daily indoor air temp. ($^\circ$F)
13	Run Program		R/S	Temp. swing/2 (convective case)
14	Run Program		R/S	Temp. swing/2 (radiative case)

SAMPLE PROBLEM

Find the interior air temperature excursions for a single zone house in the Boston climate on a clear day in March. Assume heat mirror on plastic is suspended between two hermetically sealed glass panes totaling 180 ft^2 with a U value of 0.18 BTU/hr$^\circ$Fft^2. The window daily average transmission is 57.2%. The building UA minus the window UA is 223.6 BTUH/°F. The thermal storage is 360 ft² of phase change material placed in the ceiling. Sunlight reaches the ceiling via reflectorized louvers in the windows.

INPUT	ENTER	PRESS
Average outdoor temperature	40	STO 02
Zone UA – window UA	223.6	STO 03
Average daily insolation/24 (1384 x 0.572/24)	33	STO 04
Window U	0.18	STO 05
Outdoor air temp. swing/2	10	STO 06
Mass to glass area ratio (360/180)	2	STO 07
Surface conductance	0.6	STO 08
	24	STO 09
Storage heat capacity	22	STO 10
Window area	180	STO 11

RUN	
	E

OUTPUT	DISPLAY	
Average daily indoor air temp.	63.203	R/S
Convective swing/2	25.191	R/S
Radiative swing/2	7.269	

Note: The maximum indoor air temperature for radiative coupling is 63.203 + 7.269 = 70.472°F

000	76	LBL	050	95	=	100	85	+	150	08	8
001	11	A	051	85	+	101	43	RCL	151	03	3
002	43	RCL	052	43	RCL	102	12	12	152	95	=
003	01	01	053	05	05	103	85	+.	153	42	STO
004	75	-	054	95	=	104	43	RCL	154	17	17
005	43	RCL	055	42	STO	105	15	15	155	43	RCL
006	02	02	056	28	28	106	95	=	156	45	45
007	95	=	057	43	RCL	107	34	√X	157	55	÷
008	65	×	058	01	01	108	42	STO	158	43	RCL
009	43	RCL	059	75	-	109	39	39	159	17	17
010	03	03	060	43	RCL	110	43	RCL	160	95	=
011	95	=	061	02	02	111	07	07	161	33	X²
012	42	STO	062	95	=	112	65	×	162	85	+
013	13	13	063	65	×	113	43	RCL	163	01	1
014	43	RCL	064	01	1	114	08	08	164	95	=
015	01	01	065	93	.	115	95	=	165	42	STO
016	75	-	066	06	6	116	55	÷	166	18	18
017	43	RCL	067	06	6	117	43	RCL	167	43	RCL
018	02	02	068	06	6	118	28	28	168	47	47
019	95	=	069	95	=	119	95	=	169	55	÷
020	65	×	070	33	X²	120	85	+	170	43	RCL
021	43	RCL	071	42	STO	121	02	2	171	18	18
022	05	05	072	15	15	122	95	=	172	95	=
023	95	=	073	43	RCL	123	65	×	173	85	+
024	42	STO	074	06	06	124	43	RCL	174	01	1
025	30	30	075	33	X²	125	07	07	175	95	=
026	43	RCL	076	42	STO	126	65	×	176	35	1/X
027	04	04	077	12	12	127	43	RCL	177	34	√X
028	75	-	078	43	RCL	128	08	08	178	95	=
029	43	RCL	079	01	01	129	95	=	179	42	STO
030	30	30	080	75	-	130	55	÷	180	40	40
031	95	=	081	43	RCL	131	43	RCL	181	43	RCL
032	42	STO	082	02	02	132	28	28	182	39	39
033	46	46	083	95	=	133	95	=	183	65	×
034	43	RCL	084	65	×	134	42	STO	184	43	RCL
035	13	13	085	01	1	135	47	47	185	40	40
036	55	÷	086	93	.	136	43	RCL	186	95	=
037	43	RCL	087	06	6	137	09	09	187	42	STO
038	46	46	088	06	6	138	65	×	188	41	41
039	95	=	089	06	6	139	43	RCL	189	91	R/S
040	42	STO	090	65	×	140	08	08	190	43	RCL
041	11	11	091	43	RCL	141	95	=	191	01	01
042	91	R/S	092	06	06	142	42	STO	192	75	-
043	76	LBL	093	65	×	143	45	45	193	43	RCL
044	12	B	094	01	1	144	43	RCL	194	02	02
045	43	RCL	095	93	.	145	10	10	195	95	=
046	03	03	096	04	4	146	65	×	196	55	÷
047	55	÷	097	01	1	147	06	6	197	93	.
048	43	RCL	098	04	4	148	93	.	198	06	6
049	11	11	099	95	=	149	02	2	199	95	=

200	42	STO	250	43	RCL	300	33	X²	350	03	03
201	29	29	251	02	02	301	95	=	351	85	+
202	06	6	252	95	=	302	42	STO	352	43	RCL
203	93	.	253	42	STO	303	44	44	353	05	05
204	02	2	254	34	34	304	43	RCL	354	65	×
205	08	8	255	06	6	305	43	43	355	43	RCL
206	03	3	256	93	.	306	65	×	356	11	11
207	65	×	257	02	2	307	43	RCL	357	54	)
208	43	RCL	258	08	8	308	33	33	358	85	+
209	10	10	259	03	3	309	95	=	359	43	RCL
210	95	=	260	65	×	310	85	+	360	02	02
211	42	STO	261	43	RCL	311	43	RCL	361	95	=
212	31	31	262	10	10	312	44	44	362	42	STO
213	43	RCL	263	95	=	313	95	=	363	01	01
214	09	09	264	42	STO	314	34	√X	364	91	R/S
215	65	×	265	35	35	315	95	=	365	61	GTO
216	43	RCL	266	43	RCL	316	42	STO	366	12	B
217	08	08	267	08	08	317	42	42	367	00	0
218	95	=	268	65	×	318	43	RCL	368	00	0
219	42	STO	269	43	RCL	319	41	41	369	00	0
220	32	32	270	09	09	320	55	÷			
221	43	RCL	271	95	=	321	43	RCL			
222	31	31	272	42	STO	322	39	39			
223	55	÷	273	36	36	323	95	=			
224	43	RCL	274	43	RCL	324	65	×			
225	32	32	275	35	35	325	43	RCL			
226	95	=	276	55	÷	326	42	42			
227	85	+	277	43	RCL	327	95	=			
228	01	1	278	36	36	328	91	R/S			
229	95	=	279	95	=	329	00	0			
230	65	×	280	33	X²	330	00	0			
231	43	RCL	281	85	+	331	00	0			
232	06	06	282	01	1	332	00	0			
233	95	=	283	95	=	333	00	0			
234	65	×	284	65	×	334	00	0			
235	01	1	285	93	.	335	00	0			
236	93	.	286	06	6	336	00	0			
237	04	4	287	95	=	337	00	0			
238	01	1	288	42	STO	338	00	0			
239	04	4	289	37	37	339	00	0			
240	95	=	290	43	RCL	340	76	LBL			
241	85	+	291	34	34	341	15	E			
242	43	RCL	292	55	÷	342	43	RCL			
243	29	29	293	43	RCL	343	04	04			
244	95	=	294	37	37	344	65	×			
245	42	STO	295	95	=	345	43	RCL			
246	33	33	296	42	STO	346	11	11			
247	43	RCL	297	43	43	347	55	÷			
248	01	01	298	43	RCL	348	53	(			
249	75	-	299	06	06	349	43	RCL			

Title SOLAR ANGLES AND RADIATION

Programmer Charles C. Benton   **Date** Jan 1979
Partioning (Op 17) 559.49   **Library Module** Any   **Printer** No   **Cards** 1,2,3,4

PROGRAM DESCRIPTION

Given a data base, the program calculates beam, diffuse, and total radiation upon and transmitted through a specified plane. Radiation values are given for clear sky conditions on the 21st day of the month specified. Optional output includes hourly values for solar altitude, azimuth, angle of incidence, beam and diffuse (ground plane and sky vault) radiation. Optionally, these values may be obtained for any time and day. Calculations are from ASHRAE procedures for incident radiation values. The user may specify solar time or standard time. This program does not compensate for cloudiness or shading.

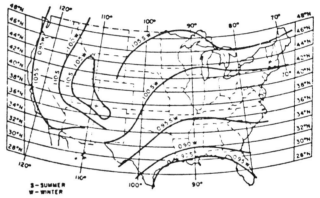

Estimated Atmospheric Clearness Numbers in the
U.S. for Nonindustrial Localities

Table A-1 Solar Radiation Intensity and Related Data BtuH/sq ft

Date	I_o	Equation of Time, min:sec	Declination, deg	A, Btuh/ sq ft	B, Air Mass^{-1}	C (Dimensionless)
Jan 21	440.1	−11:18	−20	390	0.142	0.058
Feb 21	436.5	−13:28	−10.8	385	0.144	0.060
Mar 21	430.0	− 7:19	0	376	0.156	0.071
Apr 21	422.8	+ 0:03	+11.6	360	0.180	0.097
May 21	416.5	+ 3:32	+20.0	350	0.196	0.121
June 21	413.1	− 1:48	+23.45	345	0.205	0.134
July 21	413.5	− 6:25	+20.6	344	0.207	0.136
Aug 21	417.6	− 1:18	+12.3	351	0.201	0.122
Sept 21	424.0	+ 7:30	0	365	0.177	0.092
Oct 21	431.1	+15:06	−10.5	378	0.160	0.073
Nov 21	437.6	+13:55	−19.8	387	0.149	0.063
Dec 21	441.0	+ 1:32	−23.45	391	0.142	0.057

USER INSTRUCTIONS

STEP	PROCEDURE	ENTER	PRESS	DISPLAY
1	Re-partition	5	²OP17	559.49
2	Read card sides 1,2,3,4	0		1,2,3,4
3	Enter month number (Jan = 1)	Month	A	1
4	Enter latitude	Lat.	R/S	2
5	Enter longitude	Long.	R/S	3
6	Enter Atmos. clearance	At.cl.	R/S	4
7	Enter surface tilt (90° = vertical)	Tilt	R/S	5
8	Enter surface orientation, (+ east, – west)	Orient	R/S	6
9	Enter ground reflectance	Reflt.	R/S	7
10	Enter avg. transmission factor for 0-55° angle of incidence	0-55	R/S	8
11	Enter avg. trans. fact. for 55-65°	55-65	R/S	9
12	Enter avg. trans. fact. for 65-75°	65-75	R/S	10
13	Enter avg. trans. fact. for 75-90°	75-90	R/S	0
14	Run program		B	flashes
15	Daily beam radiation transmitted		C	Beam trans.
16	Daily beam radiation incident		R/S	Beam incid.
17	Daily diffuse radiation transmitted		D	diff. trans.
18	Daily diffuse radiation incident		R/S	diff. incid.
19	Daily total radiation transmitted		E	total trans.
20	Daily total radiation incident		R/S	total incid.

OPTION NO. 1

To run a day other than the 21st of the month insert the following input steps after step no. 13 on the first page.

STEP	PROCEDURE	ENTER	PRESS	DISPLAY
1	Initialize	– –	A'	11
2	Enter equation of time	Eq. Time	R/S	12
3	Enter declination	Decl.	R/S	13
4	Enter A factor	A factor	R/S	14
5	Enter B factor	B factor	R/S	15
6	Enter C factor	C factor	R/S	0

Note: These values may be interpolated from the ASHRAE table included in the Appendix.

OPTION NO. 2

To run a specific time other than the standard even hour, insert the following step after step no. 13 on the first page.

STEP	PROCEDURE	ENTER	PRESS	DISPLAY
1	Enter time in decimal, 24 hr. format	Time	B′	0

Note: It is recommended that Option No. 4 be exercised when Option No. 2 is used.

OPTION NO. 3

To run on solar time rather than standard time, insert the following step after step 13 on the first page.

STEP	PROCEDURE	ENTER	PRESS	DISPLAY
1	Initialize	— —	C′	0

Note: This conversion is accomplished by setting the equation of time = 0 and longitude = standard meridian

OPTION NO. 4

Hourly data output is available. In addition to finding daily total radiation values, this program will provide the user with hourly values for solar position and radiation. During the normal run of the program these values will flash briefly on the display. However, by setting flag no. 1, the program will stop at each value. The program must then be restarted, by pressing R/S, to continue after each value. Flag no. 1's status may be changed by pressing D′. Do not do this after the input section of the program because it will misplace the program pointer. During the run section, change flag status by using the SFG key.

When flag no. 1 is set, the program will stop at the following values for each hour (in the following order).

1. Hour number
2. Solar altitude in degrees
3. Solar azimuth in degrees
4. Angle of incidence in degrees
5. Incident beam radiation in BTUH/SF
6. Transmitted beam radiation in BTUH/SF
7. Incident diffuse radiation in BTUH/SF
8. Transmitted diffuse radiation in BTUH/SF

This information will be presented for clear day conditions on the 21st of the month specified, beginning at 4 a.m. and running until 8 p.m. When an hour is encountered during which the sun is below the horizon, the program will skip to the next hour.

Storage Register Assignments

00	Hour Counter	14	B factor
01	Latitude	15	C factor
02	Longitude	16	Incident Beam Radiation Total
03	Atmospheric Clearance	17	Incident Diffuse Radiation Total
04	Tilt	18	Transmitted Beam Radiation Total
05	Orientation	19	Transmitted Diffuse Radiation Total
06	Ground Plane Reflectance	20	.9999999999
07	Transmission @ 0°-55° Angle of incidence	21	Operational
08	Transmission @ 55-65° Angle of incidence	22	Operational
09	Transmission @ 65-75° Angle of incidence	23	Operational
10	Transmission @ 75-90° Angle of incidence	24	Indirect Address for 26-37/Operational
11	Equation of time	25	Indirect Address for 38-49/Operational
12	Declination	26-37	Eq. of Time/A factor/C factor
13	A factor	38-49	Declination/B factor

SAMPLE PROBLEM NO. 1

Find daily total radiation values for direct, diffuse, and total radiation, both incident and transmitted for a vertical 1/8" thick glass window facing southeast at 42°N latitude, 71°W longitude during May. Atmospheric clearance is 0.85 and ground plane reflection is 0.2. Use solar time.

		ENTER	PRESS	DISPLAY
INPUT				
	Month	5	A	1
	Latitude	42°	R/S	2
	Longitude	71°	R/S	3
	Atmospheric Clearance	0.85	R/S	4
	T.H.	90°	R/S	5
	Orientation	45°	R/S	6
	Ground Plane Reflectance	0.2	R/S	7
	Transmission @ 0-55°	0.90	R/S	8
	Transmission @ 55-65°	0.82	R/S	9
	Transmission @ 65-75°	0.70	R/S	10
	Transmission @ 75-90°	0.40	R/S	0
	Adjust for Solar Time	—	C'	0
RUN*		—	B	0
OUTPUT				
	Daily total transmitted beam radiation	—	C	614.95 BTU/SF
	Daily total incident beam radiation	—	R/S	747.33 BTU/SF

Daily total transmitted diffuse
radiation   .   —   D   310.77 BTU/SF
Daily total incident diffuse
radiation   —   R/S   378.98 BTU/SF
Daily total transmitted total
radiation   —   E   925.73 BTU/SF
Daily total incident total
radiation   —   R/S   1126.31 BTU/SF

Note: RUN is finished when 21.00 enters the Display

```
000  76  LBL      050  18  18      100  42  STO      150  95   =
001  19  D'       051  85   +      101  25  25       151  42  STO
002  87  IFF      052  43  RCL     102  75   -       152  13  13
003  01  01       053  19  19      103  01   1       153  73  RC*
004  42  STO      054  95   =      104  02   2       154  25  25
005  86  STF      055  91  R/S     105  95   =       155  50  IXI
006  01  01       056  43  RCL     106  42  STO      156  22  INV
007  01   1       057  16  16      107  24  24       157  59  INT
008  91  R/S      058  85   +      108  73  RC*      158  42  STO
009  76  LBL      059  43  RCL     109  24  24       159  14  14
010  42  STO      060  17  17      110  55   ÷       160  73  RC*
011  22  INV      061  95   =      111  01   1       161  24  24
012  86  STF      062  91  R/S     112  00   0       162  50  IXI
013  01  01       063  76  LBL     113  00   0       163  22  INV
014  01   1       064  16  A'      114  00   0       164  59  INT
015  94  +/-      065  01   1      115  95   =       165  42  STO
016  91  R/S      066  06   6      116  59  INT      166  15  15
017  76  LBL      067  32  X:T     117  55   ÷       167  03   3
018  85   +       068  01   1      118  01   1       168  42  STO
019  66  PAU      069  01   1      119  00   0       169  00  00
020  22  INV      070  42  STO     120  95   =       170  01   1
021  87  IFF      071  21  21      121  42  STO      171  01   1
022  01  01       072  61  GTO     122  11  11       172  32  X:T
023  24  CE       073  23  LNX     123  73  RC*      173  01   1
024  91  R/S      074  76  LBL     124  25  25       174  42  STO
025  76  LBL      075  17  B'      125  59  INT      175  21  21
026  24  CE       076  75   -      126  55   ÷       176  76  LBL
027  92  RTN      077  01   1      127  01   1       177  23  LNX
028  76  LBL      078  95   =      128  00   0       178  91  R/S
029  35  1/X      079  42  STO     129  00   0       179  72  ST*
030  91  R/S      080  00  00      130  95   =       180  21  21
031  76  LBL      081  00   0      131  42  STO      181  01   1
032  13  C        082  91  R/S     132  12  12       182  44  SUM
033  43  RCL      083  76  LBL     133  73  RC*      183  21  21
034  18  18       084  18  C'      134  24  24       184  43  RCL
035  91  R/S      085  00   0      135  50  IXI      185  21  21
036  43  RCL      086  42  STO     136  59  INT      186  22  INV
037  16  16       087  11  11      137  55   ÷       187  67  EQ
038  91  R/S      088  01   1      138  01   1       188  23  LNX
039  76  LBL      089  05   5      139  00   0       189  00   0
040  14  D        090  42  STO     140  00   0       190  91  R/S
041  43  RCL      091  02  02      141  00   0       191  76  LBL
042  19  19       092  00   0      142  95   =       192  12  B
043  91  R/S      093  91  R/S     143  22  INV      193  58  FIX
044  43  RCL      094  76  LBL     144  59  INT      194  02  02
045  17  17       095  11  A       145  65   ×       195  00   0
046  91  R/S      096  85   +      146  01   1       196  42  STO
047  76  LBL      097  03   3      147  00   0       197  16  16
048  15  E        098  07   7      148  00   0       198  42  STO
049  43  RCL      099  95   =      149  00   0       199  17  17
```

200	42	STO	250	43	RCL	300	32	X:T	350	77	GE
201	18	18	251	11	11	301	53	(	351	33	X²
202	42	STO	252	95	=	302	43	RCL	352	01	1
203	19	19	253	65	×	303	12	12	353	94	+/-
204	76	LBL	254	93	.	304	38	SIN	354	49	PRD
205	22	INV	255	02	2	305	65	×	355	23	23
206	69	OP	256	05	5	306	43	RCL	356	76	LBL
207	20	20	257	95	=	307	01	01	357	33	X²
208	02	2	258	94	+/-	308	39	COS	358	09	9
209	01	1	259	42	STO	309	54	)	359	00	0
210	32	X:T	260	21	21	310	75	-	360	32	X:T
211	43	RCL	261	93	.	311	53	(	361	43	RCL
212	00	00	262	01	1	312	43	RCL	362	23	23
213	77	GE	263	32	X:T	313	12	12	363	71	SBR
214	35	1/X	264	53	(	314	39	COS	364	85	+
215	71	SBR	265	53	(	315	65	×	365	85	+
216	85	+	266	43	RCL	316	43	RCL	366	43	RCL
217	07	7	267	01	01	317	01	01	367	05	05
218	93	.	268	39	COS	318	38	SIN	368	95	=
219	05	5	269	65	×	319	65	×	369	50	I×I
220	32	X:T	270	43	RCL	320	43	RCL	370	39	COS
221	43	RCL	271	12	12	321	21	21	371	65	×
222	02	02	272	39	COS	322	39	COS	372	43	RCL
223	76	LBL	273	65	×	323	54	)	373	22	22
224	25	CLR	274	43	RCL	324	95	=	374	39	COS
225	75	-	275	21	21	325	55	÷	375	65	×
226	01	1	276	39	COS	326	43	RCL	376	43	RCL
227	05	5	277	54	)	327	22	22	377	04	04
228	95	=	278	85	+	328	39	COS	378	38	SIN
229	77	GE	279	53	(	329	95	=	379	54	)
230	25	CLR	280	43	RCL	330	22	INV	380	85	+
231	94	+/-	281	01	01	331	77	GE	381	43	RCL
232	65	×	282	38	SIN	332	32	X:T	382	22	22
233	04	4	283	65	×	333	01	1	383	38	SIN
234	95	=	284	43	RCL	334	76	LBL	384	65	×
235	42	STO	285	12	12	335	32	X:T	385	43	RCL
236	21	21	286	38	SIN	336	22	INV	386	04	04
237	43	RCL	287	54	)	337	39	COS	387	39	COS
238	00	00	288	54	)	338	94	+/-	388	95	=
239	75	-	289	22	INV	339	85	+	389	22	INV
240	01	1	290	38	SIN	340	01	1	390	39	COS
241	02	2	291	42	STO	341	08	8	391	22	INV
242	95	=	292	22	22	342	00	0	392	77	GE
243	65	×	293	22	INV	343	95	=	393	34	ГX
244	06	6	294	77	GE	344	42	STO	394	09	9
245	00	0	295	22	INV	345	23	23	395	00	0
246	85	+	296	71	SBR	346	29	CP	396	76	LBL
247	43	RCL	297	85	+	347	43	RCL	397	34	ГX
248	21	21	298	43	RCL	348	21	21	398	42	STO
249	85	+	299	20	20	349	22	INV	399	24	24

400	71	SBR	450	23	LNX	500	23	23	
401	85	+	451	35	1/X	501	95	=	
402	32	X:T	452	65	×	502	42	STD	
403	05	5	453	43	RCL	503	25	25	
404	05	5	454	13	13	504	43	RCL	
405	22	INV	455	65	×	505	23	23	
406	77	GE	456	43	RCL	506	65	×	
407	44	SUM	457	03	03	507	53	(	
408	43	RCL	458	95	=	508	43	RCL	
409	07	07	459	42	STD	509	15	15	
410	61	GTD	460	23	23	510	85	+	
411	45	YX	461	65	×	511	43	RCL	
412	76	LBL	462	43	RCL	512	22	22	
413	44	SUM	463	24	24	513	38	SIN	
414	06	6	464	39	CDS	514	54	)	
415	05	5	465	95	=	515	65	×	
416	22	INV	466	71	SBR	516	43	RCL	
417	77	GE	467	85	+	517	06	06	
418	52	EE	468	44	SUM	518	65	×	
419	43	RCL	469	16	16	519	43	RCL	
420	08	08	470	42	STD	520	24	24	
421	61	GTD	471	21	21	521	95	=	
422	45	YX	472	65	×	522	85	+	
423	76	LBL	473	43	RCL	523	43	RCL	
424	52	EE	474	25	25	524	25	25	
425	07	7	475	95	=	525	95	=	
426	05	5	476	44	SUM	526	71	SBR	
427	22	INV	477	18	18	527	85	+	
428	77	GE	478	71	SBR	528	44	SUM	
429	61	GTD	479	85	+	529	17	17	
430	43	RCL	480	01	1	530	65	×	
431	09	09	481	75	-	531	43	RCL	
432	61	GTD	482	43	RCL	532	08	08	
433	45	YX	483	04	04	533	95	=	
434	76	LBL	484	39	CDS	534	44	SUM	
435	61	GTD	485	54	)	535	19	19	
436	43	RCL	486	55	÷	536	71	SBR	
437	10	10	487	02	2	537	85	+	
438	76	LBL	488	95	=	538	61	GTD	
439	45	YX	489	42	STD	539	22	INV	
440	42	STD	490	24	24	540	00	0	
441	25	25	491	94	+/-	541	00	0	
442	43	RCL	492	85	+	542	00	0	
443	14	14	493	01	1	543	00	0	
444	55	÷	494	95	=	544	00	0	
445	43	RCL	495	65	×	545	00	0	
446	22	22	496	43	RCL	546	00	0	
447	38	SIN	497	15	15	547	00	0	
448	95	=	498	65	×	548	00	0	
449	22	INV	499	43	RCL	549	00	0	

DATA REGISTERS:

.9999999999	20
0.	21
0.	22
0.	23
0.	24
0.	25
-113390.058	26
-135385.06	27
-73376.071	28
1360.097	29
35350.121	30
-18345.134	31
-64344.136	32
-13351.122	33
75365.092	34
151378.073	35
139387.063	36
15391.057	37
-2000.142	38
-1080.144	39
0.156	40
1160.18	41
2000.196	42
2345.205	43
2060.207	44
1230.201	45
0.177	46
-1050.16	47
-1980.149	48
-2345.142	49

LABELS:

001	19	D'
010	42	STD
018	85	+
026	24	CE
029	35	1/X
032	13	C
040	14	D
048	15	E
064	16	A'
075	17	B'
084	18	C'
095	11	A
177	23	LNX
192	12	B
205	22	INV
224	25	CLR
335	32	X:T
357	33	X²
397	34	ГX
413	44	SUM
424	52	EE
435	61	GTD
439	45	YX

Title   AVERAGE DAILY RADIATION III
Programmer Jim Rosen   **Date** Jan. 23, 1980
Partitioning (Op 17) 719.29   **Library Module** Any   **Printer** Yes   **Card** 1,2,3,4

PROGRAM DESCRIPTION

Given a data base, this program calculates the average daily insolation striking a surface of any orientation. The daily radiation is broken down into its beam, diffuse and reflected components, in order to facilitate determining the quantity transmitted through a glazing system.

The necessary data is all entered with the user defined labels. To re-run the program, all the values need not be re-entered. Simply enter the values that differ from the previous run and then press C' to re-run the program. Note that the average horizontal radiation is restricted to the specified units and that English and metric units are entered with different keys.

This program follows the method outlined by S.A. Klein[1]. It uses the relationships reported by Page[1] to calculate the daily diffuse radiation.

USER INSTRUCTIONS

STEP	PROCEDURE	ENTER	PRESS	DISPLAY
1	Partition calculator	3	OP 17	719.29
2	Read card sides 1,2,3,4	0		1,2,3,4
3	Enter tilt (90° = vertical)	Tilt	A	Tilt
4	Enter absolute value of azimuth angle (0° = south, 90° = east or west, 180° = north)	Azimuth	B	Azimuth
5	Enter ground reflectance ($0 \leqslant \rho \leqslant 1$)	Gr. refl.	C	Gr. refl.
6	Enter latitude (degrees)	Latitude	D	Latitude
7	Enter month number (Jan = 1, Feb = 2)	Month	E	Varies
8	Enter monthly average daily total radiation on a horizontal surface			
	— English Units (BTU/ft^2)	Rad. (E)	A'	428
	— Metric Units (Kj/M^2)	Rad. (SI)	B'	4871
9	Run program		C'	
	Non-Printer Version Only:			
9	Run program		C'	Beam radiation
10	Run program		R/S	Diffuse rad.
11	Run program		R/S	Reflected rad.
12	Run program		R/S	Total radiation

[1]S.A. Klein, "Calculation of Monthly Average Insolation on Tilted Surfaces," *Solar Energy*, Vol. 19, No. 4, 1977.

SAMPLE PROBLEM

For the months of January and February, calculate the average daily radiation striking a vertical south facing surface in Boston. A ground reflectance of .2 is assumed.

	English Units (BTU/Ft²)				*Metric Units (Kj/M²)*	
	ENTER	*PRESS*			*ENTER*	*PRESS*
INPUT						
TILT	90.	A		TILT	90.	A
AZIM	0.	B		AZIM	0.	B
REFL	0.2	C		REFL	0.2	C
LAT	42.2	D		LAT	42.2	D
MON	1.	E		MON	1.	E
AVE	475.5	A′		AVE	5396.	B′
RUN		C′				C′
OUTPUT						
BEAM	550.0	R/S		BEAM	6223.7	R/S
DIFF	130.8	R/S		DIFF	1488.0	R/S
REFL	47.6	R/S		REFL	539.6	R/S
TOTL	728.4			TOTL	8251.3	
INPUT						
MON	2.	E		MON	2.	E
AVE	709.6	A′		AVE	8053.	B′
RUN		C′				C′
OUTPUT						
BEAM	600.0	R/S		BEAM	6789.8	R/S
DIFF	183.4	R/S		DIFF	2087.1	R/S
REFL	71.0	R/S		REFL	805.3	R/S
TOTL	854.4			TOTL	9682.2	

Storage Register Assignments

00	$\bar{H}_d/\bar{H}$
01	–
02	$A^2 + 1$
03	W_s
04	$\sin \delta$
05	$\cos \delta$
06	37242737: alpha for TILT
07	13462430: alpha for AZIM
08	35172127: alpha for REFL
09	13421700: alpha for AVE
10	A
11	B
12	n = recommended day of the year for each month
13	solar constant
14	16242121: alpha for DIFF
15	$\sqrt{A^2 - B + 1}$
16	$\bar{R}_b$
17	30323100: alpha for MON
18	27133700: alpha for LAT
19	$--$
20	total radiation
21	$\bar{H}$ = monthly average daily total radiation on horizontal surface
22	$\bar{K}_T$ = fraction of extraterrestrial radiation
23	ϕ = latitude
24	ρ = ground reflectance
25	s = tilt of surface from horizontal
26	σ = surface azimuth angle
27	δ = declination
28	W_{ss}
29	W_{sr}

000	76	LBL	044	08	08	088	95	=
001	11	A	045	69	OP	089	42	STO
002	42	STO	046	04	04	090	12	12
003	25	25	047	43	RCL	091	91	R/S
004	43	RCL	048	24	24	092	76	LBL
005	06	06	049	69	OP	093	16	A'
006	69	OP	050	06	06	094	42	STO
007	04	04	051	91	R/S	095	21	21
008	43	RCL	052	76	LBL	096	25	CLR
009	25	25	053	14	D	097	43	RCL
010	69	OP	054	42	STO	098	09	09
011	06	06	055	23	23	099	69	OP
012	91	R/S	056	43	RCL	100	04	04
013	76	LBL	057	18	18	101	43	RCL
014	12	B	058	69	OP	102	21	21
015	42	STO	059	04	04	103	69	OP
016	26	26	060	43	RCL	104	06	06
017	43	RCL	061	23	23	105	04	4
018	07	07	062	69	OP	106	02	2
019	69	OP	063	06	06	107	08	8
020	04	04	064	91	R/S	108	42	STO
021	43	RCL	065	76	LBL	109	13	13
022	26	26	066	15	E	110	91	R/S
023	69	OP	067	42	STO	111	76	LBL
024	06	06	068	12	12	112	17	B'
025	00	0	069	43	RCL	113	42	STO
026	32	X:T	070	17	17	114	21	21
027	43	RCL	071	69	OP	115	25	CLR
028	26	26	072	04	04	116	43	RCL
029	67	EQ	073	43	RCL	117	09	09
030	38	SIN	074	12	12	118	69	OP
031	91	R/S	075	69	OP	119	04	04
032	76	LBL	076	06	06	120	43	RCL
033	38	SIN	077	75	-	121	21	21
034	93	.	078	01	1	122	69	OP
035	01	1	079	95	=	123	06	06
036	42	STO	080	65	×	124	04	4
037	26	26	081	03	3	125	08	8
038	91	R/S	082	00	0	126	07	7
039	76	LBL	083	93	.	127	01	1
040	13	C	084	02	2	128	42	STO
041	42	STO	085	85	+	129	13	13
042	24	24	086	01	1	130	91	R/S
043	43	RCL	087	06	6	131	76	LBL

Program Listing* to change program into non-printer version, simply replace the pause instruction at Steps 315, 344, 379 and 400 with R/S.

132	18	C'	176	03	03	220	43	RCL
133	98	ADV	177	42	STO	221	27	27
134	02	2	178	02	02	222	39	COS
135	03	3	179	42	STO	223	65	×
136	93	.	180	28	28	224	43	RCL
137	04	4	181	94	+/−	225	03	03
138	05	5	182	42	STO	226	38	SIN
139	65	×	183	29	29	227	85	+
140	53	(	184	02	2	228	43	RCL
141	03	3	185	04	4	229	03	03
142	06	6	186	55	÷	230	65	×
143	00	0	187	89	π	231	89	π
144	65	×	188	65	×	232	55	÷
145	53	(	189	43	RCL	233	01	1
146	02	2	190	13	13	234	08	8
147	08	8	191	65	×	235	00	0
148	04	4	192	53	(	236	65	×
149	85	+	193	01	1	237	43	RCL
150	43	RCL	194	85	+	238	23	23
151	12	12	195	93	.	239	38	SIN
152	54	)	196	00	0	240	65	×
153	55	÷	197	03	3	241	43	RCL
154	03	3	198	03	3	242	27	27
155	06	6	199	65	×	243	38	SIN
156	05	5	200	53	(	244	54	)
157	54	)	201	03	3	245	95	=
158	38	SIN	202	06	6	246	35	1/X
159	95	=	203	00	0	247	65	×
160	42	STO	204	65	×	248	43	RCL
161	27	27	205	43	RCL	249	21	21
162	53	(	206	12	12	250	95	=
163	43	RCL	207	55	÷	251	42	STO
164	23	23	208	03	3	252	22	22
165	30	TAN	209	06	6	253	43	RCL
166	94	+/−	210	05	5	254	27	27
167	65	×	211	54	)	255	38	SIN
168	43	RCL	212	39	COS	256	95	=
169	27	27	213	54	)	257	42	STO
170	30	TAN	214	65	×	258	04	04
171	54	)	215	53	(	259	43	RCL
172	22	INV	216	43	RCL	260	27	27
173	39	COS	217	23	23	261	39	COS
174	95	=	218	39	COS	262	95	=
175	42	STO	219	65	×	263	42	STO

264	05	05		308	58	FIX	352	05	5
265	61	GTO		309	01	01	353	01	1
266	50	IxI		310	22	INV	354	07	7
267	76	LBL		311	77	GE	355	02	2
268	23	LNX		312	45	YX	356	01	1
269	00	0		313	76	LBL	357	02	2
270	32	X:T		314	78	Σ+	358	07	7
271	01	1 *		315	66	PAU	359	69	OP
272	75	-		316	69	OP	360	04	04
273	01	1		317	06	06	361	43	RCL
274	93	.		318	22	INV	362	24	24
275	01	1		319	58	FIX	363	65	x
276	03	3		320	42	STO	364	53	(
277	65	x		321	20	20	365	01	1
278	43	RCL		322	43	RCL	366	75	-
279	22	22		323	14	14	367	43	RCL
280	95	=		324	69	OP	368	25	25
281	42	STO		325	04	04	369	39	COS
282	00	00		326	43	RCL	370	54	)
283	01	1		327	00	00	371	55	÷
284	04	4		328	65	x	372	02	2
285	01	1		329	53	(	373	65	x
286	07	7		330	01	1	374	43	RCL
287	01	1		331	85	+	375	21	21
288	03	3		332	43	RCL	376	95	=
289	03	3		333	25	25	377	58	FIX
290	00	0		334	39	COS	378	01	01
291	69	OP		335	54	)	*379	66	PAU
292	04	04		336	55	÷	380	69	OP
293	53	(		337	02	2	381	06	06
294	53	(		338	65	x	382	22	INV
295	01	1		339	43	RCL	383	58	FIX
296	75	-		340	21	21	384	44	SUM
297	43	RCL		341	95	=	385	20	20
298	00	00		342	58	FIX	386	03	3
299	54	)		343	01	01	387	07	7
300	65	x *		344	66	PAU	388	03	3
301	43	RCL		345	69	OP	389	02	2
302	16	16		346	06	06	390	03	3
303	54	)		347	22	INV	391	07	7
304	65	x		348	58	FIX	392	02	2
305	43	RCL		349	44	SUM	393	07	7
306	21	21		350	20	20	394	69	OP
307	95	=		351	03	3	395	04	04

Program Listing* R/S, *NOT* Pause for non-printer version.

396	43	RCL	440	30	TAN	484	15	15
397	20	20	441	54	)	485	53	(
398	58	FIX	442	42	STO	486	43	RCL
399	01	01	443	10	10	487	10	10
*400	66	PAU	444	53	(	488	65	×
401	69	OP	445	43	RCL	489	43	RCL
402	06	06	446	27	27	490	11	11
403	98	ADV	447	30	TAN	491	85	+
404	98	ADV	448	65	×	492	43	RCL
405	98	ADV	449	53	(	493	15	15
406	22	INV	450	43	RCL	494	54	)
407	58	FIX	451	23	23	495	55	÷
408	91	R/S	452	39	COS	496	53	(
409	76	LBL	453	55	÷	497	43	RCL
410	45	Y×	454	43	RCL	498	10	10
411	00	0	455	26	26	499	33	X²
412	61	GTO	456	30	TAN	500	85	+
413	78	Σ+	457	75	-	501	01	1
414	76	LBL	458	43	RCL	502	54	)
415	50	I×I	459	23	23	503	42	STO
416	43	RCL	460	38	SIN	504	02	02
417	03	03	461	55	÷	505	95	=
418	32	X:T	462	53	(	506	22	INV
419	53	(	463	43	RCL	507	39	COS
420	43	RCL	464	26	26	508	77	GE
421	23	23	465	38	SIN	509	70	RAD
422	39	COS	466	65	×	510	94	+/-
423	55	÷	467	43	RCL	511	42	STO
424	53	(	468	25	25	512	29	29
425	43	RCL	469	30	TAN	513	76	LBL
426	26	26	470	95	=	514	70	RAD
427	38	SIN	471	42	STO	515	53	(
428	65	×	472	11	11	516	43	RCL
429	43	RCL	473	33	X²	517	10	10
430	25	25	474	94	+/-	518	65	×
431	30	TAN	475	85	+	519	43	RCL
432	54	)	476	43	RCL	520	11	11
433	85	+	477	10	10	521	75	-
434	43	RCL	478	33	X²	522	43	RCL
435	23	23	479	85	+	523	15	15
436	38	SIN	480	01	1	524	54	)
437	55	÷	481	95	=	525	55	÷
438	43	RCL	482	34	ГX	526	43	RCL
439	26	26	483	42	STO	527	02	02

Program Listing* R/S, *NOT* Pause for non-printer version.

528	95	=		572	43	RCL		616	54	)
529	22	INV		573	25	25		617	85	+
530	39	COS		574	38	SIN		618	53	(
531	77	GE		575	65	×		619	43	RCL
532	48	EXC		576	43	RCL		620	05	05
533	42	STO		577	26	26		621	65	×
534	28	28		578	39	COS		622	43	RCL
535	76	LBL		579	54	)		623	26	26
536	48	EXC		580	65	×		624	39	COS
537	53	(		581	89	π		625	65	×
538	43	RCL		582	55	÷		626	43	RCL
539	25	25		583	01	1		627	23	23
540	39	COS		584	08	8		628	38	SIN
541	65	×		585	00	0		629	65	×
542	43	RCL		586	65	×		630	43	RCL
543	04	04		587	53	(		631	25	25
544	65	×		588	43	RCL		632	38	SIN
545	43	RCL		589	28	28		633	54	)
546	23	23		590	75	−		634	65	×
547	38	SIN		591	43	RCL		635	53	(
548	54	)		592	29	29		636	43	RCL
549	65	×		593	54	)		637	28	28
550	89	π		594	85	+		638	38	SIN
551	55	÷		595	53	(		639	75	−
552	01	1		596	43	RCL		640	43	RCL
553	08	8		597	23	23		641	29	29
554	00	0		598	39	COS		642	38	SIN
555	65	×		599	65	×		643	54	)
556	53	(		600	43	RCL		644	75	−
557	43	RCL		601	05	05		645	53	(
558	28	28		602	65	×		646	43	RCL
559	75	−		603	43	RCL		647	05	05
560	43	RCL		604	25	25		648	65	×
561	29	29		605	39	COS		649	43	RCL
562	54	)		606	54	)		650	25	25
563	75	−		607	65	×		651	38	SIN
564	53	(		608	53	(		652	65	×
565	43	RCL		609	43	RCL		653	43	RCL
566	04	04		610	28	28		654	26	26
567	65	×		611	38	SIN		655	38	SIN
568	43	RCL		612	75	−		656	54	)
569	23	23		613	43	RCL		657	65	×
570	39	COS		614	29	29		658	53	(
571	65	×		615	38	SIN		659	43	RCL

660	28	28		704	91	R/S		
661	39	COS		705	00	0		
662	75	-		706	00	0		
663	43	RCL		707	00	0		
664	29	29		708	00	0		
665	39	COS		709	00	0		
666	95	=		710	00	0		
667	55	÷		711	00	0		
668	53	(		712	00	0		
669	02	2		713	00	0		
670	65	×		714	00	0		
671	53	(		715	00	0		
672	43	RCL		716	00	0		
673	23	23		717	00	0		
674	39	COS		718	00	0		
675	65	×		719	00	0		
676	43	RCL						
677	05	05						
678	65	×						
679	43	RCL						
680	03	03						
681	38	SIN						
682	85	+						
683	89	π						
684	55	÷						
685	01	1						
686	08	8						
687	00	0						
688	65	×						
689	43	RCL						
690	03	03						
691	65	×						
692	43	RCL						
693	23	23						
694	38	SIN						
695	65	×						
696	43	RCL						
697	04	04						
698	95	=						
699	42	STO						
700	16	16						
701	25	CLR						
702	61	GTO						
703	23	LNX						

STORAGE REGISTERS

0.	00
0.	01
0.	02
0.	03
0.	04
0.	05
37242737.	06
13462430.	07
35172127.	08
13421700.	09
0.	10
0.	11
0.	12
0.	13
16242121.	14
0.	15
0.	16
30323100.	17
27133700.	18
0.	19
0.	20
0.	21
0.	22
0.	23
0.	24
0.	25
0.	26
0.	27
0.	28
0.	29

Program Listing   Jim Rosen, January 23, 1980.

Climatic
Data

TABLE OF MONTHLY AVERAGE SOLAR RADIATION, TEMPERATURE, AND DEGREE-DAYS

HS = normal daily value of total hemispheric solar radiation on a horizontal surface (Btu/ft^2 day).

VS = normal daily value of total solar radiation on a vertical, south-facing surface (Btu/ft^2 day).

TA = $(T_{min} + T_{max})/2$, where T_{min} and T_{max} are monthly (or annual) normals of daily minimum and maximum ambient temperature (F).

Dxx = monthly (or annual) normal of heating degree-days below the base temperature xx ($^\circ$F)

Values of HS, TA, and D65 were taken from Reference 1. "Normals" are mean values for the period 1941 to 1970. Degree-days from base temperatures other than 65°F were calculated by the method described by Thom,[2,3] based on the values of TA and D65 from Reference 1.

For the Canadian cities, solar radiation data was compiled at Los Alamos Scientific Laboratory (LASL) from *Card Deck 480 Solar Radiation – Summary of Day*,

Reprinted from: *Passive Solar Design Handbook, Volume Two*, U.S. Department of Energy, DOE/CS-0127/2, 1980

National Weather Records Center, ESSA (October 1969). Ambient temperatures were computed from the degree-day data (some of which is from the *ASHRAE Systems Handbook*), using

$$TA = 65 - DD/N$$

where N is the number of days in the month (or year).

For all cities, values of VS were computed using the following correlation, which was developed by R. D. McFarland at LASL:

$$\frac{VS}{HS} = \frac{.2260 - .002512X + .0003075X^2}{.599 - .005462X + .00026011X^2 - .000003387X^3}$$

where X = Lat – Dec
  Lat = Latitude (degrees)
 and Dec = sun's mid-month declination (degrees).
This is based on a ground reflectance of 0.3.

REFERENCES

1. *Input Data for Solar Systems* by Cinquemani, Owenby, and Baldwin, National Climatic Center, Asheville, NC (Nov. 1978.)

2. H. C. S. Thom, "The Rational Relationship Between Heating Degree-Days and Temperature," *Monthly Weather Review,* Vol. 82, No. 1 (Jan. 1954).

3. H. C. S. Thom, "Normal Degree-Days Below Any Base," *Monthly Weather Review*, Vol. 82, No. 5 (May 1954).

YUMA, ARIZONA — LAT = 32.7, ELEV 207

	JAN	FEB	MAR	APR	MAY	JUN	JUL	AUG	SEP	OCT	NOV	DEC	YEAR
HS	1096	1443	1919	2413	2728	2814	2453	2329	2051	1623	1215	1000	1924
VS	1550	1637	1607	1393	1215	1145	1031	1181	1476	1658	1618	1494	17006
TA	55.4	59.8		71.0	78.7	85.8	93.0	92.8	87.1	75.0	63.3	56.3	73.7
D50	28					0	0	0	0		12	22	64
D55	87	33	11			0	0	0	1		44	74	218
D60	177	93	41	24		0	0	0		5	108	158	520
D65	308	192	97	73	11	1	0	0		46	276	308	1010
D70	455	303	212						36	228	215	427	1724

FORT SMITH, ARKANSAS — LAT = 35.3, ELEV 463

	JAN	FEB	MAR	APR	MAY	JUN	JUL	AUG	SEP	OCT	NOV	DEC	YEAR
HS	744	999	1312	1616	1912	2089	2065	1877	1518	1201	851	682	1404
VS	1130	1218	1187	1010	908	892	917	1026	1170	1321	1217	1094	13091
TA	39.0	43.3	50.3	62.2	70.1	78.0	82.2	81.4	74.0	63.2	50.4	41.5	61.3
D50	346	204	85	15						11	81	274	996
D55	497	331	177	56				4		36	169	421	1622
D60	636	472	308	139	17	1		4	2	136	298	577	2305
D65	805	608	471	246	88	12	3		41	228	498	729	3305
D70	961	748	611								588	884	4409

LITTLE ROCK, ARKANSAS — LAT = 34.7, ELEV 266

	JAN	FEB	MAR	APR	MAY	JUN	JUL	AUG	SEP	OCT	NOV	DEC	YEAR
HS	731	1003	1313	1611	1929	2106	2032	1860	1518	1228	847	674	1404
VS	1092	1203	1167	988	902	888	890	999	1162	1328	1192	1064	12875
TA	39.5	42.9	50.3	61.7	69.0	78.1	81.0	80.6	73.3	62.4	50.3	42.0	61.0
D50	331	212	83							14	81	270	984
D55	482	342	185	66				4		40	189	334	1577
D60	636	472	308	140	21			5	2	149	298	571	2214
D65	791	619	470	233	91	11	4		41	243	441	725	3354
D70	946	759	611								591	880	4447

BAKERSFIELD, CALIFORNIA — LAT = 35.4, ELEV 492

	JAN	FEB	MAR	APR	MAY	JUN	JUL	AUG	SEP	OCT	NOV	DEC	YEAR
HS	766	1102	1595	2095	2509	2749	2683	2421	1992	1516	942	677	1749
VS	1166	1348	1447	1313	1195	1176	1195	1328	1557	1608	1351	1089	15573
TA	47.5	52.4	56.7	62.7	69.8	76.9	83.9	81.6	76.6	66.9	56.0	48.0	64.9
D50	131	50	14	3							21	124	348
D55	270	135	68	13						17	124	379	809
D60	393	220	149	41	7	2				55	156	379	1372
D65	543	353	266	140	22	4			18	143	296	530	2185
D70	698	493	418	233	92				41	248	422	685	3224

DAGGETT, CALIFORNIA — LAT = 34.9, ELEV 1929

	JAN	FEB	MAR	APR	MAY	JUN	JUL	AUG	SEP	OCT	NOV	DEC	YEAR
HS	958	1281	1772	2274	2591	2766	2603	2383	2008	1516	1085	876	1843
VS	1439	1545	1584	1404	1218	1172	1146	1288	1546	1649	1535	1390	16914
TA	47.3	52.0	57.2	64.3	72.1	80.1	87.0	85.5	79.2	68.1	55.5	48.0	66.4
D50	144	63	23	4		2	0	0	0		30	132	396
D55	308	135	83	25	14				7	14	188	238	809
D60	428	287	155	41	51	3		1	7	57	296	403	1806
D65	611	423	271	118	65	9	5		23	130	527	595	2203
D70	766	563	416	200	132				107	202	682	750	3165

FRESNO, CALIFORNIA — LAT = 36.8, ELEV 328

	JAN	FEB	MAR	APR	MAY	JUN	JUL	AUG	SEP	OCT	NOV	DEC	YEAR
HS	657	1012	1566	2093	2484	2733	2685	2423	1985	1429	888	574	1711
VS	1040	1286	1480	1370	1228	1206	1237	1386	1618	1639	1323	960	15573
TA	45.3	49.9	53.9	60.3	67.4	73.9	80.6	78.3	71.8	64.2	53.5	46.4	62.3
D50	176	81	37	25						8	40	165	507
D55	308	287	209	51	14			11		29	210	293	1036
D60	611	423	344	182	51	2		1	7	90	345	595	1721
D65	766	563	500	298	132	9	5		37	202	496	750	2650
D70													3797

LONG BEACH, CALIFORNIA — LAT = 33.8, ELEV 56

	JAN	FEB	MAR	APR	MAY	JUN	JUL	AUG	SEP	OCT	NOV	DEC	YEAR
HS	928	1215	1610	1938	2064	2140	2300	2100	1701	1326	1003	847	1598
VS	1353	1421	1394	1157	941	888	988	1099	1266	1398	1377	1304	14587
TA	54.2		57.6	60.6	64.1	67.3	72.0	73.3	71.8	66.9	60.6	55.1	63.6
D50	79		35	10	1					6	10	59	250
D55	189	116	116	38	18				1	48	55	155	740
D60	339	273	247	148	71	23			19	110	195	295	1606
D65	490	406	397	284	192	110	35	24	88	122	284	450	2834

BIRMINGHAM, ALABAMA — LAT = 33.6, ELEV 630

	JAN	FEB	MAR	APR	MAY	JUN	JUL	AUG	SEP	OCT	NOV	DEC	YEAR
HS	707	967	1296	1673	1857	1918	1810	1724	1077	1211	858	1012	1345
VS	1025	1125	1115	992	845	793	774	897		1270	1171	1012	12096
TA	44.2		53.3	63.2	70.5	77.4	79.9	79.0	73.9	63.3	52.1	45.2	62.4
D50	216	144	61	6	1	0	0	0	0	6	75	193	702
D55	346	246	135	20	3	0	0	0		61	151	308	1240
D60	493	372	237	60	12	0	0	0	5	137	258	463	1961
D65	654	517	382	116	20	24	14	16	52	237	391	614	2844
D70	800	647	520	232	100						539	769	3950

MOBILE, ALABAMA — LAT = 30.7, ELEV 220

	JAN	FEB	MAR	APR	MAY	JUN	JUL	AUG	SEP	OCT	NOV	DEC	YEAR
HS	828	1100	1407	1722	1872	1868	1715	1641	1468	1299	955	759	1385
VS	1109	1180	1110	936	798	738	696	788	981	1253	1204	1074	11865
TA	51.2	54.0	59.4	67.9	74.0	80.3	81.6	81.5	77.5	68.9	58.5	52.6	67.4
D50	97	54	19						0	2	22	73	270
D55	180	119	55	8						7	63	149	581
D60	304	204	130	40	2					21	135	252	1056
D65	451	330	221	76	7	15	10	11	28	135	248	391	1656
D70	585	452	343	145	51					133	356	533	2664

MONTGOMERY, ALABAMA — LAT = 32.3, ELEV 203

	JAN	FEB	MAR	APR	MAY	JUN	JUL	AUG	SEP	OCT	NOV	DEC	YEAR
HS	752	1013	1341	1729	1897	1972	1841	1746	1468	1262	915	719	1388
VS	1052	1136	1110	986	837	797	768	876	1044	1275	1205	1062	12148
TA	47.5	50.6	56.5	66.5	72.4	78.9	81.0	80.0	75.8	65.5	55.0	48.5	64.8
D50	148	88	30	3					0	1	41	131	445
D55	285	166	85	12	2					11	103	231	866
D60	428	292	185	58	7				2	93	203	305	1552
D65	584	419	299	76	8	16	10	11	32	180	306	512	2269
D70			424	186	72						454	667	3295

PHOENIX, ARIZONA — LAT = 33.4, ELEV 1112

	JAN	FEB	MAR	APR	MAY	JUN	JUL	AUG	SEP	OCT	NOV	DEC	YEAR
HS	1021	1374	1814	2355	2676	2739	2486	2293	2015	1576	1150	932	1869
VS	1472	1589	1552	1388	1211	1128	1059	1186	1482	1643	1561	1419	16692
TA	51.2	55.1	59.7	67.7	76.0	84.6	91.2	89.1	83.8	72.2	59.8	52.5	70.3
D50	162	78	30	3				0	0	5	34	137	459
D55	285	166	105	13	2					17	103	189	866
D60	428	292	185	58	7				3	93	182	388	1552
D65	584	419	327	130	24	1				180	306	544	2269
D70											314		2411

PRESCOTT, ARIZONA — LAT = 34.6, ELEV 5023

	JAN	FEB	MAR	APR	MAY	JUN	JUL	AUG	SEP	OCT	NOV	DEC	YEAR
HS	1016	1335	1775	2275	2629	2762	2309	2092	1954	1543	1140	927	1813
VS	1514	1597	1575	1391	1226	1163	1010	1121	1491	1664	1599	1459	16809
TA	30.1	40.5	44.3	52.9	60.4	69.1	75.0	73.0	68.1	57.2	38.6	38.8	55.1
D50	555	308	335	127					7	48	114	356	1436
D55	710	540	487	248	78	18		1	29	124	262	509	3284
D65	865	686	642	398	165	33	18		91	254	576	818	4456
D70	1020	826	797	540	302	91		38	107	398	726	973	5837

TUCSON, ARIZONA — LAT = 32.1, ELEV 2556

	JAN	FEB	MAR	APR	MAY	JUN	JUL	AUG	SEP	OCT	NOV	DEC	YEAR
HS	1099	1397	1864	2363	2671	2730	2341	2183	1928	1602	1208	996	1872
VS	1529	1597	1534	1339	1173	1100	973	1089	1399	1650	1583	1464	16388
TA	50.0	53.0	57.6	65.3	73.6	83.8	86.3	84.3	79.5	70.1	58.5	67.4	67.8
D50	166	106	56	8						2	44	165	525
D55	292	201	155	26					0	29	114	293	1036
D60	442	333	243	81	45			1		182	221	403	1752
D65	593	463	388	169	124	4			91	254	350	559	2673

WINSLOW, ARIZONA — LAT = 35.0, ELEV 4882

	JAN	FEB	MAR	APR	MAY	JUN	JUL	AUG	SEP	OCT	NOV	DEC	YEAR
HS	985	1327	1780	2283	2595	2712	2347	2141	1928	1513	1119	894	1802
VS	1184	1305	1596	1413	1223	1151	1035	1160	1489	1650	1587	1422	16817
TA	32.6	39.0	45.7	53.7	62.7	72.1	78.0	76.1	69.5	57.3	43.2	55.3	55.3
D50	540	446	321	103	10			2	6	52	217	503	1800
D55	694	585	472	205	45	12			19	129	507	857	3631
D65	849	725	626	348	124	14	9		88	252	654	967	4733
D70	1159	865	781	490	238	55		17		396	804	1122	6025

LOS ANGELES, CALIFORNIA LAT = 33.9 ELEV = 105

	JAN	FEB	MAR	APR	MAY	JUN	JUL	AUG	SEP	OCT	NOV	DEC	YEAR
HS	926	1214	1619	1951	2060	2119	2307	2079	1681	1317	1004	848	1594
VS	1353	1424	1405	1168	944	880	993	1091	1255	1392	1382	1309	14599
TA	54.5	55.6	56.5	58.8	61.9	64.5	68.5	69.5	68.7	65.2	60.5	56.9	61.7
D50	21	13	11	5	2	1	0	0	0	0	2	9	64
D55	83	59	53	26	9	4	1	1	1	3	15	47	299
D60	186	143	138	91	47	20	5	4	5	17	65	129	849
D65	331	270	267	195	114	71	19	15	23	77	158	279	1819
D70	481	404	419	338	257	180	99	83	93	168	289	407	3216

MOUNT SHASTA, CALIFORNIA LAT = 41.3 ELEV = 3586

	JAN	FEB	MAR	APR	MAY	JUN	JUL	AUG	SEP	OCT	NOV	DEC	YEAR
HS	561	857	1250	1756	2186	2436	2577	2213	1735	1155	659	505	1491
VS	1005	1232	1344	1319	1232	1205	1341	1453	1616	1501	1111	957	15316
TA	33.6	37.8	40.4	46.3	53.3	60.0	67.8	66.0	61.2	51.4	41.7	35.5	49.6
D50	509	344	303	143	37	4	0	1	3	61	257	451	2112
D55	663	482	454	268	109	22	2	3	15	146	400	605	3169
D60	818	622	608	412	221	78	9	17	62	274	549	760	4430
D65	973	762	763	561	371	178	37	64	145	422	699	915	5890
D70	1128	902	918	711	518	304	118	154	271	577	849	1070	7520

NEEDLES, CALIFORNIA LAT = 34.8 ELEV = 886

	JAN	FEB	MAR	APR	MAY	JUN	JUL	AUG	SEP	OCT	NOV	DEC	YEAR
HS	985	1353	1825	2317	2652	2791	2541	2278	2015	1537	1124	913	1861
VS	1476	1627	1627	1426	1243	1180	1116	1227	1547	1667	1586	1445	17166
TA	51.6	56.5	61.6	70.4	79.6	88.3	95.4	93.3	86.9	74.3	60.7	52.7	72.6
D50	80	25	8	1	0	0	0	0	0	0	9	65	188
D55	161	74	27	3	0	0	0	0	0	1	32	141	439
D60	278	147	80	10	0	0	0	0	0	4	90	249	858
D65	421	261	150	42	0	0	0	0	0	10	163	381	1428
D70	572	382	278	94	13	1	0	0	2	46	292	538	2219

OAKLAND, CALIFORNIA LAT = 37.7 ELEV = 7

	JAN	FEB	MAR	APR	MAY	JUN	JUL	AUG	SEP	OCT	NOV	DEC	YEAR
HS	708	1017	1456	1922	2211	2350	2322	2053	1701	1212	822	647	1535
VS	1148	1325	1413	1293	1121	1059	1094	1207	1425	1426	1255	1109	14875
TA	48.6	51.9	53.7	56.1	58.9	61.9	63.1	63.5	64.5	61.1	55.3	49.9	57.4
D50	77	25	12	4	1	0	0	0	0	0	5	55	179
D55	202	101	75	36	11	2	1	1	1	4	47	164	646
D60	354	228	199	128	72	26	16	13	8	37	148	314	1543
D65	508	367	350	270	193	114	80	74	59	135	291	468	2909
D70	663	507	505	417	344	244	216	205	170	277	441	623	4613

RED BLUFF, CALIFORNIA LAT = 40.1 ELEV = 354

	JAN	FEB	MAR	APR	MAY	JUN	JUL	AUG	SEP	OCT	NOV	DEC	YEAR
HS	570	892	1354	1910	2375	2600	2672	2311	1845	1227	706	511	1581
VS	988	1241	1407	1383	1291	1245	1344	1462	1659	1542	1151	937	15651
TA	45.2	50.0	53.2	59.5	67.4	75.5	82.3	79.9	75.3	65.0	53.7	46.4	62.8
D50	189	92	58	12	2	0	0	0	0	3	50	165	572
D55	316	175	132	42	6	1	0	0	0	11	120	283	1086
D60	462	290	236	107	22	3	0	0	0	39	217	426	1802
D65	614	420	366	218	64	8	0	0	0	82	339	577	2688
D70	769	561	523	325	146	33	6	12	35	194	491	732	3827

SACRAMENTO, CALIFORNIA LAT = 38.5 ELEV = 26

	JAN	FEB	MAR	APR	MAY	JUN	JUL	AUG	SEP	OCT	NOV	DEC	YEAR
HS	597	939	1458	2004	2435	2684	2688	2368	1907	1315	782	538	1643
VS	990	1251	1448	1382	1263	1233	1294	1426	1636	1582	1221	943	15667
TA	45.1	49.8	53.0	58.3	64.3	70.5	75.2	74.1	71.5	63.3	53.0	45.8	60.3
D50	183	86	50	12	2	0	0	0	0	3	49	168	554
D55	315	172	125	45	9	1	0	0	1	12	121	295	1097
D60	464	292	235	116	37	6	0	0	5	47	227	442	1871
D65	617	426	372	227	120	20	0	0	5	101	360	595	2843
D70	772	566	528	355	202	82	29	38	68	227	511	750	4129

SAN DIEGO, CALIFORNIA LAT = 32.7 ELEV = 30

	JAN	FEB	MAR	APR	MAY	JUN	JUL	AUG	SEP	OCT	NOV	DEC	YEAR
HS	976	1266	1632	1937	2003	2062	2186	2057	1717	1373	1063	904	1598
VS	1381	1436	1367	1118	892	839	919	1043	1236	1403	1416	1351	14399
TA	55.2	56.7	58.0	60.7	63.3	65.5	69.6	71.4	69.9	66.1	60.8	56.7	62.9
D50	9	4	3	1	0	0	0	0	0	0	1	5	23
D55	58	33	23	7	2	1	0	0	0	1	7	37	170
D60	160	111	95	49	20	8	1	0	1	6	48	123	623
D65	314	237	219	144	79	52	6	0	16	43	140	257	1507
D70	459	373	372	281	213	147	68	41	61	137	278	413	2841

SAN FRANCISCO, CALIFORNIA LAT = 37.6 ELEV = 16

	JAN	FEB	MAR	APR	MAY	JUN	JUL	AUG	SEP	OCT	NOV	DEC	YEAR
HS	708	1009	1455	1920	2226	2377	2392	2116	1742	1226	821	642	1553
VS	1145	1311	1408	1288	1126	1068	1124	1240	1455	1438	1250	1097	14951
TA	48.3	51.2	53.0	55.3	58.3	61.6	62.5	63.0	64.1	61.0	55.3	49.7	56.9
D50	82	32	17	5	1	0	0	0	0	0	5	58	202
D55	210	117	88	47	15	3	2	1	1	4	47	170	705
D60	363	247	219	148	82	30	21	17	10	39	148	320	1643
D65	518	386	372	291	210	120	93	84	66	137	291	474	3042
D70	673	526	527	441	363	253	234	219	181	280	441	629	4768

SANTA MARIA, CALIFORNIA LAT = 34.9 ELEV = 236

	JAN	FEB	MAR	APR	MAY	JUN	JUL	AUG	SEP	OCT	NOV	DEC	YEAR
HS	854	1141	1582	1921	2141	2349	2341	2106	1730	1353	974	804	1608
VS	1283	1376	1415	1186	1006	995	1030	1138	1332	1472	1378	1276	14886
TA	50.5	52.0	52.8	54.9	57.1	59.6	62.1	62.3	62.6	60.4	56.1	51.8	56.9
D50	51	28	22	9	3	1	0	0	0	1	5	33	155
D55	150	103	97	58	30	10	3	3	3	7	41	118	624
D60	296	226	226	161	112	63	30	27	24	53	131	256	1604
D65	450	364	378	303	245	167	112	102	94	159	270	409	3053
D70	605	504	533	453	400	313	247	241	225	299	417	564	4801

COLORADO SPRINGS, COLORADO LAT = 38.8 ELEV = 6171

	JAN	FEB	MAR	APR	MAY	JUN	JUL	AUG	SEP	OCT	NOV	DEC	YEAR
HS	891	1178	1550	1931	2129	2369	2212	2025	1759	1359	944	782	1594
VS	1490	1582	1552	1344	1114	1097	1073	1231	1522	1648	1486	1382	16521
TA	28.6	31.3	35.3	46.2	55.5	64.6	70.7	69.1	60.9	50.5	37.5	31.0	48.4
D50	663	524	457	145	19	1	0	0	3	74	377	589	2853
D55	818	664	611	271	74	5	1	1	17	166	525	744	3896
D60	973	804	766	415	166	25	4	6	66	300	675	899	5098
D65	1128	944	921	564	301	103	9	13	155	456	825	1054	6473
D70	1283	1084	1076	714	451	181	71	96	279	605	975	1209	8023

DENVER, COLORADO LAT = 39.7 ELEV = 5331

	JAN	FEB	MAR	APR	MAY	JUN	JUL	AUG	SEP	OCT	NOV	DEC	YEAR
HS	840	1127	1530	1879	2135	2351	2273	2044	1727	1300	883	732	1568
VS	1440	1551	1572	1344	1147	1114	1130	1277	1535	1616	1424	1327	16478
TA	29.9	32.8	37.0	47.5	57.0	66.0	73.0	71.6	62.8	52.0	39.4	32.6	50.1
D50	623	482	406	130	18	1	0	0	3	63	324	540	2592
D55	778	622	559	240	63	5	0	0	14	143	469	695	3588
D60	933	762	713	379	143	23	0	0	51	261	618	849	4733
D65	1088	902	868	525	253	80	0	0	120	408	768	1004	6016
D70	1243	1042	1023	675	406	158	50	69	232	559	918	1159	7535

EAGLE, COLORADO LAT = 39.6 ELEV = 6512

	JAN	FEB	MAR	APR	MAY	JUN	JUL	AUG	SEP	OCT	NOV	DEC	YEAR
HS	754	1078	1502	1933	2255	2509	2384	2084	1767	1307	869	691	1594
VS	1289	1480	1539	1379	1208	1185	1182	1298	1566	1621	1398	1249	16393
TA	18.0	23.3	31.1	41.9	51.3	58.9	65.9	63.7	55.6	44.8	30.9	20.3	42.2
D50	992	748	586	245	38	1	0	0	6	168	573	921	4278
D55	1147	888	741	393	129	13	0	1	46	317	723	1076	5474
D60	1302	1028	896	543	271	72	5	14	142	471	873	1231	6849
D65	1457	1168	1051	693	425	190	43	79	285	626	1023	1386	8426
D70	1612	1308	1206	843	580	333	139	200	432	781	1173	1541	10147

GRAND JUNCTION, COLORADO LAT = 39.1 ELEV = 4839

	JAN	FEB	MAR	APR	MAY	JUN	JUL	AUG	SEP	OCT	NOV	DEC	YEAR
HS	791	1119	1553	1986	2380	2598	2465	2182	1834	1345	918	731	1659
VS	1334	1515	1569	1395	1256	1212	1206	1339	1602	1645	1457	1303	16830
TA	26.6	33.6	41.2	51.7	62.2	71.3	78.7	75.4	67.2	54.9	39.8	29.5	52.7
D50	726	460	283	63	4	0	0	0	1	30	312	636	2514
D55	880	599	430	142	16	1	0	0	3	91	457	791	3412
D60	1035	739	583	260	58	5	0	0	15	186	606	946	4434
D65	1190	879	738	404	133	20	0	0	60	324	756	1101	5605
D70	1345	1019	893	550	255	69	10	26	133	470	906	1256	6931

PUEBLO, COLORADO LAT = 38.3 ELEV = 4721

	JAN	FEB	MAR	APR	MAY	JUN	JUL	AUG	SEP	OCT	NOV	DEC	YEAR
HS	894	1172	1564	1956	2162	2434	2312	2102	1779	1361	954	782	1623
VS	1474	1552	1544	1340	1115	1113	1107	1258	1517	1628	1481	1363	16493
TA	30.1	34.7	40.0	51.7	61.1	70.7	76.4	74.5	66.2	54.5	40.8	33.0	52.8
D50	617	429	315	56	3	0	0	0	1	27	282	527	2258
D55	772	569	466	136	17	1	0	0	3	91	427	682	3163
D60	927	708	620	257	67	4	0	0	16	191	576	837	4203
D65	1082	848	775	405	148	28	0	0	55	335	726	992	5394
D70	1237	988	930	549	283	70	15	27	146	481	876	1147	6751

ORLANDO, FLORIDA   LAT = 28.5   ELEV = 118

	JAN	FEB	MAR	APR	MAY	JUN	JUL	AUG	SEP	OCT	NOV	DEC	YEAR
HS	1259	1587	1898	1998	1837	1800	1667	1667	947	1304	1196	1226	18687
VS	1259	1167	1305	983	883	708	708	752	947	1300	1306	1233	12295
TA	60.3	61.5	65.9	71.3	76.4	80.2	81.4	81.8	80.0	74.3	66.9	61.0	71.8
D50	42	29	17	3	0	0	0	0	0	0	0	32	139
D55	105	79	57	10	0	0	0	0	0	0	30	87	126
D60	197	184	94	13	0	0	0	0	0	17	75	170	348
D70	316	256	181	88	33	13	9	9	13	51	162	316	733

TALLAHASSEE, FLORIDA   LAT = 30.4   ELEV = 69

	JAN	FEB	MAR	APR	MAY	JUN	JUL	AUG	SEP	OCT	NOV	DEC	YEAR
HS	877	1138	1479	1823	1936	1883	1748	1675	1491	1318	1008	810	1533
VS	1165	1210	1156	982	820	711	706	798	1001	1260	1296	1141	12281
TA	52.6	54.8	60.1	67.9	74.8	80.0	81.1	81.1	78.1	69.3	58.9	53.2	67.7
D50	73	42	13	2	0	0	0	0	0	5	18	53	215
D55	150	102	45	7	0	0	0	0	0	17	55	140	501
D60	256	185	106	23	0	0	0	0	0	31	124	241	951
D70	542	429	316	140	47	14	11	11	22	122	304	376	2523

TAMPA, FLORIDA   LAT = 28.0   ELEV = 10

	JAN	FEB	MAR	APR	MAY	JUN	JUL	AUG	SEP	OCT	NOV	DEC	YEAR
HS	1011	1259	1594	1908	1998	1847	1753	1653	1492	1346	1060	935	1492
VS	1257	1250	1158	959	810	711	686	741	929	1200	1108	1228	11451
TA	60.4	61.8	66.4	72.0	77.2	81.0	81.9	82.2	80.8	74.7	66.6	61.6	72.2
D50	16	17	14	1	0	0	0	0	0	0	7	36	47
D55	46	31	41	3	0	0	0	0	0	5	33	93	141
D60	110	81	85	11	0	0	0	0	0	17	36	169	369
D70	316	253	253	84	32	13	11	10	14	53	164	285	1421

WEST PALM BEACH, FLORIDA

	JAN	FEB	MAR	APR	MAY	JUN	JUL	AUG	SEP	OCT	NOV	DEC	YEAR
HS	1000	1233	1556	1814	1845	1706	1779	1663	1419	1224	1060	958	1438
VS	1199	1179	1086	880	843	651	687	889	849	1050	1196	1214	12136
TA	65.5	66.1	69.8	73.0	77.5	80.5	81.9	82.3	81.5	77.2	71.0	66.8	74.5
D50	8	6	2	0	0	0	0	0	0	0	2	6	24
D55	23	23	10	0	0	0	0	0	0	0	7	24	92
D60	83	65	25	5	0	0	0	0	0	6	22	58	299
D70	178	150	100	43	18	8	5	5	6	20	80	152	765

ATLANTA, GEORGIA   LAT = 33.6   ELEV = 1033

	JAN	FEB	MAR	APR	MAY	JUN	JUL	AUG	SEP	OCT	NOV	DEC	YEAR
HS	718	969	1304	1686	1854	1914	1812	1708	1422	1200	883	674	1345
VS	1083	1127	1122	1000	843	791	768	889	1052	1258	1205	1032	12136
TA	42.4	45.0	51.1	61.1	69.1	75.6	78.0	77.5	72.3	62.4	51.4	43.5	60.8
D50	297	161	67	11	0	0	0	0	2	11	142	217	758
D55	393	284	153	16	7	0	0	0	11	49	266	360	1350
D60	546	421	283	65	27	0	0	0	18	137	512	667	2150
D70	856	701	560	274	98	19	9	11	49	246	558	732	4228

AUGUSTA, GEORGIA   LAT = 33.4   ELEV = 148

	JAN	FEB	MAR	APR	MAY	JUN	JUL	AUG	SEP	OCT	NOV	DEC	YEAR
HS	751	1015	1338	1728	1865	1904	1803	1667	1410	1220	916	721	1362
VS	1083	1174	1144	1019	810	784	750	862	1037	1272	1244	1098	12329
TA	45.8	48.3	54.6	63.8	71.7	78.2	80.4	79.6	74.2	64.1	53.7	46.4	63.4
D50	208	105	38	13	0	0	0	0	0	12	116	161	539
D55	297	208	105	45	6	0	0	0	2	44	214	281	1033
D60	443	333	199	90	30	0	0	0	11	116	425	512	1709
D70	750	608	480	211	73	15	11	11	41	211	491	577	3631

MACON, GEORGIA   LAT = 32.7   ELEV = 361

	JAN	FEB	MAR	APR	MAY	JUN	JUL	AUG	SEP	OCT	NOV	DEC	YEAR
HS	769	1020	1363	1736	1885	1919	1785	1718	1439	1247	940	729	1379
VS	1088	1157	1142	1002	781	781	750	871	1036	1274	1089	1089	12281
TA	47.8	50.4	56.2	65.8	73.5	79.6	81.4	80.9	75.8	65.7	55.2	48.3	65.1
D50	138	86	26	3	0	0	0	0	0	3	95	129	838
D55	245	166	80	30	4	0	0	0	0	32	182	233	420
D60	384	280	162	66	6	6	8	9	30	370	578	1240	
D70	689	550	423	170	53	12	8	9	30	178	447	673	3240

HARTFORD, CONNECTICUT   LAT = 41.9   ELEV = 180

	JAN	FEB	MAR	APR	MAY	JUN	JUL	AUG	SEP	OCT	NOV	DEC	YEAR
HS	877	1015	1078	1305	1508	1686	1449	1422	1054	942	807	742	1687
VS	1115	1138	1181	980	900	886	951	951	1123	1305	1123	745	11377
TA	26.8	35.6	47.7	58.3	67.8	72.7	70.4	62.1	52.6	41.3	28.2	49.1	
D50	781	650	601	226	101	6	0	2	34	114	412	745	3948
D55	936	790	756	347	226	24	0	12	106	237	561	831	5075
D60	1246	930	911	519	226	24	12	67	224	384	711	986	6350
D70	1401	1210	1066	669	364	107	36	67	224	540	861	1141	7881

WILMINGTON, DELAWARE   LAT = 39.7   ELEV = 79

	JAN	FEB	MAR	APR	MAY	JUN	JUL	AUG	SEP	OCT	NOV	DEC	YEAR
HS	571	827	1149	1480	1710	1883	1823	1615	1318	984	645	489	1208
VS	979	1138	1167	1059	919	892	884	1009	1172	1223	1040	886	12405
TA	32.0	33.6	41.6	52.3	62.4	71.1	75.0	74.1	67.0	57.2	45.6	34.7	54.0
D50	558	460	268	123	17	0	0	0	2	50	156	475	2829
D55	713	599	417	240	47	1	0	0	9	129	285	629	3818
D60	868	739	571	381	128	3	0	9	32	254	430	784	5075
D70	1023	879	725	531	246	59	18	29	113	394	729	939	6295

WASHINGTON, DC   LAT = 38.9   ELEV = 289

	JAN	FEB	MAR	APR	MAY	JUN	JUL	AUG	SEP	OCT	NOV	DEC	YEAR
HS	572	815	1130	1459	1718	1901	1817	1617	1340	1004	651	481	1208
VS	959	1097	1130	1019	902	882	884	986	1163	1221	1027	852	12123
TA	32.1	33.8	41.8	53.1	62.6	71.4	75.3	73.6	66.9	55.9	44.7	34.0	53.7
D50	555	454	262	109	10	0	0	0	1	68	179	497	2004
D55	710	594	411	219	45	1	0	3	12	156	313	651	2869
D60	865	734	564	357	131	3	0	20	43	291	460	806	3864
D70	1020	874	719	507	240	63	20	34	131	395	609	961	5010

APALACHICOLA, FLORIDA   LAT = 29.7   ELEV = 20

	JAN	FEB	MAR	APR	MAY	JUN	JUL	AUG	SEP	OCT	NOV	DEC	YEAR
HS	853	1126	1474	1879	2091	1998	1814	1688	1535	1371	1040	818	1474
VS	1111	1247	1298	1027	874	781	710	789	1285	1275	1275	1126	12267
TA	53.7	55.8	60.7	68.1	74.9	80.0	81.4	81.5	78.6	70.8	61.1	55.2	68.5
D50	125	84	38	14	0	0	0	0	0	2	30	101	382
D55	225	161	94	18	3	0	0	0	0	10	85	191	783
D60	368	290	175	57	10	1	0	0	3	52	158	318	1361
D70	508	401	302	108	128	15	11	10	16	92	282	462	2261

DAYTONA BEACH, FLORIDA   LAT = 29.2   ELEV = 39

	JAN	FEB	MAR	APR	MAY	JUN	JUL	AUG	SEP	OCT	NOV	DEC	YEAR
HS	958	1213	1548	1884	1968	1826	1784	1682	1478	1251	1035	870	1458
VS	1199	1247	1193	980	815	710	708	777	955	1155	1252	1181	12177
TA	58.4	59.6	63.9	69.7	75.0	79.4	81.0	81.1	79.5	73.0	65.1	59.6	70.5
D50	60	42	17	0	0	0	0	0	0	6	12	46	183
D55	133	103	54	14	0	0	0	0	0	20	46	114	463
D60	225	161	94	17	0	0	0	0	0	47	97	191	1127
D70	368	290	222	108	50	16	11	10	61	189	334	457	1677

JACKSONVILLE, FLORIDA   LAT = 30.5   ELEV = 30

	JAN	FEB	MAR	APR	MAY	JUN	JUL	AUG	SEP	OCT	NOV	DEC	YEAR
HS	900	1164	1522	1856	1956	1885	1763	1694	1442	1223	996	818	1438
VS	1199	1241	1193	980	830	743	708	809	970	1244	1249	1151	12289
TA	54.6	56.3	61.2	68.1	74.3	79.2	81.0	81.0	78.2	70.5	61.2	55.4	68.4
D50	47	29	10	33	0	0	0	0	0	1	10	40	138
D55	133	81	33	7	0	0	0	0	0	19	32	102	372
D60	208	162	105	24	5	0	0	0	0	32	90	390	1277
D70	481	389	291	108	135	6	11	11	20	101	281	457	2241

MIAMI, FLORIDA   LAT = 25.8   ELEV = 361

	JAN	FEB	MAR	APR	MAY	JUN	JUL	AUG	SEP	OCT	NOV	DEC	YEAR
HS	1057	1314	1603	1859	1844	1708	1763	1630	1456	1303	1119	1019	1473
VS	1236	1224	1208	1019	725	743	708	696	848	1260	1231	1260	11605
TA	67.2	67.8	71.3	75.0	78.0	81.0	82.3	82.9	81.7	77.8	72.0	68.3	75.5
D50	18	13	1	0	0	0	0	0	0	0	1	11	55
D55	53	67	6	0	0	0	0	0	0	0	3	56	206
D60	142	118	76	31	15	6	4	4	5	15	61	122	599

SAVANNAH, GEORGIA — LAT = 32.1, ELEV = 52

	JAN	FEB	MAR	APR	MAY	JUN	JUL	AUG	SEP	OCT	NOV	DEC	YEAR
HS	795	1044	1398	1761	1852	1844	1783	1621	1364	1222	941	754	1364
VS	1106	1165	1150	998	813	743	741	808	964	1222	1233	1108	12052
TA	49.9	52.1	58.0	66.1	73.0	79.1	81.0	80.6	76.2	67.1	57.1	50.4	293
D50	100	61	16							5	20	92	293
D55	192	133	55	7						60	183	308	1188
D60	336	236	135	26					25	60	253	458	1952
D65	483	379	255	63	6				25	147	391	608	2917
D70	624	502	378	161	53	12	7	8					

BOISE, IDAHO — LAT = 43.6, ELEV = 2867

	JAN	FEB	MAR	APR	MAY	JUN	JUL	AUG	SEP	OCT	NOV	DEC	YEAR
HS	485	840	1304	1827	2277	2463	2613	2196	1737	1203	628	437	1495
VS	927	1286	1496	1472	1376	1300	1455	1547	1730	1575	1129	885	16177
TA	29.0	35.5	41.1	49.0	57.4	64.8	74.5	72.2	63.1	52.1	39.8	32.1	2420
D50	651	408	288	110	19	2			5	67	314	556	4335
D55	806	546	437	209	63	9			56	266	469	711	4336
D60	953	686	587	330	141	35		12	141	406	607	860	5833
D65	1116	826	741	480	252	97	10	32	227	756	1020	7315	
D70	1271	966	896	630	395	188	39	95					

LEWISTON, IDAHO — LAT = 46.4, ELEV = 1437

	JAN	FEB	MAR	APR	MAY	JUN	JUL	AUG	SEP	OCT	NOV	DEC	YEAR
HS	340	609	1020	1257	1842	2015	2336	1931	1435	860	413	286	1210
VS	705	1007	1265	1257	1213	1156	1416	1482	1548	1285	803	629	13764
TA	31.2	38.1	42.9	50.3	58.1	65.2	73.4	71.5	63.3	51.8	40.5	34.8	51.7
D50	583	337	288	84	13	1			13	65	293	477	2090
D55	738	477	437	177	49	7		5	45	190	443	623	3042
D60	893	613	539	299	123	29		17	124	409	735	781	4171
D65	1048	753	685	441	232	84	6	70	219	565	885	936	5464
D70	1203	893	840	591	373	179	45	259	6955				

POCATELLO, IDAHO — LAT = 42.9, ELEV = 4478

	JAN	FEB	MAR	APR	MAY	JUN	JUL	AUG	SEP	OCT	NOV	DEC	YEAR
HS	539	882	1371	1820	2280	2480	2600	2239	1769	1203	689	477	1529
VS	1010	1325	1542	1436	1348	1283	1418	1544	1726	1633	1214	982	16426
TA	23.2	29.4	35.4	45.3	54.4	61.3	71.0	69.5	59.4	46.7	35.7	26.4	46.7
D50	881	601	486	234	69	13	1	3	48	210	430	627	3322
D55	1036	741	658	376	169	53	8	19	98	413	579	782	5666
D60	1141	857	763	442	194	56		20	183	515	729	936	7063
D65	1296	997	918	591	336	138	10	92	322	670	879	1091	8651
D70	1451	1137	1073	741	484	255	62		1029				

CHICAGO, ILLINOIS — LAT = 41.8, ELEV = 623

	JAN	FEB	MAR	APR	MAY	JUN	JUL	AUG	SEP	OCT	NOV	DEC	YEAR
HS	507	759	1107	1459	1789	2007	1994	1719	1354	996	566	401	1215
VS	921	1106	1207	1113	1023	1006	1006	1146	1280	1276	967	771	12845
TA	24.3	27.4	36.8	49.0	60.0	70.5	75.4	73.7	65.2	54.4	40.4	28.5	50.6
D50	797	640	546	187	36	6		8	33	106	299	667	3018
D55	952	773	565	313	99	26		11	57	183	465	867	3991
D60	1107	857	763	442	194	56		20	183	344	589	977	4940
D65	1262	997	918	591	336	138	10	79	316	485	738	1132	6127
D70	1417	1137	1073	741	484	255	62	189	456	888	1287	7537	

MOLINE, ILLINOIS — LAT = 41.4, ELEV = 594

	JAN	FEB	MAR	APR	MAY	JUN	JUL	AUG	SEP	OCT	NOV	DEC	YEAR
HS	535	812	1171	1515	1754	1969	1939	1715	1357	996	595	433	1224
VS	961	1171	1271	1100	991	976	1012	1129	1268	1298	1006	823	12942
TA	22.3	27.4	30.4	50.6	61.0	70.5	75.1	72.9	64.4	54.4	39.2	26.6	49.8
D50	884	681	566	167	36	6		6	33	106	302	723	3197
D55	1039	820	744	313	99	26		11	57	183	465	867	5178
D60	1107	960	906	436	208	79		11	106	344	624	1035	5510
D65	1349	1100	963	582	320	26	20	189	485	774	1345	6395	
D70	1504	1240	1063	1196	297	94	924		7786				

SPRINGFIELD, ILLINOIS — LAT = 39.8, ELEV = 614

	JAN	FEB	MAR	APR	MAY	JUN	JUL	AUG	SEP	OCT	NOV	DEC	YEAR
HS	554	836	1168	1519	1895	2097	2058	1806	1454	1068	677	490	1301
VS	1006	1180	1321	1205	1069	1100	1026	1132	1296	1332	1095	891	13231
TA	26.7	30.4	39.4	45.7	57.4	67.2	76.0	74.0	56.4	56.8	26.6	18.5	52.7
D50	723	549	537	79	15	1				85	174	493	3034
D55	877	689	486	126	59	14		5	28	174	303	792	4338
D60	1032	829	639	363	132	46	16	165	457	792	6559		
D70	1187	1109	949	508	229	135	74		605	1092	1547	9415	

EVANSVILLE, INDIANA — LAT = 38.0, ELEV = 387

	JAN	FEB	MAR	APR	MAY	JUN	JUL	AUG	SEP	OCT	NOV	DEC	YEAR
HS	574	823	1151	1501	1783	1983	1920	1835	1403	1087	682	499	1262
VS	939	1081	1126	1019	912	903	923	1035	1186	1289	912	462	12306
TA	32.6	35.9	44.3	56.7	65.7	74.7	77.8	76.2	69.1	58.0	44.9	35.8	2630
D50	541	398	206	71	8	1			12	54	186	453	1830
D55	695	536	340	150	30	3			34	128	312	611	2630
D60	849	675	489	263	95	37	5	34	109	236	455	766	3556
D65	1004	815	653	403	175		17	26	372	603	921	4629	
D70	1159	956	797							509	753	1076	5879

FORT WAYNE, INDIANA — LAT = 41.0, ELEV = 827

	JAN	FEB	MAR	APR	MAY	JUN	JUL	AUG	SEP	OCT	NOV	DEC	YEAR
HS	455	698	982	1361	1672	1842	1787	1594	1177	924	516	369	1165
VS	809	995	1047	1013	934	903	922	1037	1174	1274	563	413	11123
TA	25.3	27.6	36.5	49.3	59.6	69.5	73.0	71.3	64.5	53.6	40.2	28.6	49.9
D50	766	541	421	98	32	5			8	112	446	664	2927
D55	921	767	574	194	96	18		5	31	218	594	818	3874
D60	1076	907	729	326	216	57	5	12	90	363	744	973	4963
D65	1231	1047	884	471	328	23	71	189	509	894	1128	6209	
D70	1386	1187	621	48				1283	7650				

INDIANAPOLIS, INDIANA — LAT = 39.7, ELEV = 807

	JAN	FEB	MAR	APR	MAY	JUN	JUL	AUG	SEP	OCT	NOV	DEC	YEAR
HS	496	747	1037	1398	1688	1868	1806	1643	1325	977	579	417	1165
VS	850	1028	1066	1000	907	885	898	1027	1177	1215	579	417	11742
TA	27.8	30.7	39.7	52.3	62.2	71.7	75.0	73.2	66.3	55.7	41.7	30.9	52.3
D50	685	477	328	139	20	1			7	88	264	593	2511
D55	840	681	477	248	66	6			25	175	403	747	3403
D60	995	820	630	387	159	55		9	63	302	550	902	4421
D65	1150	960	784	532	259	71	11	157	446	699	1057	5577	
D70	1305	1100	939		35	54			849	1212	6960		

SOUTH BEND, INDIANA — LAT = 41.7, ELEV = 774

	JAN	FEB	MAR	APR	MAY	JUN	JUL	AUG	SEP	OCT	NOV	DEC	YEAR
HS	416	660	992	1385	1722	1922	1852	1666	1291	1909	497	340	1138
VS	754	959	1079	1057	964	961	975	1107	1297	1909	497	340	11782
TA	24.0	26.3	35.3	48.1	58.4	68.6	72.3	71.0	63.8	53.4	39.6	27.6	48.8
D50	806	664	458	226	48	1		4	12	122	464	676	3112
D55	961	804	611	362	122	12		9	43	226	612	831	4084
D60	1116	944	766	507	245	35	6	62	98	368	762	986	5199
D65	1271	1084	921	657	657	114	81	209	516	762	1141	6462	
D70	1426	1224									1296	7938	

BURLINGTON, IOWA — LAT = 40.8, ELEV = 702

	JAN	FEB	MAR	APR	MAY	JUN	JUL	AUG	SEP	OCT	NOV	DEC	YEAR
HS	577	859	1165	1538	1876	2121	2085	1828	1456	1360	664	491	1306
VS	1023	1235	1235	1385	1041	1035	1097	1182	1300	1360	1104	891	13005
TA	22.9	27.3	36.1	51.8	61.8	71.4	75.4	73.9	65.4	55.3	39.8	27.6	50.8
D50	859	636	411	159	23	2			9	95	315	695	3018
D55	1150	776	562	275	77	16		5	32	185	458	849	3930
D60	1150	916	716	416	172	35		13	70	320	607	1004	4969
D65	1305	1056	871	562	271	98	16	98	271	516	756	1159	6149
D70	1460	1196	1026				33		177			1314	8129

DES MOINES, IOWA — LAT = 41.5, ELEV = 965

	JAN	FEB	MAR	APR	MAY	JUN	JUL	AUG	SEP	OCT	NOV	DEC	YEAR
HS	541	861	1180	1577	1867	2125	2097	1833	1405	1010	658	443	1288
VS	1047	1245	1276	1177	1058	1057	1143	1207	1379	1395	658	884	14181
TA	19.4	24.2	33.9	49.8	60.9	70.5	75.1	73.3	64.3	54.1	37.8	20.1	48.8
D50	1104	723	502	200	33	3		5	14	116	378	829	3491
D55	1259	862	655	325	99	10		18	45	211	518	930	4435
D60	1259	1002	809	465	186	26		58	94	350	666	1085	5510
D65	1569	1142	964	616	297	94	39	204	489	816	1240	6710	
D70			1119					302	605	1395	8129		

MASON CITY, IOWA — LAT = 43.1, ELEV = 1224

	JAN	FEB	MAR	APR	MAY	JUN	JUL	AUG	SEP	OCT	NOV	DEC	YEAR
HS	554	836	1168	1519	1895	2214	2084	1833	1405	1010	600	443	1288
VS	1044	1272	1327	1205	1100	1100	1143	1272	1379	1379	600	884	14181
TA	14.2	18.5	29.0	45.7	57.4	67.2	71.3	69.9	60.2	50.5	33.6	20.1	44.8
D50	1110	882	651	288	58	7		5	28	85	642	927	4338
D55	1265	1022	806	431	164	16	2	14	174	303	792	1082	5373
D60	1420	1162	961	585	280	64	13	73	165	457	1237	6559	
D65	1575	1402	1271	729	394	135	94		302	605	1392	7901	
D70	1730										1547	9915	

BATON ROUGE, LOUISIANA — LAT = 30.5 — ELEV = 75

	JAN	FEB	MAR	APR	MAY	JUN	JUL	AUG	SEP	OCT	NOV	DEC	YEAR
HS	788	1038	1170	1681	1871	1926	1746	1677	1464	1301	920	737	1378
VS	1045	1124	1081	1278	794	759	706	801	985	1248	1153	1037	11642
TA	51.0	53.9	59.7	68.4	74.8	80.3	82.0	81.0	77.5	68.5	58.5	52.9	67.4
D50	90	46	17	5	0	0	0	0	0	17	53	63	232
D55	174	111	43	17	0	0	0	0	0	54	124	139	530
D60	294	199	109	43	0	0	0	0	0	124	217	245	1006
D65	451	335	208	109	42	0	7	8	22	217	398	381	1670
D70	590	453	330	208	127	11	7	8	129	350	491	532	2601

LAKE CHARLES, LOUISIANA — LAT = 30.1 — ELEV = 10

	JAN	FEB	MAR	APR	MAY	JUN	JUL	AUG	SEP	OCT	NOV	DEC	YEAR
HS	728	1010	1313	1570	1849	1970	1788	1657	1485	1381	917	706	1365
VS	959	1065	1017	1093	779	773	719	783	987	1262	1137	982	11348
TA	52.3	55.1	60.3	68.9	75.2	80.7	82.4	82.0	78.4	70.0	60.2	54.3	68.3
D50	181	100	44	6	0	0	0	0	0	16	44	124	207
D55	265	181	108	19	0	0	0	0	16	54	217	217	481
D60	415	306	200	108	26	0	0	0	112	112	398	398	897
D65	551	422	317	200	108	19	10	112	310	310	491	491	1998
D70	590	453	409	308	127	45	8	118	310	310	491	532	2427

NEW ORLEANS, LOUISIANA — LAT = 30.0 — ELEV = 10

	JAN	FEB	MAR	APR	MAY	JUN	JUL	AUG	SEP	OCT	NOV	DEC	YEAR
HS	835	1112	1415	1780	1968	2004	1813	1717	1514	1335	973	779	1437
VS	1097	1169	1093	948	827	786	728	809	1003	1203	1081	1086	12005
TA	52.9	55.5	60.7	68.6	75.1	80.4	81.9	81.9	78.2	69.8	60.1	54.8	68.3
D50	73	39	15	2	0	0	0	0	0	17	16	54	197
D55	150	96	42	7	0	0	0	0	0	44	116	208	497
D60	252	173	108	42	0	0	0	0	0	116	179	327	887
D65	403	279	200	108	48	0	6	11	24	179	313	476	2167
D70	533	409	308	308	547	15	6	11	118	313	490	646	3152

SHREVEPORT, LOUISIANA — LAT = 32.5 — ELEV = 259

	JAN	FEB	MAR	APR	MAY	JUN	JUL	AUG	SEP	OCT	NOV	DEC	YEAR
HS	762	1038	1341	1613	1886	2065	2014	1877	1554	1303	929	731	1426
VS	1072	1171	1117	925	836	838	843	947	1206	1230	1086	1086	12500
TA	47.2	50.5	56.8	66.4	73.4	80.2	83.2	83.0	77.4	67.5	56.2	49.2	65.9
D50	154	90	31	9	0	0	0	0	0	26	90	120	428
D55	264	169	81	31	0	0	0	0	6	87	206	315	832
D60	403	291	161	81	16	0	0	0	65	170	315	490	1832
D65	552	416	291	163	87	23	21	84	170	247	477	646	3157
D70	707	547	408	291	178	81	84	178	315	477	606	646	3152

CARIBOU, MAINE — LAT = 46.9 — ELEV = 623

	JAN	FEB	MAR	APR	MAY	JUN	JUL	AUG	SEP	OCT	NOV	DEC	YEAR
HS	419	724	1133	1414	1578	1757	1762	1501	1103	688	366	310	1063
VS	881	1214	1424	1257	1055	1023	1084	1170	1206	1138	691	691	12770
TA	10.7	12.9	23.6	36.7	49.7	59.6	64.9	62.3	54.1	43.8	31.4	16.1	38.8
D50	1373	1179	973	549	183	23	10	46	206	350	558	708	5408
D55	1528	1319	1128	699	323	82	21	84	350	503	708	858	8061
D60	1683	1459	1283	849	474	170	84	132	477	658	858	1008	9632
D65	1838	1599	1438	999	629	315	178	247	629	812	1158	1158	11363

PORTLAND, MAINE — LAT = 43.6 — ELEV = 62

	JAN	FEB	MAR	APR	MAY	JUN	JUL	AUG	SEP	OCT	NOV	DEC	YEAR
HS	450	682	970	1304	1567	1712	1659	1461	1153	822	459	363	1051
VS	860	1044	1113	970	947	879	894	929	1153	1138	735	735	11722
TA	21.5	22.9	31.8	42.2	52.7	62.2	68.0	66.4	58.7	49.1	38.6	25.7	45.0
D50	884	759	564	225	108	6	1	5	87	343	459	735	3958
D55	1039	899	719	370	232	38	5	32	200	493	642	825	6039
D60	1194	1039	874	519	383	106	27	92	340	648	792	1063	9198
D65	1349	1179	1029	669	536	239	102	135	519	648	942	1218	9142
D70	1504	1319	1184	819	648	648	135	247	648	812	1158	1373	—

BALTIMORE, MARYLAND — LAT = 39.2 — ELEV = 154

	JAN	FEB	MAR	APR	MAY	JUN	JUL	AUG	SEP	OCT	NOV	DEC	YEAR
HS	587	840	1162	1488	1714	1879	1894	1599	1165	998	660	499	1215
VS	992	1140	1177	907	879	879	894	1050	1165	1330	892	825	12353
TA	33.4	34.8	42.8	53.8	63.7	72.4	76.6	74.9	68.5	57.1	45.0	35.9	54.5
D50	515	449	236	36	8	0	0	0	8	27	185	357	1831
D55	692	613	371	110	36	0	0	0	36	110	274	507	2662
D60	825	766	534	203	105	8	0	0	105	252	418	766	3623
D65	980	906	688	340	212	49	25	110	252	567	567	921	4729
D70	1135	1046	843	487	487	105	105	195	375	717	750	1066	6042

SIOUX CITY, IOWA — LAT = 42.4 — ELEV = 1102

	JAN	FEB	MAR	APR	MAY	JUN	JUL	AUG	SEP	OCT	NOV	DEC	YEAR
HS	644	945	1170	1578	1901	2124	2122	1844	1427	1038	665	543	1340
VS	1052	1248	1298	1226	1107	1083	1140	1253	1467	1390	917	822	—
TA	18.0	23.4	33.2	49.4	60.9	70.3	75.0	73.0	63.4	51.3	36.3	23.5	48.4
D50	992	745	523	201	32	1	0	5	17	134	562	822	3680
D55	1147	885	676	328	90	10	5	54	113	239	711	977	4634
D60	1302	1025	831	474	189	33	10	113	378	518	861	1132	5726
D65	1457	1165	986	619	297	95	36	224	378	738	1011	1287	6953
D70	1612	1305	—	—	—	—	—	—	—	590	1135	—	8382

DODGE CITY, KANSAS — LAT = 37.8 — ELEV = 2582

	JAN	FEB	MAR	APR	MAY	JUN	JUL	AUG	SEP	OCT	NOV	DEC	YEAR
HS	827	1122	1476	1886	2090	2358	2295	2055	1687	1301	894	732	1560
VS	1345	1466	1436	1273	1063	1065	1084	1212	1417	1535	1369	1258	15523
TA	30.8	35.2	41.2	54.0	64.0	73.7	79.2	78.1	68.9	57.9	42.8	33.4	54.9
D50	596	417	289	48	15	0	0	20	63	139	373	670	2132
D55	750	555	432	116	50	0	0	44	139	287	518	825	2980
D60	905	695	584	244	118	13	0	108	373	518	666	980	3945
D65	960	834	738	388	216	55	15	247	373	816	980	1082	5016
D70	1215	974	893	—	—	—	—	—	—	590	1135	—	6318

GOODLAND, KANSAS — LAT = 39.4 — ELEV = 3688

	JAN	FEB	MAR	APR	MAY	JUN	JUL	AUG	SEP	OCT	NOV	DEC	YEAR
HS	789	1089	1424	1829	2062	2357	2319	2046	1642	1268	857	695	1529
VS	1341	1441	1451	1297	1098	1048	1104	1172	1564	1535	1371	1258	15777
TA	27.6	31.5	36.3	48.7	58.9	69.1	75.0	74.1	64.3	52.8	38.5	30.1	50.6
D50	695	519	445	113	52	1	0	6	45	240	497	618	2819
D55	850	658	581	217	152	14	0	42	140	388	652	772	3784
D60	1004	798	735	357	291	55	0	81	291	540	807	927	4885
D65	1159	938	890	497	429	133	35	163	291	535	795	1082	—
D70	1314	1078	1045	640	—	—	—	—	—	—	—	1237	7547

TOPEKA, KANSAS — LAT = 39.1 — ELEV = 886

	JAN	FEB	MAR	APR	MAY	JUN	JUL	AUG	SEP	OCT	NOV	DEC	YEAR
HS	681	941	1257	1642	1915	2126	2128	1910	1516	1147	772	695	1385
VS	1148	1274	1270	1153	1011	1004	1011	1172	1516	1403	1225	1039	14051
TA	28.0	31.5	41.2	54.5	64.5	73.5	78.0	77.2	68.2	57.6	42.9	31.8	54.3
D50	683	467	291	113	16	2	0	6	31	148	497	566	2819
D55	837	605	433	217	52	9	0	21	148	371	497	720	3175
D60	992	745	588	357	118	14	0	81	240	515	695	874	5243
D65	1147	885	743	497	216	55	0	163	292	666	795	1029	3642
D70	1302	1025	893	640	353	115	33	204	535	813	1029	1184	6527

WICHITA, KANSAS — LAT = 37.6 — ELEV = 1339

	JAN	FEB	MAR	APR	MAY	JUN	JUL	AUG	SEP	OCT	NOV	DEC	YEAR
HS	784	1058	1405	1782	2036	2264	2238	2032	1616	1250	871	690	1502
VS	1268	1375	1359	1195	1030	1052	1041	1191	1466	1466	1326	1179	14809
TA	31.3	36.3	43.6	56.0	66.1	75.8	80.7	79.7	70.6	59.4	44.8	34.5	56.6
D50	581	389	231	83	11	1	0	3	23	115	460	558	2725
D55	735	525	363	161	35	11	0	27	102	211	606	708	3642
D60	890	664	511	307	106	36	0	84	319	460	756	858	4887
D65	1045	804	666	447	197	52	29	211	323	558	756	946	5897
D70	1200	944	819	558	308	122	52	286	383	792	907	1101	6887

LEXINGTON, KENTUCKY — LAT = 38.0 — ELEV = 988

	JAN	FEB	MAR	APR	MAY	JUN	JUL	AUG	SEP	OCT	NOV	DEC	YEAR
HS	546	779	1099	1479	1747	1897	1850	1685	1362	1044	657	485	1219
VS	893	1023	1076	1004	861	861	850	999	1238	1238	1012	762	11868
TA	32.9	35.1	43.6	55.1	64.7	73.0	76.1	75.0	68.6	57.8	44.6	35.5	55.1
D50	531	414	223	90	10	1	0	13	192	232	464	605	1865
D55	685	552	360	161	32	11	0	58	332	464	699	858	2686
D60	840	692	511	307	106	32	38	115	452	699	858	1008	3632
D65	995	831	666	447	197	48	38	232	538	792	1008	1218	—
D70	1150	972	819	558	—	—	—	—	—	—	—	—	6026

LOUISVILLE, KENTUCKY — LAT = 38.2 — ELEV = 489

	JAN	FEB	MAR	APR	MAY	JUN	JUL	AUG	SEP	OCT	NOV	DEC	YEAR
HS	545	789	1102	1467	1720	1903	1837	1680	1361	1042	653	488	1216
VS	896	1042	1085	1002	868	867	868	1003	1243	1243	1011	750	11917
TA	33.3	35.8	44.0	55.9	64.8	73.3	76.9	75.9	69.1	57.2	45.0	35.6	55.6
D50	531	414	223	28	8	0	0	8	130	232	449	600	1816
D55	685	552	360	90	38	8	0	52	274	449	600	750	2662
D60	828	682	498	165	105	8	0	110	452	600	911	911	3663
D65	983	818	661	286	195	52	22	340	340	688	911	911	4645
D70	1138	958	806	426	—	—	—	—	—	—	—	1066	5927

BOSTON, MASSACHUSETTS LAT = 42.4 ELEV = 16

	JAN	FEB	MAR	APR	MAY	JUN	JUL	AUG	SEP	OCT	NOV	DEC	YEAR
HS	475	710	1016	1326	1620	1817	1749	1486	1260	890	503	403	1105
VS	878	1052	1127	1030	944	927	940	1009	1212	1192	874	788	11972
TA	29.2	30.4	38.1	48.6	58.6	68.0	73.3	71.3	64.5	55.4	45.2	33.0	51.3
D50	645	549	371	96	5	0	0	0	1	16	163	527	2374
D55	800	689	524	203	29	1	0	0	4	70	297	682	3300
D60	955	829	679	344	99	7	0	2	21	164	445	837	4381
D65	1110	969	834	492	218	27	0	8	76	301	594	992	5621
D70	1265	1109	989	642	355	106	32	57	180	453	744	1147	7080

ALPENA, MICHIGAN LAT = 45.1 ELEV = 689

	JAN	FEB	MAR	APR	MAY	JUN	JUL	AUG	SEP	OCT	NOV	DEC	YEAR
HS	362	617	1028	1407	1720	1879	1885	1583	1156	743	382	270	1086
VS	722	984	1230	1186	1088	1037	1098	1168	1202	1071	716	571	12072
TA	17.8	18.3	26.2	40.1	50.5	60.9	65.5	64.2	56.3	47.3	34.9	23.4	42.1
D50	998	888	738	303	79	4	1	2	17	132	454	825	4440
D55	1153	1028	893	448	169	19	5	7	65	250	603	980	5621
D60	1308	1168	1048	597	301	71	22	32	147	396	753	1135	6978
D65	1463	1308	1203	747	455	150	75	110	265	549	903	1290	8518
D70	1618	1448	1358	897	605	280	169	200	413	704	1053	1445	10190

DETROIT, MICHIGAN LAT = 42.4 ELEV = 627

	JAN	FEB	MAR	APR	MAY	JUN	JUL	AUG	SEP	OCT	NOV	DEC	YEAR
HS	417	680	1000	1399	1716	1866	1835	1575	1253	876	478	343	1120
VS	771	1008	1109	1087	999	952	986	1069	1205	1173	831	671	11861
TA	25.5	26.9	35.4	48.1	58.4	69.1	73.3	71.9	64.5	54.3	41.1	29.6	49.9
D50	760	647	454	116	10	0	0	0	2	33	276	633	2931
D55	915	787	608	223	42	2	0	1	7	100	419	787	3890
D60	1070	927	763	360	115	8	0	4	31	199	567	942	4986
D65	1225	1067	918	507	238	26	0	11	80	342	717	1097	6228
D70	1380	1207	1073	657	364	100	43	61	188	488	867	1252	7679

FLINT, MICHIGAN LAT = 43.0 ELEV = 764

	JAN	FEB	MAR	APR	MAY	JUN	JUL	AUG	SEP	OCT	NOV	DEC	YEAR
HS	383	636	957	1339	1658	1813	1797	1555	1195	829	429	309	1075
VS	720	958	1080	1059	983	941	983	1076	1170	1129	758	615	11470
TA	22.3	23.8	32.6	45.9	55.8	65.8	69.7	68.2	61.0	51.2	38.3	26.8	46.8
D50	859	734	540	153	19	1	0	0	4	66	354	719	3449
D55	1014	874	694	280	72	4	1	2	17	152	502	874	4485
D60	1169	1014	849	424	161	18	6	9	67	280	651	1029	5677
D65	1324	1154	1004	573	306	65	14	36	147	433	801	1184	7041
D70	1479	1294	1159	723	442	155	89	113	277	583	951	1339	8604

GRAND RAPIDS, MICHIGAN LAT = 42.9 ELEV = 804

	JAN	FEB	MAR	APR	MAY	JUN	JUL	AUG	SEP	OCT	NOV	DEC	YEAR
HS	370	648	1014	1412	1755	1956	1914	1676	1262	858	446	311	1135
VS	694	973	1141	1114	1038	1012	1044	1156	1232	1165	786	617	11970
TA	23.2	24.5	33.1	46.5	57.1	67.4	71.5	70.0	62.4	52.0	38.7	27.4	47.8
D50	831	714	525	145	15	1	0	0	3	59	343	701	3337
D55	986	854	679	265	58	3	1	1	13	140	490	856	4345
D60	1141	994	834	407	138	13	4	6	52	260	639	1011	5499
D65	1296	1134	989	555	270	44	8	27	114	409	789	1166	6801
D70	1451	1274	1144	705	403	128	66	88	241	559	939	1321	8317

SAULT STE. MARIE, MICHIGAN LAT = 46.5 ELEV = 725

	JAN	FEB	MAR	APR	MAY	JUN	JUL	AUG	SEP	OCT	NOV	DEC	YEAR
HS	325	603	1029	1383	1688	1811	1835	1523	1049	673	332	253	1042
VS	675	1000	1279	1215	1115	1042	1115	1173	1134	1008	648	558	11962
TA	14.2	15.2	24.0	38.2	49.0	58.7	63.8	63.2	55.3	46.2	32.8	20.1	40.0
D50	1110	974	806	357	98	7	1	2	20	150	516	927	4969
D55	1265	1114	961	504	203	33	7	8	75	280	666	1082	6198
D60	1420	1254	1116	654	344	100	33	39	165	429	816	1237	7607
D65	1575	1394	1271	804	496	200	96	125	291	583	966	1392	9193
D70	1730	1534	1426	954	651	342	208	224	442	738	1116	1547	10912

TRAVERSE CITY, MICHIGAN LAT = 44.7 ELEV = 630

	JAN	FEB	MAR	APR	MAY	JUN	JUL	AUG	SEP	OCT	NOV	DEC	YEAR
HS	311	567	1001	1405	1729	1912	1910	1609	1165	754	377	257	1083
VS	614	895	1184	1170	1080	1042	1099	1173	1197	1075	699	537	11765
TA	20.8	20.7	28.7	42.7	52.8	63.7	68.7	67.5	59.4	49.8	36.9	25.9	44.8
D50	905	820	660	231	45	2	0	0	6	87	395	747	3899
D55	1060	960	815	371	121	8	2	2	28	184	543	902	4997
D60	1215	1100	970	519	236	34	8	11	91	321	693	1057	6257
D65	1370	1240	1125	669	387	104	33	66	178	471	843	1212	7698
D70	1525	1380	1280	819	534	205	105	126	322	626	993	1367	9284

DULUTH, MINNESOTA LAT = 46.8 ELEV = 1417

	JAN	FEB	MAR	APR	MAY	JUN	JUL	AUG	SEP	OCT	NOV	DEC	YEAR
HS	389	673	1034	1373	1643	1767	1854	1547	1095	725	381	292	1064
VS	816	1125	1296	1217	1095	1026	1137	1202	1194	1095	750	649	12603
TA	8.5	12.1	23.5	38.6	49.4	59.0	65.6	64.1	54.4	45.3	28.4	14.4	38.6
D50	1287	1061	822	345	91	6	1	1	26	170	648	1104	5560
D55	1442	1201	977	492	192	29	4	6	88	306	798	1259	6792
D60	1597	1341	1132	642	332	94	18	29	186	457	948	1414	8189
D65	1751	1481	1287	792	484	194	67	104	318	611	1098	1569	9756
D70	1907	1621	1442	942	639	333	163	200	469	766	1248	1724	11452

INTERNATIONAL FALLS, MINNESOTA LAT = 48.6 ELEV = 1184

	JAN	FEB	MAR	APR	MAY	JUN	JUL	AUG	SEP	OCT	NOV	DEC	YEAR
HS	356	663	1046	1444	1716	1853	1921	1618	1121	704	345	272	1088
VS	787	1165	1378	1349	1209	1137	1245	1327	1286	1117	715	639	13354
TA	1.9	7.0	20.6	38.2	50.1	60.4	65.8	63.2	53.0	43.5	24.9	8.7	36.5
D50	1491	1204	911	357	81	4	1	2	40	216	753	1280	6341
D55	1646	1344	1066	505	176	20	4	9	112	360	903	1435	7580
D60	1801	1484	1221	654	312	74	18	39	222	512	1053	1590	8983
D65	1956	1624	1376	804	462	168	66	112	364	667	1203	1745	10547
D70	2111	1764	1531	954	617	293	160	224	510	822	1353	1900	12241

MINNEAPOLIS-ST. PAUL, MINNESOTA LAT = 44.9 ELEV = 837

	JAN	FEB	MAR	APR	MAY	JUN	JUL	AUG	SEP	OCT	NOV	DEC	YEAR
HS	464	764	1103	1442	1737	1927	1970	1687	1255	860	480	353	1170
VS	921	1212	1312	1208	1092	1057	1140	1237	1297	1233	895	742	13346
TA	12.2	16.5	28.3	45.1	57.1	66.9	71.9	70.2	60.0	50.0	32.4	18.6	44.1
D50	1172	938	673	178	18	1	0	0	8	93	529	973	4584
D55	1327	1078	828	305	63	4	1	2	30	186	678	1128	5631
D60	1482	1218	983	449	143	18	5	8	90	318	828	1283	6824
D65	1637	1358	1138	597	271	65	11	21	173	472	978	1438	8159
D70	1792	1498	1293	747	403	142	66	90	308	620	1128	1593	9680

ROCHESTER, MINNESOTA LAT = 43.9 ELEV = 1319

	JAN	FEB	MAR	APR	MAY	JUN	JUL	AUG	SEP	OCT	NOV	DEC	YEAR
HS	477	753	1082	1410	1696	1902	1909	1662	1250	870	494	370	1156
VS	920	1163	1252	1146	1034	1013	1072	1182	1255	1214	895	756	12901
TA	12.9	16.9	27.8	44.5	56.2	66.0	70.1	68.6	59.3	49.6	32.6	18.9	43.6
D50	1150	927	688	188	20	1	0	0	8	95	523	964	4565
D55	1305	1067	843	320	71	5	1	2	33	192	672	1119	5631
D60	1460	1207	998	466	156	20	6	10	97	328	822	1274	6845
D65	1615	1347	1153	615	292	78	21	35	185	485	972	1429	8227
D70	1770	1487	1308	765	430	155	87	112	326	633	1122	1584	9779

JACKSON, MISSISSIPPI LAT = 32.3 ELEV = 331

	JAN	FEB	MAR	APR	MAY	JUN	JUL	AUG	SEP	OCT	NOV	DEC	YEAR
HS	753	1026	1369	1708	1941	2024	1909	1780	1509	1271	902	709	1409
VS	1053	1151	1133	974	856	818	796	893	1073	1284	1188	1048	12268
TA	47.1	49.8	56.1	65.7	72.7	79.4	81.7	81.2	76.0	65.8	55.3	48.9	65.0
D50	158	102	35	3	1	0	0	0	0	3	40	128	471
D55	268	184	94	12	2	0	0	0	0	12	102	224	898
D60	407	298	177	37	7	0	0	0	0	38	187	355	1506
D65	569	442	313	74	6	0	0	0	0	91	301	504	2300
D70	710	567	436	179	71	16	9	11	35	183	445	655	3318

MERIDIAN, MISSISSIPPI LAT = 32.3 ELEV = 308

	JAN	FEB	MAR	APR	MAY	JUN	JUL	AUG	SEP	OCT	NOV	DEC	YEAR
HS	744	1012	1328	1662	1860	1963	1823	1739	1454	1258	897	699	1370
VS	1041	1135	1099	948	821	794	760	872	1034	1271	1182	1033	11989
TA	46.9	49.8	56.1	65.4	72.4	79.2	81.2	80.7	75.3	64.8	54.2	47.9	64.5
D50	163	103	36	4	1	0	0	0	0	5	52	146	510
D55	274	185	95	13	2	0	0	0	0	16	120	249	955
D60	413	298	178	41	8	0	0	0	0	48	211	384	1582
D65	575	443	312	79	7	0	0	0	0	111	331	530	2388
D70	717	567	437	186	76	17	11	13	42	205	478	686	3434

COLUMBIA, MISSOURI LAT = 38.8 ELEV = 886

	JAN	FEB	MAR	APR	MAY	JUN	JUL	AUG	SEP	OCT	NOV	DEC	YEAR
HS	611	875	1179	1526	1880	2089	2116	1878	1450	1101	703	522	1328
VS	1022	1175	1181	1062	984	967	1027	1142	1255	1335	1106	923	13177
TA	29.3	33.6	41.7	55.0	64.4	73.0	77.3	76.0	68.3	58.0	43.9	32.8	54.4
D50	642	461	275	37	4	0	0	0	1	19	212	535	2186
D55	797	600	417	99	13	1	0	1	5	60	341	689	3022
D60	952	739	569	187	44	5	0	2	17	135	485	843	3979
D65	1107	879	730	314	117	11	0	5	42	247	633	998	5083
D70	1262	1019	877	453	207	58	22	30	126	379	783	1153	6370

KANSAS CITY, MISSOURI LAT = 39.3 ELEV = 1033

	JAN	FEB	MAR	APR	MAY	JUN	JUL	AUG	SEP	OCT	NOV	DEC	YEAR
HS	648	895	1203	1575	1873	2080	2102	1862	1452	1092	737	561	1340
VS	1098	1218	1222	1113	994	975	1034	1149	1276	1343	1176	1005	13604
TA	27.1	32.3	40.7	54.2	64.1	73.0	77.5	76.5	68.0	57.6	42.3	31.3	53.7
D50	710	497	303	46	4	0	0	0	1	22	252	581	2417
D55	865	636	447	114	15	1	0	0	5	67	387	735	3273
D60	1020	776	599	206	49	5	0	0	19	144	533	890	4242
D65	1175	916	753	336	127	15	0	0	50	259	681	1045	5357
D70	1330	1056	908	477	216	60	22	28	133	391	831	1200	6651

SAINT LOUIS, MISSOURI LAT = 38.7 ELEV = 564

	JAN	FEB	MAR	APR	MAY	JUN	JUL	AUG	SEP	OCT	NOV	DEC	YEAR
HS	627	886	1205	1564	1871	2092	2049	1816	1459	1100	718	531	1327
VS	1045	1186	1203	1085	976	966	991	1100	1259	1330	1127	936	13207
TA	31.3	35.1	43.3	56.5	65.8	74.9	78.6	77.2	69.6	59.1	45.0	34.6	55.9
D50	581	421	237	29	3	0	0	0	1	16	191	481	1961
D55	735	558	371	83	11	1	0	0	4	52	313	633	2762
D60	890	697	520	162	36	4	0	0	14	122	454	788	3686
D65	1045	837	682	272	103	10	0	0	35	224	600	942	4750
D70	1200	977	828	410	181	42	19	26	110	349	750	1097	5989

SPRINGFIELD, MISSOURI LAT = 37.2 ELEV = 1270

	JAN	FEB	MAR	APR	MAY	JUN	JUL	AUG	SEP	OCT	NOV	DEC	YEAR
HS	684	926	1235	1604	1882	2075	2063	1873	1481	1144	775	603	1362
VS	1094	1190	1181	1063	941	924	960	1084	1222	1327	1167	1019	13173
TA	32.9	37.0	44.0	56.5	65.1	73.6	77.8	77.1	69.3	59.0	45.5	36.0	56.1
D50	532	369	217	27	3	0	0	0	1	15	178	438	1779
D55	686	505	350	79	11	1	0	0	4	49	298	590	2573
D60	840	644	498	158	38	4	0	2	13	120	438	744	3501
D65	995	784	660	275	94	10	0	6	35	227	585	899	4570
D70	1150	924	806	410	192	52	20	24	111	350	735	1054	5828

BILLINGS, MONTANA LAT = 45.8 ELEV = 3570

	JAN	FEB	MAR	APR	MAY	JUN	JUL	AUG	SEP	OCT	NOV	DEC	YEAR
HS	486	763	1189	1526	1913	2174	2384	2022	1470	987	561	421	1325
VS	990	1241	1450	1313	1236	1225	1418	1524	1559	1451	1073	909	15388
TA	21.9	27.4	32.6	44.6	54.5	62.6	71.8	70.1	58.9	49.3	35.7	26.8	46.3
D50	871	633	540	190	36	4	0	0	11	105	431	719	3541
D55	1026	773	695	319	102	15	1	2	41	203	580	874	4630
D60	1181	913	849	464	198	55	5	8	108	338	729	1029	5878
D65	1336	1053	1004	612	333	131	10	15	221	487	879	1184	7265
D70	1491	1193	1159	762	482	238	68	92	339	642	1029	1339	8835

CUT BANK, MONTANA LAT = 48.6 ELEV = 3839

	JAN	FEB	MAR	APR	MAY	JUN	JUL	AUG	SEP	OCT	NOV	DEC	YEAR
HS	402	688	1128	1485	1883	2045	2287	1897	1352	871	480	334	1238
VS	889	1209	1486	1387	1327	1254	1483	1556	1551	1382	995	784	15303
TA	16.2	22.4	26.8	39.5	49.6	56.5	64.4	62.6	53.2	44.1	29.7	21.4	40.5
D50	1048	773	719	318	85	12	1	2	34	198	609	887	4686
D55	1203	913	874	466	185	55	5	9	105	341	759	1042	5955
D60	1358	1053	1029	615	326	136	25	42	215	493	909	1197	7398
D65	1513	1193	1184	765	477	267	82	125	368	648	1059	1352	9033
D70	1668	1333	1339	915	633	406	190	239	504	803	1209	1507	10745

DILLON, MONTANA LAT = 45.2 ELEV = 5210

	JAN	FEB	MAR	APR	MAY	JUN	JUL	AUG	SEP	OCT	NOV	DEC	YEAR
HS	526	846	1279	1639	1989	2143	2392	2023	1521	1023	602	450	1370
VS	1053	1353	1534	1385	1262	1186	1397	1497	1585	1479	1132	954	15818
TA	20.2	25.5	29.6	41.1	50.4	57.5	66.4	64.6	54.7	45.0	31.8	23.9	42.6
D50	924	686	633	276	84	14	1	2	30	183	547	809	4188
D55	1079	826	787	419	174	52	4	8	91	317	696	964	5418
D60	1234	966	942	567	305	127	19	32	184	466	846	1119	6809
D65	1389	1106	1097	717	453	238	54	85	325	620	996	1274	8354
D70	1544	1246	1252	867	608	378	153	193	460	775	1146	1429	10051

GLASGOW, MONTANA LAT = 48.2 ELEV = 2297

	JAN	FEB	MAR	APR	MAY	JUN	JUL	AUG	SEP	OCT	NOV	DEC	YEAR
HS	388	671	1105	1488	1828	2047	2193	1863	1340	877	479	334	1218
VS	848	1166	1440	1374	1272	1240	1404	1510	1520	1376	981	775	14907
TA	9.2	15.2	25.2	42.8	54.2	62.0	70.5	69.0	57.2	46.4	29.0	17.1	41.5
D50	1265	974	769	234	40	5	0	1	18	158	630	1020	5114
D55	1420	1114	924	370	108	19	2	3	61	279	780	1175	6256
D60	1575	1254	1079	517	206	64	7	11	138	425	930	1330	7537
D65	1730	1394	1234	666	344	151	15	30	263	577	1080	1485	8969
D70	1885	1534	1389	816	491	254	88	112	388	732	1230	1640	10559

GREAT FALLS, MONTANA LAT = 47.5 ELEV = 3661

	JAN	FEB	MAR	APR	MAY	JUN	JUL	AUG	SEP	OCT	NOV	DEC	YEAR
HS	420	720	1170	1489	1848	2101	2329	1933	1378	925	498	336	1262
VS	899	1227	1495	1347	1259	1246	1460	1534	1533	1424	1000	763	15187
TA	20.5	26.6	30.5	43.4	53.3	60.8	69.3	67.4	57.3	48.3	34.6	26.5	44.9
D50	915	655	605	215	44	5	0	1	14	117	463	729	3761
D55	1070	795	760	352	117	21	2	3	54	225	612	884	4893
D60	1225	935	915	499	225	74	8	14	130	367	762	1039	6191
D65	1380	1075	1070	648	367	162	18	42	260	524	912	1194	7652
D70	1535	1215	1225	798	519	284	100	132	384	673	1062	1349	9274

HELENA, MONTANA LAT = 46.6 ELEV = 3898

	JAN	FEB	MAR	APR	MAY	JUN	JUL	AUG	SEP	OCT	NOV	DEC	YEAR
HS	419	709	1145	1487	1860	2040	2334	1930	1412	926	521	364	1262
VS	873	1179	1428	1310	1232	1177	1423	1490	1531	1391	1019	805	14859
TA	18.1	25.4	30.6	42.7	52.2	59.2	67.9	66.2	55.5	45.3	31.7	23.3	43.2
D50	989	689	602	232	56	8	1	1	23	175	549	828	4151
D55	1144	829	756	372	135	32	3	4	78	307	699	983	5342
D60	1299	969	911	520	254	97	12	19	165	457	849	1138	6689
D65	1454	1109	1066	669	401	194	33	57	304	611	999	1293	8190
D70	1609	1249	1221	819	552	329	122	155	436	766	1149	1448	9855

LEWISTOWN, MONTANA LAT = 47.0 ELEV = 4147

	JAN	FEB	MAR	APR	MAY	JUN	JUL	AUG	SEP	OCT	NOV	DEC	YEAR
HS	420	692	1128	1444	1807	2059	2288	1901	1372	905	502	363	1240
VS	886	1163	1422	1287	1212	1203	1412	1486	1505	1374	993	812	14756
TA	19.1	23.8	27.5	40.1	49.6	56.6	65.5	64.4	54.0	45.5	32.2	24.5	41.9
D50	958	734	698	306	102	21	2	3	41	177	535	791	4367
D55	1113	874	853	449	198	70	8	10	109	305	684	946	5617
D60	1268	1014	1008	598	330	150	29	39	205	452	834	1101	7026
D65	1423	1154	1163	747	477	265	70	94	348	605	984	1256	8586
D70	1578	1294	1318	897	633	405	177	202	482	760	1134	1411	10289

MILES CITY, MONTANA LAT = 46.4 ELEV = 2634

	JAN	FEB	MAR	APR	MAY	JUN	JUL	AUG	SEP	OCT	NOV	DEC	YEAR
HS	457	745	1185	1542	1896	2146	2293	1977	1444	961	551	399	1300
VS	947	1232	1469	1351	1248	1231	1389	1517	1557	1436	1072	877	15327
TA	15.4	21.6	30.2	45.3	56.3	64.9	74.4	72.5	59.9	48.8	32.4	22.0	45.3
D50	1073	795	615	190	37	5	1	1	16	134	531	868	4265
D55	1228	935	769	308	95	16	2	3	47	230	679	1023	5334
D60	1383	1075	924	446	177	47	6	9	111	359	828	1178	6544
D65	1538	1215	1079	591	288	117	9	16	217	508	978	1333	7889
D70	1693	1355	1234	741	432	199	54	78	318	658	1128	1488	9378

MISSOULA, MONTANA LAT = 46.9 ELEV = 3189

	JAN	FEB	MAR	APR	MAY	JUN	JUL	AUG	SEP	OCT	NOV	DEC	YEAR
HS	312	574	981	1382	1782	1933	2327	1881	1358	813	410	267	1168
VS	656	962	1233	1228	1192	1126	1432	1466	1485	1231	809	596	13416
TA	20.8	27.2	33.3	43.9	52.2	58.9	66.6	65.0	55.3	44.1	32.3	24.7	43.7
D50	905	638	518	194	42	4	0	0	15	195	531	784	3828
D55	1060	778	673	335	122	24	2	3	66	340	681	939	5023
D60	1215	918	828	483	248	88	10	17	159	493	831	1094	6385
D65	1370	1058	983	633	397	201	39	71	301	648	981	1249	7931
D70	1525	1198	1138	783	552	335	134	172	441	803	1131	1404	9617

GRAND ISLAND, NEBRASKA LAT = 41.0 ELEV = 1857

	JAN	FEB	MAR	APR	MAY	JUN	JUL	AUG	SEP	OCT	NOV	DEC	YEAR
HS	661	917	1265	1692	1972	2242	2216	1939	1509	1138	738	569	1405
VS	1175	1308	1349	1260	1101	1100	1143	1261	1394	1466	1234	1070	14859
TA	22.3	27.7	35.5	49.9	60.7	70.7	76.3	75.0	64.4	53.7	38.2	27.0	50.1
D50	859	625	453	103	10	1	0	0	4	54	362	713	3186
D55	1014	765	606	192	35	3	1	1	14	127	506	868	4130
D60	1169	904	760	315	95	10	2	3	45	226	655	1023	5208
D65	1324	1044	915	461	184	35	6	5	107	362	804	1178	6425
D70	1479	1184	1070	604	303	92	30	41	203	508	954	1333	7801

NORTH OMAHA, NEBRASKA LAT = 41.4 ELEV = 1325

	JAN	FEB	MAR	APR	MAY	JUN	JUL	AUG	SEP	OCT	NOV	DEC	YEAR
HS	634	892	1222	1558	1873	2122	2106	1858	1373	1050	644	511	1320
VS	1139	1286	1318	1174	1058	1052	1099	1223	1283	1368	1089	972	14062
TA	20.2	25.5	34.6	50.0	60.9	70.2	75.1	73.7	64.4	54.4	37.9	25.7	49.4
D50	924	686	480	99	9	1	0	0	3	44	369	754	3369
D55	1079	826	633	187	31	3	1	1	13	112	515	908	4309
D60	1234	966	788	311	89	10	3	4	43	207	663	1063	5381
D65	1389	1106	942	456	186	33	7	10	99	342	813	1218	6601
D70	1544	1246	1097	601	296	96	38	52	200	486	963	1373	7992

NORTH PLATTE, NEBRASKA LAT = 41.1 ELEV = 2785

	JAN	FEB	MAR	APR	MAY	JUN	JUL	AUG	SEP	OCT	NOV	DEC	YEAR
HS	692	958	1333	1724	1988	2266	2277	1989	1565	1177	759	605	1445
VS	1233	1370	1425	1287	1113	1114	1178	1298	1449	1521	1273	1141	15403
TA	23.4	28.1	34.3	47.8	58.3	68.0	74.3	73.0	62.3	51.0	36.2	26.8	48.6
D50	825	614	490	138	20	2	0	0	7	92	419	720	3326
D55	980	753	643	241	60	6	1	2	24	176	565	874	4325
D60	1135	893	797	373	134	20	4	6	71	295	714	1029	5473
D65	1290	1033	952	522	238	65	7	8	141	439	864	1184	6743
D70	1445	1173	1107	667	371	135	49	64	253	590	1014	1339	8206

SCOTTSBLUFF, NEBRASKA LAT = 41.9 ELEV = 3957

	JAN	FEB	MAR	APR	MAY	JUN	JUL	AUG	SEP	OCT	NOV	DEC	YEAR
HS	676	950	1307	1668	1933	2237	2284	1999	1599	1145	723	575	1425
VS	1232	1389	1430	1276	1109	1125	1209	1337	1516	1512	1239	1109	15482
TA	24.9	29.5	34.3	46.2	56.5	65.9	73.7	71.6	61.2	50.2	36.2	27.6	48.2
D50	778	575	489	163	27	2	0	1	8	100	418	695	3256
D55	933	714	642	279	81	9	0	2	28	190	565	850	4293
D60	1088	854	797	418	163	30	0	8	83	316	714	1004	5475
D65	1243	994	952	564	280	91	0	8	160	459	864	1159	6774
D70	1398	1134	1107	714	423	169	52	80	279	615	1014	1314	8299

ELKO, NEVADA LAT = 40.8 ELEV = 5075

	JAN	FEB	MAR	APR	MAY	JUN	JUL	AUG	SEP	OCT	NOV	DEC	YEAR
HS	689	1034	1463	1900	2303	2534	2623	2316	1893	1322	812	617	1625
VS	1218	1467	1551	1406	1278	1236	1345	1497	1738	1694	1350	1153	16934
TA	23.2	29.2	35.0	43.5	51.9	59.6	69.5	67.0	57.6	46.9	34.8	25.9	45.4
D50	831	583	467	216	67	9	1	1	16	147	458	747	3541
D55	986	722	620	350	147	34	2	5	55	265	606	902	4696
D60	1141	862	775	496	265	97	9	19	130	409	756	1057	6018
D65	1296	1002	930	645	406	190	27	60	248	561	906	1212	7483
D70	1451	1142	1085	795	562	319	102	145	376	716	1056	1367	9117

ELY, NEVADA LAT = 39.3 ELEV = 6253

	JAN	FEB	MAR	APR	MAY	JUN	JUL	AUG	SEP	OCT	NOV	DEC	YEAR
HS	819	1141	1606	2009	2311	2513	2447	2230	1935	1408	926	723	1672
VS	1388	1553	1632	1420	1227	1178	1204	1376	1700	1731	1477	1296	17182
TA	23.6	27.9	32.8	41.3	50.0	57.7	67.2	65.5	56.7	46.0	34.0	26.2	44.1
D50	818	619	534	268	81	9	0	1	13	154	481	738	3716
D55	973	759	688	412	178	42	2	4	55	285	630	893	4922
D60	1128	899	843	561	315	116	11	19	135	435	780	1048	6291
D65	1283	1039	998	711	470	241	23	62	265	589	930	1203	7814
D70	1438	1179	1153	861	620	371	130	166	400	744	1080	1358	9500

LAS VEGAS, NEVADA LAT = 36.1 ELEV = 2178

	JAN	FEB	MAR	APR	MAY	JUN	JUL	AUG	SEP	OCT	NOV	DEC	YEAR
HS	978	1339	1823	2319	2646	2778	2588	2355	2037	1540	1085	880	1864
VS	1518	1669	1688	1485	1284	1207	1172	1319	1626	1732	1586	1443	17730
TA	44.2	49.1	54.8	63.8	73.3	82.3	89.6	87.4	80.1	67.1	53.3	45.2	65.8
D50	216	110	45	5	0	0	0	0	0	2	59	193	631
D55	346	197	111	17	2	0	0	0	0	8	131	318	1129
D60	493	315	202	53	6	0	0	0	0	27	229	463	1788
D65	645	451	324	126	10	0	0	0	0	74	357	614	2601
D70	800	586	475	218	61	7	1	2	13	156	503	769	3591

LOVELOCK, NEVADA LAT = 40.1 ELEV = 3904

	JAN	FEB	MAR	APR	MAY	JUN	JUL	AUG	SEP	OCT	NOV	DEC	YEAR
HS	804	1165	1656	2165	2555	2749	2784	2484	2027	1451	929	714	1790
VS	1394	1621	1721	1568	1389	1316	1400	1571	1823	1824	1515	1309	18451
TA	28.9	35.2	40.1	48.5	57.5	65.6	14.3	71.3	62.7	51.2	38.4	30.8	50.4
D50	654	416	316	116	17	2	0	0	4	77	353	596	2551
D55	809	555	464	216	59	7	0	1	15	162	499	750	3538
D60	964	695	617	350	137	27	0	6	55	285	648	905	4688
D65	1119	834	772	495	255	86	0	17	126	428	798	1060	5990
D70	1274	974	927	645	392	169	1727	76	236	583	948	1215	9166

RENO, NEVADA LAT = 39.5 ELEV = 4400

	JAN	FEB	MAR	APR	MAY	JUN	JUL	AUG	SEP	OCT	NOV	DEC	YEAR
HS	800	1150	1649	2159	2523	2701	2692	2406	1998	1431	912	705	1761
VS	1364	1574	1685	1535	1347	1273	1331	1494	1766	1769	1463	1271	17872
TA	31.9	37.1	40.3	46.8	54.6	61.5	69.3	66.9	60.2	50.3	40.1	33.0	49.4
D50	561	363	305	131	24	2	0	0	4	74	301	527	2292
D55	716	501	456	253	85	12	1	2	19	169	448	682	3345
D60	871	641	611	397	186	55	5	11	73	305	597	837	4590
D65	1026	781	766	546	328	145	17	50	168	456	747	992	6022
D70	1181	921	921	696	478	261	90	133	298	611	897	1147	7635

TONOPAH, NEVADA LAT = 38.1 ELEV = 5423

	JAN	FEB	MAR	APR	MAY	JUN	JUL	AUG	SEP	OCT	NOV	DEC	YEAR
HS	918	1274	1777	2251	2577	2788	2703	2438	2043	1520	1031	827	1845
VS	1505	1678	1744	1533	1322	1268	1287	1451	1732	1808	1592	1433	18354
TA	30.2	34.6	39.6	48.1	56.9	65.3	73.0	70.7	63.5	52.1	39.8	31.9	50.5
D50	614	432	329	118	17	1	0	0	2	60	312	562	2448
D55	769	571	479	224	63	6	0	1	10	140	457	716	3436
D60	924	711	633	361	143	26	0	6	41	258	606	871	4580
D65	1079	851	787	512	269	92	0	13	108	407	756	1026	5900
D70	1234	991	942	657	409	171	48	80	214	556	906	1181	7389

WINNEMUCCA, NEVADA LAT = 40.9 ELEV = 4340

	JAN	FEB	MAR	APR	MAY	JUN	JUL	AUG	SEP	OCT	NOV	DEC	YEAR
HS	690	1028	1472	1967	2362	2569	2678	2348	1907	1322	809	618	1648
VS	1223	1462	1565	1460	1315	1257	1377	1522	1756	1699	1349	1158	17143
TA	28.2	34.1	37.6	45.1	53.8	61.7	71.0	67.8	59.2	48.3	37.3	30.4	47.9
D50	676	446	388	176	40	4	0	1	9	119	384	608	2851
D55	831	585	540	304	110	18	1	3	35	226	532	763	3949
D60	986	725	695	449	213	64	5	13	101	367	681	918	5216
D65	1141	865	849	597	359	149	6	42	199	518	831	1073	6629
D70	1296	1005	1004	747	503	260	76	127	329	673	981	1228	8230

CONCORD, NEW HAMPSHIRE LAT = 43.2 ELEV = 344

	JAN	FEB	MAR	APR	MAY	JUN	JUL	AUG	SEP	OCT	NOV	DEC	YEAR
HS	459	686	974	1317	1582	1705	1675	1455	1140	817	463	362	1053
VS	868	1039	1105	1048	944	890	921	1013	1122	1118	823	725	11615
TA	20.6	22.6	32.3	44.2	55.1	64.7	69.7	67.2	59.5	49.3	38.0	24.8	45.6
D50	911	767	549	185	14	0	0	0	3	81	361	781	3653
D55	1066	907	704	326	68	2	0	1	17	188	510	936	4726
D60	1221	1047	859	474	167	16	3	7	75	333	660	1091	5954
D65	1376	1187	1014	624	315	58	16	45	182	487	810	1246	7360
D70	1531	1327	1169	774	462	172	75	119	317	642	960	1401	8949

NEWARK, NEW JERSEY LAT = 40.7 ELEV = 30

	JAN	FEB	MAR	APR	MAY	JUN	JUL	AUG	SEP	OCT	NOV	DEC	YEAR
HS	552	793	1109	1449	1687	1795	1760	1565	1273	951	596	454	1165
VS	973	1122	1173	1069	934	873	900	1008	1165	1215	988	846	12267
TA	31.4	32.6	40.6	51.7	61.9	71.4	76.4	74.6	67.8	57.5	46.2	34.5	53.9
D50	577	488	297	55	2	0	0	0	0	10	145	481	2056
D55	732	627	447	135	13	0	0	0	2	46	271	636	2908
D60	887	767	602	257	54	0	0	0	9	124	415	791	3905
D65	1042	907	756	399	143	0	0	0	34	243	564	946	5034
D70	1197	1047	911	549	260	59	15	26	115	389	714	1101	6382

ALBUQUERQUE, NEW MEXICO LAT = 35.0 ELEV = 5312

	JAN	FEB	MAR	APR	MAY	JUN	JUL	AUG	SEP	OCT	NOV	DEC	YEAR
HS	1016	1342	1768	2228	2538	2679	2489	2290	1972	1547	1134	928	1827
VS	1530	1623	1586	1379	1196	1137	1098	1241	1523	1687	1608	1477	17086
TA	35.2	40.0	45.8	55.8	65.3	74.6	78.7	76.6	70.1	58.2	44.5	36.2	56.8
D50	459	281	145	7	0	0	0	0	0	3	173	428	1497
D55	614	420	287	49	1	0	0	0	0	22	316	583	2292
D60	769	560	440	140	9	0	0	0	1	93	465	738	3216
D65	924	700	595	282	58	0	0	0	7	218	615	893	4292
D70	1079	840	750	426	158	12	2	5	59	366	765	1048	5511

CLAYTON, NEW MEXICO LAT = 36.4 ELEV = 4970

	JAN	FEB	MAR	APR	MAY	JUN	JUL	AUG	SEP	OCT	NOV	DEC	YEAR
HS	962	1241	1652	2039	2222	2418	2284	2097	1802	1433	1028	861	1670
VS	1506	1560	1544	1318	1087	1057	1042	1185	1452	1626	1515	1424	16314
TA	33.1	36.1	40.4	50.8	60.0	69.2	73.6	72.4	65.0	54.8	42.3	35.1	52.7
D50	524	390	303	67	4	0	0	0	1	24	240	463	2017
D55	679	529	454	154	22	1	0	0	4	84	383	617	2928
D60	834	669	608	282	81	6	0	2	22	182	531	772	3988
D65	989	809	763	431	172	38	0	5	73	324	681	927	5212
D70	1144	949	918	576	314	91	34	47	172	472	831	1082	6630

FARMINGTON, NEW MEXICO LAT = 36.7 ELEV = 5502

	JAN	FEB	MAR	APR	MAY	JUN	JUL	AUG	SEP	OCT	NOV	DEC	YEAR
HS	944	1281	1693	2133	2452	2665	2478	2252	1934	1479	1047	837	1766
VS	1490	1624	1596	1391	1209	1173	1138	1284	1572	1692	1556	1396	17121
TA	28.6	35.0	40.6	49.7	59.5	67.9	75.0	72.6	64.6	52.9	39.2	30.1	51.3
D50	663	420	294	73	3	0	0	0	0	32	326	617	2428
D55	818	560	447	172	18	1	0	0	3	106	474	772	3371
D60	973	700	601	311	79	5	0	1	17	227	624	927	4465
D65	1128	840	756	465	184	36	0	6	67	375	774	1082	5713
D70	1283	980	911	609	327	102	15	35	175	530	924	1237	7130

LOS ALAMOS, NEW MEXICO (LASL DATA) LAT = 35.9 ELEV = 7380

	JAN	FEB	MAR	APR	MAY	JUN	JUL	AUG	SEP	OCT	NOV	DEC	YEAR
HS	952	1279	1568	1929	2071	2132	1889	1759	1656	1267	1037	880	1535
VS	1470	1586	1444	1228	999	922	851	979	1314	1417	1507	1435	15153
TA	29.0	32.1	37.8	45.8	55.2	65.1	68.2	65.9	60.4	50.3	38.2	30.4	48.3
D50	651	501	379	142	11	0	0	0	1	61	355	608	2710
D55	806	641	533	278	62	1	0	1	10	160	504	763	3760
D60	961	781	688	426	162	11	3	9	57	303	654	918	4974
D65	1117	929	856	560	304	87	18	44	147	448	796	1053	6359
D70	1271	1061	998	726	459	159	95	145	290	611	954	1228	7997

ROSWELL, NEW MEXICO LAT = 33.4 ELEV = 3619

	JAN	FEB	MAR	APR	MAY	JUN	JUL	AUG	SEP	OCT	NOV	DEC	YEAR
HS	1046	1373	1807	2218	2459	2610	2441	2242	1913	1527	1131	952	1810
VS	1508	1588	1546	1308	1113	1075	1040	1160	1407	1592	1535	1450	16321
TA	38.1	42.9	49.3	59.7	68.5	77.0	79.2	77.9	70.4	59.6	46.9	39.3	59.1
D50	371	209	92	5	0	0	0	0	0	5	131	335	1149
D55	524	341	195	24	1	0	0	0	1	25	251	487	1849
D60	679	479	335	83	7	0	0	0	4	87	395	642	2711
D65	834	619	487	185	20	0	0	0	17	195	543	797	3697
D70	989	759	642	313	106	11	6	9	73	326	693	952	4878

TRUTH OR CONSEQUENCES, NEW MEXICO LAT = 33.2 ELEV = 4859

	JAN	FEB	MAR	APR	MAY	JUN	JUL	AUG	SEP	OCT	NOV	DEC	YEAR
HS	1118	1451	1886	2338	2557	2650	2365	2216	1940	1579	1217	1003	1860
VS	1603	1669	1604	1370	1152	1087	1004	1140	1418	1637	1643	1519	16846
TA	40.0	44.9	50.2	59.5	59.5	76.9	79.3	77.4	71.6	61.3	48.7	40.8	59.9
D50	315	163	79	5	6	0	0	0	0	3	100	291	963
D55	466	287	173	26	27	0	0	0	1	16	204	441	1641
D60	620	424	309	88	91	0	0	0	3	63	342	595	2535
D65	775	563	459	188	19	0	0	0	5	144	489	750	3392
D70	930	703	614	319	330	13	6	11	57	277	639	905	4804

TUCUMCARI, NEW MEXICO LAT = 35.2 ELEV = 4039

	JAN	FEB	MAR	APR	MAY	JUN	JUL	AUG	SEP	OCT	NOV	DEC	YEAR
HS	1009	1297	1712	2098	2314	2484	2349	2164	1829	1443	1073	910	1723
VS	1528	1577	1544	1307	1096	1059	1041	1180	1421	1583	1530	1456	16322
TA	37.0	41.1	46.7	56.9	65.6	75.1	78.4	76.7	69.6	58.7	46.2	38.6	57.6
D50	405	256	141	13	1	0	0	0	0	8	147	357	1328
D55	558	390	266	54	4	0	0	0	1	35	271	509	2090
D60	713	529	414	133	20	1	0	0	6	105	415	664	3000
D65	868	669	567	260	57	7	0	0	20	217	564	818	4047
D70	1023	809	722	395	165	23	8	14	87	354	714	973	5288

ZUNI, NEW MEXICO LAT = 35.1 ELEV = 6447

	JAN	FEB	MAR	APR	MAY	JUN	JUL	AUG	SEP	OCT	NOV	DEC	YEAR
HS	986	1297	1688	2167	2473	2602	2264	2078	1895	1496	1088	893	1744
VS	1489	1573	1518	1346	1168	1107	1001	1130	1468	1636	1547	1425	16408
TA	30.3	34.6	39.6	48.1	56.6	65.4	71.4	69.4	63.3	52.5	40.1	32.0	50.3
D50	611	431	324	96	7	0	0	0	0	33	299	558	2361
D55	766	571	478	213	45	2	0	0	4	111	447	713	3349
D60	921	711	632	358	130	11	0	2	25	238	597	868	4493
D65	1076	851	787	507	264	68	0	13	91	388	747	1023	5815
D70	1231	991	942	657	416	153	47	77	208	543	897	1178	7341

ALBANY, NEW YORK LAT = 42.7 ELEV = 292

	JAN	FEB	MAR	APR	MAY	JUN	JUL	AUG	SEP	OCT	NOV	DEC	YEAR
HS	456	688	986	1335	1570	1730	1725	1499	1170	817	457	356	1066
VS	850	1028	1103	1047	923	890	935	1027	1135	1103	801	702	11544
TA	21.5	23.5	33.4	46.9	57.7	67.5	72.0	69.6	61.9	51.4	39.6	25.9	47.6
D50	884	742	515	136	12	1	0	0	3	66	317	747	3424
D55	1039	882	670	253	49	3	1	1	15	150	463	902	4428
D60	1194	1022	825	395	125	12	3	7	58	276	612	1057	5586
D65	1349	1162	980	543	253	39	9	22	135	422	762	1212	6888
D70	1504	1302	1135	693	384	125	58	93	253	577	912	1367	8403

BINGHAMTON, NEW YORK LAT = 42.2 ELEV = 1637

	JAN	FEB	MAR	APR	MAY	JUN	JUL	AUG	SEP	OCT	NOV	DEC	YEAR
HS	386	576	861	1242	1496	1681	1659	1425	1131	779	414	297	996
VS	709	849	950	959	866	852	886	962	1082	1037	716	578	10446
TA	22.0	22.8	31.3	44.7	55.1	64.8	69.1	67.3	60.2	50.3	38.2	25.4	46.0
D50	868	762	580	176	18	1	0	0	3	72	356	763	3598
D55	1023	902	735	312	75	4	1	1	17	167	504	918	4657
D60	1178	1042	890	459	172	20	5	9	71	304	654	1073	5875
D65	1333	1182	1045	609	320	75	21	40	172	456	804	1228	7285
D70	1488	1322	1200	759	462	173	91	123	298	611	954	1383	8863

BUFFALO, NEW YORK LAT = 42.9 ELEV = 705

	JAN	FEB	MAR	APR	MAY	JUN	JUL	AUG	SEP	OCT	NOV	DEC	YEAR
HS	349	546	888	1315	1596	1804	1776	1513	1152	784	403	283	1034
VS	654	820	999	1037	944	933	968	1043	1124	1064	710	562	10859
TA	23.7	24.4	32.1	44.9	55.1	65.7	70.1	68.4	61.6	51.5	39.8	27.9	47.1
D50	815	717	555	170	17	0	0	0	2	52	309	685	3322
D55	970	857	710	306	72	2	0	1	10	137	456	840	4363
D60	1125	997	865	453	170	13	3	5	49	269	606	995	5551
D65	1280	1137	1020	603	321	58	12	33	138	419	756	1150	6927
D70	1435	1277	1175	753	462	151	72	101	257	574	906	1305	8468

MASSENA, NEW YORK LAT = 44.9 ELEV = 207

	JAN	FEB	MAR	APR	MAY	JUN	JUL	AUG	SEP	OCT	NOV	DEC	YEAR
HS	391	620	977	1343	1613	1779	1751	1484	1124	736	388	294	1042
VS	776	984	1162	1125	1014	976	1014	1088	1162	1055	723	618	11697
TA	14.5	16.7	27.6	42.2	54.1	64.3	64.3	66.7	59.2	48.5	35.9	20.1	43.2
D50	1101	932	694	242	27	1	1	0	5	103	424	927	4456
D55	1256	1072	849	385	93	5	5	2	25	214	573	1082	5561
D60	1411	1212	1004	534	198	24	25	12	88	359	723	1237	6827
D65	1566	1352	1159	684	350	78	22	57	192	512	873	1392	8237
D70	1721	1492	1314	834	493	187	193	136	327	667	1023	1547	9934

NEW YORK (CENTRAL PARK), NEW YORK LAT = 40.8 ELEV = 187

	JAN	FEB	MAR	APR	MAY	JUN	JUL	AUG	SEP	OCT	NOV	DEC	YEAR
HS	500	721	1037	1364	1636	1710	1688	1483	1214	895	533	404	1099
VS	884	1023	1100	1009	908	834	866	959	1115	1147	886	755	11485
TA	32.2	33.4	41.1	52.1	62.3	71.6	76.6	74.9	68.4	58.7	47.4	35.5	54.5
D50	552	465	282	50	2	0	0	0	0	7	122	451	1931
D55	707	605	432	127	11	0	0	0	1	33	238	605	2759
D60	862	745	586	246	49	0	0	0	7	103	380	760	3737
D65	1017	885	741	387	137	0	0	0	29	209	528	915	4848
D70	1172	1025	896	537	248	56	14	23	104	353	678	1070	6177

ROCHESTER, NEW YORK LAT = 43.1 ELEV = 554

	JAN	FEB	MAR	APR	MAY	JUN	JUL	AUG	SEP	OCT	NOV	DEC	YEAR
HS	364	559	903	1339	1606	1817	1781	1519	1160	782	404	281	1043
VS	686	844	1022	1063	956	945	977	1054	1139	1067	716	561	11029
TA	24.0	24.8	33.0	46.1	56.5	66.9	71.2	69.3	62.3	52.3	40.5	28.3	47.9
D50	806	706	528	152	18	1	0	0	3	55	292	673	3233
D55	961	846	682	275	66	3	1	2	13	133	436	828	4247
D60	1116	986	837	419	149	15	4	8	53	251	585	983	5405
D65	1271	1126	992	567	285	46	9	26	126	398	735	1138	6719
D70	1426	1266	1147	717	421	136	70	99	243	549	885	1293	8252

SYRACUSE, NEW YORK LAT = 43.1 ELEV = 407

	JAN	FEB	MAR	APR	MAY	JUN	JUL	AUG	SEP	OCT	NOV	DEC	YEAR
HS	385	571	890	1324	1578	1778	1758	1504	1165	777	399	285	1034
VS	726	862	1007	1051	939	925	964	1043	1143	1061	707	569	10997
TA	23.6	24.6	33.2	46.5	56.8	66.9	71.5	69.7	62.8	52.5	41.0	28.1	48.1
D50	818	711	521	141	14	1	0	0	2	49	277	679	3215
D55	973	851	676	263	58	3	1	1	10	126	421	834	4218
D60	1128	991	831	407	140	13	3	6	44	244	570	989	5366
D65	1283	1131	986	555	272	46	11	18	120	392	720	1144	6678
D70	1438	1271	1141	705	411	133	62	89	228	543	870	1299	8192

ASHEVILLE, NORTH CAROLINA LAT = 35.4 ELEV = 2169

	JAN	FEB	MAR	APR	MAY	JUN	JUL	AUG	SEP	OCT	NOV	DEC	YEAR
HS	722	971	1306	1668	1804	1854	1776	1627	1361	1147	849	658	1312
VS	1099	1187	1185	1045	859	793	791	892	1064	1265	1217	1059	12458
TA	37.9	39.4	45.9	55.9	63.7	70.6	73.5	72.8	66.7	56.8	46.3	38.7	55.7
D50	377	300	157	17	1	0	0	0	0	13	143	353	1362
D55	531	437	288	66	7	1	0	0	3	56	268	506	2162
D60	685	577	438	152	33	4	0	0	13	138	412	660	3112
D65	840	717	592	279	100	14	0	0	50	269	561	815	4237
D70	995	857	747	424	210	70	35	43	135	411	711	970	5609

CAPE HATTERAS, NORTH CAROLINA LAT = 35.3 ELEV = 7

	JAN	FEB	MAR	APR	MAY	JUN	JUL	AUG	SEP	OCT	NOV	DEC	YEAR
HS	686	952	1326	1774	1962	2036	1921	1705	1470	1137	873	659	1375
VS	1042	1161	1200	1108	932	869	853	932	1146	1251	1248	1057	12800
TA	45.3	45.8	50.6	58.9	67.0	74.3	78.0	77.5	73.7	65.2	56.0	47.7	61.7
D50	167	140	68	5	0	0	0	0	0	1	14	116	512
D55	305	262	160	27	2	0	0	0	0	3	60	235	1055
D60	456	398	296	92	10	0	0	0	0	18	146	383	1800
D65	611	538	458	188	47	0	0	0	0	76	277	536	2731
D70	766	678	602	335	130	24	7	9	29	170	421	691	3860

CHARLOTTE, NORTH CAROLINA LAT = 35.2 ELEV = 768

	JAN	FEB	MAR	APR	MAY	JUN	JUL	AUG	SEP	OCT	NOV	DEC	YEAR
HS	719	971	1317	1695	1856	1921	1831	1695	1416	1173	865	672	1344
VS	1089	1181	1188	1056	879	819	811	924	1100	1287	1234	1075	12643
TA	42.1	44.0	50.6	60.8	68.8	75.9	78.5	77.7	72.0	61.7	51.0	42.5	60.5
D50	255	184	74	4	0	0	0	0	0	3	66	243	828
D55	402	311	164	18	1	0	0	0	0	14	150	390	1451
D60	555	449	297	69	7	0	0	0	2	58	277	543	2257
D65	710	588	461	145	34	0	0	0	10	152	420	698	3218
D70	865	728	602	282	102	17	8	10	52	266	570	853	4355

GREENSBORO, NORTH CAROLINA LAT = 36.1 ELEV = 886

	JAN	FEB	MAR	APR	MAY	JUN	JUL	AUG	SEP	OCT	NOV	DEC	YEAR
HS	715	970	1313	1683	1868	1953	1864	1697	1418	1141	839	659	1343
VS	1110	1209	1216	1078	906	848	844	950	1132	1284	1226	1081	12885
TA	38.7	40.6	47.8	58.6	67.1	74.4	77.2	76.0	69.7	59.2	48.3	39.6	58.1
D50	354	270	123	9	1	0	0	0	0	7	111	328	1202
D55	506	405	237	37	3	0	0	0	1	33	216	478	1916
D60	660	543	381	106	14	0	0	0	6	99	354	633	2797
D65	815	683	544	203	59	0	0	0	24	209	501	787	3825
D70	970	823	688	346	136	30	14	19	88	339	651	942	5047

RALEIGH-DURHAM, NORTH CAROLINA LAT = 35.9 ELEV = 440

	JAN	FEB	MAR	APR	MAY	JUN	JUL	AUG	SEP	OCT	NOV	DEC	YEAR
HS	694	943	1276	1644	1808	1864	1776	1611	1377	1105	812	636	1295
VS	1071	1169	1175	1046	873	806	800	897	1093	1236	1180	1037	12384
TA	40.5	42.2	49.2	59.5	67.4	74.4	77.5	76.5	70.6	60.2	50.0	41.2	59.1
D50	300	227	95	5	0	0	0	0	0	4	79	280	990
D55	451	360	198	26	2	0	0	0	1	21	172	429	1659
D60	605	499	338	87	11	0	0	0	4	79	304	583	2509
D65	760	638	502	180	48	0	0	0	12	186	450	738	3514
D70	915	778	645	319	126	26	10	14	71	309	600	893	4706

BISMARCK, NORTH DAKOTA LAT = 46.8 ELEV = 1647

	JAN	FEB	MAR	APR	MAY	JUN	JUL	AUG	SEP	OCT	NOV	DEC	YEAR
HS	467	776	1168	1459	1848	2060	2184	1877	1354	908	507	373	1248
VS	979	1297	1464	1293	1232	1196	1340	1458	1477	1371	997	830	14935
TA	8.2	13.5	25.1	43.0	54.4	63.8	70.8	69.2	57.5	46.8	28.9	15.6	41.4
D50	1296	1022	772	230	40	3	0	1	18	152	633	1066	5235
D55	1451	1162	927	365	108	13	2	3	60	270	783	1221	6364
D60	1606	1302	1082	511	204	45	8	12	135	413	933	1376	7627
D65	1761	1442	1237	660	339	122	18	35	252	564	1083	1531	9044
D70	1916	1582	1392	810	486	211	86	111	380	719	1233	1686	10612

FARGO, NORTH DAKOTA LAT = 46.9 ELEV = 899

	JAN	FEB	MAR	APR	MAY	JUN	JUL	AUG	SEP	OCT	NOV	DEC	YEAR
HS	415	706	1098	1476	1835	1994	2120	1825	1304	874	457	337	1203
VS	873	1184	1380	1312	1227	1161	1304	1422	1426	1324	902	752	14267
TA	5.9	10.7	24.2	42.3	54.6	64.7	70.7	69.2	57.9	47.0	28.6	13.0	40.8
D50	1367	1100	800	243	31	1	0	0	12	140	642	1147	5485
D55	1522	1240	955	384	95	7	1	2	47	260	792	1302	6607
D60	1677	1380	1110	532	192	29	5	8	120	406	942	1457	7858
D65	1832	1520	1265	681	334	97	13	33	234	558	1092	1612	9271
D70	1987	1660	1420	831	479	184	78	102	366	713	1242	1767	10829

MINOT, NORTH DAKOTA LAT = 48.3 ELEV = 1713

	JAN	FEB	MAR	APR	MAY	JUN	JUL	AUG	SEP	OCT	NOV	DEC	YEAR
HS	384	656	1044	1461	1846	1975	2098	1800	1277	850	438	310	1178
VS	841	1143	1364	1353	1289	1200	1348	1463	1453	1338	900	721	14413
TA	7.9	12.8	23.6	41.1	52.8	62.0	68.8	67.2	56.2	46.1	27.9	14.7	40.1
D50	1305	1042	819	280	60	6	1	1	26	168	663	1094	5465
D55	1460	1182	973	420	136	21	4	6	79	289	813	1249	6633
D60	1615	1322	1128	568	244	68	14	21	160	434	963	1404	7943
D65	1770	1462	1283	717	384	150	27	70	286	586	1113	1559	9407
D70	1925	1602	1438	867	535	257	119	147	418	741	1263	1714	11025

AKRON-CANTON, OHIO LAT = 40.9 ELEV = 1237

	JAN	FEB	MAR	APR	MAY	JUN	JUL	AUG	SEP	OCT	NOV	DEC	YEAR
HS	428	649	964	1357	1668	1839	1787	1596	1272	908	505	353	1110
VS	759	923	1025	1007	929	900	919	1035	1171	1167	842	662	11338
TA	26.3	27.7	36.2	48.5	58.7	68.3	71.7	70.3	63.7	53.3	40.7	29.4	49.6
D50	735	625	430	108	9	0	0	0	2	42	286	639	2876
D55	890	764	583	212	38	2	1	1	9	115	431	794	3839
D60	1045	904	738	349	108	10	4	5	37	224	579	949	4951
D65	1200	1044	893	495	231	33	9	16	101	369	729	1104	6224
D70	1355	1184	1048	645	354	111	62	83	207	518	879	1259	7705

CINCINNATI, OHIO LAT = 39.1 ELEV = 889

	JAN	FEB	MAR	APR	MAY	JUN	JUL	AUG	SEP	OCT	NOV	DEC	YEAR
HS	500	738	1027	1398	1672	1837	1771	1634	1312	990	588	432	1158
VS	843	999	1037	982	883	857	866	1002	1146	1211	933	770	11529
TA	31.1	33.3	41.7	53.9	63.2	72.1	75.6	74.4	67.8	56.8	43.8	33.7	54.0
D50	587	469	272	44	4	0	0	0	1	22	211	507	2117
D55	741	608	416	112	15	1	0	0	4	72	343	661	2973
D60	896	748	568	209	53	5	0	0	17	152	488	815	3951
D65	1051	888	722	341	138	9	0	0	44	271	636	970	5070
D70	1206	1028	877	485	233	65	30	40	130	413	786	1125	6419

CLEVELAND, OHIO LAT = 41.4 ELEV = 804

	JAN	FEB	MAR	APR	MAY	JUN	JUL	AUG	SEP	OCT	NOV	DEC	YEAR
HS	388	601	922	1349	1681	1843	1828	1583	1239	867	466	318	1091
VS	697	867	994	1017	950	914	954	1042	1158	1130	788	605	11114
TA	26.9	27.9	36.1	48.3	58.3	67.9	71.4	70.0	63.9	53.8	41.6	30.3	49.7
D50	716	619	433	112	11	1	0	0	2	38	262	611	2804
D55	871	759	586	217	43	3	1	1	9	108	404	766	3768
D60	1026	899	741	355	116	11	4	6	36	212	552	921	4879
D65	1181	1039	896	501	244	40	9	17	95	354	702	1076	6154
D70	1336	1179	1051	651	366	119	68	88	202	503	852	1231	7646

COLUMBUS, OHIO LAT = 40.0 ELEV = 833

	JAN	FEB	MAR	APR	MAY	JUN	JUL	AUG	SEP	OCT	NOV	DEC	YEAR
HS	459	677	980	1353	1647	1813	1755	1641	1282	945	538	387	1123
VS	793	939	1016	977	893	866	880	1035	1150	1185	875	707	11315
TA	28.4	30.3	39.2	51.2	61.1	70.4	73.6	71.9	65.2	54.2	41.7	30.7	51.5
D50	670	552	339	67	4	0	0	0	1	33	259	599	2524
D55	825	692	491	150	19	1	0	1	5	100	401	753	3438
D60	980	832	645	272	71	5	0	3	24	201	549	908	4491
D65	1135	972	800	418	176	13	0	8	76	342	699	1063	5702
D70	1290	1112	955	564	284	78	39	59	171	491	849	1218	7111

DAYTON, OHIO LAT = 39.9 ELEV = 1004

	JAN	FEB	MAR	APR	MAY	JUN	JUL	AUG	SEP	OCT	NOV	DEC	YEAR
HS	489	725	1025	1403	1699	1874	1810	1645	1318	969	564	407	1161
VS	843	1003	1059	1010	918	892	905	1034	1178	1211	915	742	11712
TA	28.1	30.4	39.0	51.4	61.6	71.3	74.6	73.0	66.3	55.5	41.8	30.9	52.0
D50	679	549	346	68	4	0	0	0	1	25	257	593	2523
D55	834	689	497	149	19	1	0	1	5	83	399	747	3422
D60	989	829	651	268	67	5	0	3	20	173	547	902	4453
D65	1144	969	806	413	166	13	0	7	63	307	696	1057	5641
D70	1299	1109	961	559	272	69	32	49	150	451	846	1212	7009

TOLEDO, OHIO LAT = 41.6 ELEV = 692

	JAN	FEB	MAR	APR	MAY	JUN	JUL	AUG	SEP	OCT	NOV	DEC	YEAR
HS	435	680	997	1384	1717	1878	1849	1616	1276	911	498	355	1133
VS	786	986	1081	1049	976	936	970	1071	1199	1193	847	679	11774
TA	24.8	27.1	35.8	48.4	58.8	68.9	72.3	70.8	63.8	53.0	39.6	28.0	49.3
D50	781	641	442	113	10	0	0	0	2	49	318	682	3040
D55	936	781	596	216	40	2	1	1	10	124	463	837	4007
D60	1091	921	750	352	110	9	4	6	39	234	612	992	5120
D65	1246	1061	905	498	229	32	5	18	99	379	762	1147	6381
D70	1401	1201	1060	648	352	105	57	79	206	528	912	1302	7852

YOUNGSTOWN, OHIO LAT = 41.3 ELEV = 1184

	JAN	FEB	MAR	APR	MAY	JUN	JUL	AUG	SEP	OCT	NOV	DEC	YEAR
HS	385	586	890	1278	1586	1759	1734	1506	1194	851	456	315	1045
VS	690	843	957	960	894	870	902	989	1112	1106	769	597	10688
TA	25.7	26.7	35.3	47.7	57.6	67.0	70.7	69.2	62.7	52.6	40.3	28.8	48.7
D50	753	652	457	120	12	1	0	0	2	49	297	657	3001
D55	908	792	611	231	49	3	1	1	11	126	442	812	3988
D60	1063	932	766	372	126	14	4	7	46	242	591	967	5130
D65	1218	1072	921	519	258	42	9	22	118	384	741	1122	6426
D70	1373	1212	1076	669	387	133	75	99	231	540	891	1277	7963

OKLAHOMA CITY, OKLAHOMA LAT = 35.4 ELEV = 1302

	JAN	FEB	MAR	APR	MAY	JUN	JUL	AUG	SEP	OCT	NOV	DEC	YEAR
HS	801	1055	1400	1725	1918	2144	2128	1950	1554	1233	901	725	1461
VS	1220	1290	1270	1081	913	917	947	1069	1215	1360	1292	1166	13742
TA	36.8	41.3	48.2	60.4	68.3	76.8	81.5	81.1	73.0	62.4	49.2	40.0	59.9
D50	413	255	126	8	1	0	0	0	0	5	106	319	1232
D55	565	386	232	29	4	0	0	0	1	18	201	467	1903
D60	719	524	371	87	14	0	0	0	4	62	331	621	2734
D65	874	664	532	180	36	0	0	0	12	148	474	775	3695
D70	1029	804	676	298	124	20	6	7	52	253	624	930	4823

TULSA, OKLAHOMA — LAT = 36.2 — ELEV = 676

	JAN	FEB	MAR	APR	MAY	JUN	JUL	AUG	SEP	OCT	NOV	DEC	YEAR
HS	732	978	1305	1603	1822	2021	2030	1865	1473	1164	827	659	1373
VS	1139	1223	1212	1030	886	880	921	1048	1180	1313	1212	1084	13127
TA	36.6	41.2	48.3	60.8	68.8	77.3	82.1	81.4	73.3	62.9	49.4	39.8	60.2
D50	419	258	126	7	1	0	0	0	0	4	104	325	1245
D55	571	389	230	28	3	0	0	0	1	17	197	473	1910
D60	726	527	369	83	13	0	0	0	4	57	326	627	2731
D65	880	666	528	176	28	0	0	0	10	143	468	781	3680
D70	1035	806	673	287	117	19	5	6	50	241	618	936	4796

ASTORIA, OREGON — LAT = 46.1 — ELEV = 23

	JAN	FEB	MAR	APR	MAY	JUN	JUL	AUG	SEP	OCT	NOV	DEC	YEAR
HS	315	545	866	1253	1608	1626	1746	1499	1183	713	387	261	1000
VS	647	894	1065	1088	1049	924	1048	1140	1265	1056	746	568	11492
TA	40.6	43.6	44.4	47.8	52.3	56.5	60.0	60.3	58.4	52.8	46.5	42.8	50.5
D50	292	183	180	92	26	4	1	1	2	21	120	226	1147
D55	446	320	329	219	106	34	8	7	16	95	256	378	2215
D60	601	459	484	366	241	120	57	52	81	226	405	533	3626
D65	756	599	639	516	394	255	163	151	201	378	555	688	5295
D70	911	739	794	666	549	405	311	302	348	533	705	843	7106

BURNS, OREGON — LAT = 43.6 — ELEV = 4170

	JAN	FEB	MAR	APR	MAY	JUN	JUL	AUG	SEP	OCT	NOV	DEC	YEAR
HS	490	792	1187	1649	2052	2280	2460	2083	1620	1043	593	430	1390
VS	937	1213	1362	1328	1240	1204	1369	1468	1613	1443	1066	871	15113
TA	25.2	31.0	36.1	44.2	52.2	59.0	68.4	66.1	58.2	47.3	35.8	27.9	46.0
D50	769	532	433	195	57	8	0	1	11	134	428	685	3253
D55	924	672	586	329	136	35	2	5	43	251	576	840	4399
D60	1079	812	741	475	254	101	10	20	114	396	726	995	5725
D65	1234	952	896	624	402	205	30	68	226	549	876	1150	7212
D70	1389	1092	1051	774	552	335	115	158	358	704	1026	1305	8858

MEDFORD, OREGON — LAT = 42.4 — ELEV = 1299

	JAN	FEB	MAR	APR	MAY	JUN	JUL	AUG	SEP	OCT	NOV	DEC	YEAR
HS	407	737	1133	1639	2034	2278	2475	2121	1589	982	504	337	1353
VS	752	1092	1257	1273	1185	1162	1330	1440	1528	1315	876	659	13869
TA	36.6	41.3	44.8	50.2	57.3	64.3	71.7	70.4	64.4	53.4	43.5	37.7	53.0
D50	417	251	184	78	12	1	0	0	1	38	210	384	1576
D55	571	385	321	169	51	6	1	1	6	110	348	537	2505
D60	725	524	472	299	130	29	3	4	28	219	496	691	3621
D65	880	664	626	444	250	94	11	21	89	360	645	846	4930
D70	1035	804	781	594	396	190	59	78	188	515	795	1001	6436

NORTH BEND, OREGON — LAT = 43.4 — ELEV = 16

	JAN	FEB	MAR	APR	MAY	JUN	JUL	AUG	SEP	OCT	NOV	DEC	YEAR
HS	438	704	1058	1510	1857	1994	2108	1786	1377	893	525	381	1219
VS	833	1072	1207	1209	1115	1046	1166	1251	1363	1229	938	767	13197
TA	44.6	46.6	46.9	49.1	53.1	56.9	59.0	59.7	58.4	54.9	50.1	46.5	52.2
D50	202	133	119	77	26	4	2	2	3	13	61	142	784
D55	332	244	254	185	98	34	16	14	22	67	159	270	1696
D60	480	377	406	328	220	115	79	71	88	170	299	420	3053
D65	632	515	561	477	369	243	188	168	201	313	447	574	4688
D70	788	655	716	627	524	393	342	321	349	468	597	729	6508

PENDLETON, OREGON — LAT = 45.7 — ELEV = 1496

	JAN	FEB	MAR	APR	MAY	JUN	JUL	AUG	SEP	OCT	NOV	DEC	YEAR
HS	348	614	1044	1503	1925	2144	2396	1994	1502	908	438	293	1259
VS	707	996	1270	1289	1240	1204	1421	1498	1588	1331	835	631	14010
TA	32.0	38.9	43.8	50.9	58.5	65.6	73.5	71.5	64.0	52.6	41.4	35.7	52.4
D50	558	314	209	68	8	1	0	0	1	47	266	445	1917
D55	713	451	351	153	37	4	0	1	7	124	410	599	2848
D60	868	591	503	279	108	19	2	3	31	241	558	753	3957
D65	1023	731	657	423	220	70	6	13	97	384	708	908	5240
D70	1178	871	812	573	360	160	37	62	197	540	858	1063	6710

PORTLAND, OREGON — LAT = 45.6 — ELEV = 39

	JAN	FEB	MAR	APR	MAY	JUN	JUL	AUG	SEP	OCT	NOV	DEC	YEAR
HS	310	554	895	1308	1663	1772	2037	1674	1217	724	388	260	1067
VS	628	896	1085	1119	1068	992	1205	1254	1283	1058	738	558	11884
TA	38.1	42.8	45.7	50.6	56.7	62.0	67.1	66.6	62.2	53.8	45.3	40.7	52.6
D50	371	210	158	67	12	2	0	0	2	29	162	293	1307
D55	524	343	293	156	53	10	2	2	9	98	295	444	2230
D60	679	482	444	286	136	48	10	12	45	206	442	598	3389
D65	834	622	598	432	264	128	48	56	119	347	591	753	4792
D70	989	762	753	582	413	247	128	139	242	503	741	908	6407

REDMOND, OREGON — LAT = 44.3 — ELEV = 3084

	JAN	FEB	MAR	APR	MAY	JUN	JUL	AUG	SEP	OCT	NOV	DEC	YEAR
HS	491	775	1190	1683	2079	2287	2446	2069	1584	999	572	424	1383
VS	958	1210	1392	1385	1283	1232	1391	1489	1609	1409	1048	876	15282
TA	30.2	35.8	38.6	38.6	51.3	58.2	65.7	63.8	57.7	48.4	39.0	33.4	47.2
D50	614	399	356	345	62	8	1	1	9	107	333	515	2750
D55	769	538	509	493	148	37	4	7	42	218	481	670	3913
D60	924	678	663	642	277	107	18	32	116	362	630	825	5274
D65	1079	818	818	618	425	220	55	102	233	515	780	980	6643
D70	1234	958	973	942	580	356	161	208	371	670	930	1135	8517

SALEM, OREGON — LAT = 44.9 — ELEV = 200

	JAN	FEB	MAR	APR	MAY	JUN	JUL	AUG	SEP	OCT	NOV	DEC	YEAR
HS	332	588	947	1370	1738	1849	2142	1775	1328	769	410	277	1127
VS	659	933	1126	1148	1093	1014	1240	1301	1372	1103	764	582	12336
TA	38.8	42.9	45.2	49.8	55.7	61.2	66.6	66.1	61.9	53.2	45.2	40.9	52.3
D50	348	204	163	68	10	1	0	0	1	26	158	285	1265
D55	502	340	306	168	57	8	1	1	6	97	296	437	2220
D60	657	479	459	308	151	48	7	9	39	217	444	592	3411
D65	812	619	614	456	295	133	43	53	120	366	594	747	4852
D70	967	759	769	606	444	267	130	141	247	521	744	902	6496

ALLENTOWN, PENNSYLVANIA — LAT = 40.6 — ELEV = 384

	JAN	FEB	MAR	APR	MAY	JUN	JUL	AUG	SEP	OCT	NOV	DEC	YEAR
HS	527	763	1078	1410	1637	1777	1765	1546	1238	926	568	430	1139
VS	926	1076	1137	1037	903	862	900	993	1130	1180	939	799	11883
TA	27.8	29.4	38.1	49.9	60.1	69.5	74.1	71.7	64.7	54.1	42.3	30.7	51.0
D50	688	577	372	85	6	0	0	0	1	33	242	599	2604
D55	843	717	525	178	25	1	0	1	6	101	383	753	3534
D60	998	857	679	308	85	7	0	3	27	203	531	908	4607
D65	1153	997	834	453	190	21	0	6	85	344	681	1063	5827
D70	1308	1137	989	603	313	91	33	62	182	494	831	1218	7262

ERIE, PENNSYLVANIA — LAT = 42.1 — ELEV = 738

	JAN	FEB	MAR	APR	MAY	JUN	JUL	AUG	SEP	OCT	NOV	DEC	YEAR
HS	346	577	920	1359	1646	1847	1833	1455	1201	827	416	278	1059
VS	634	848	1012	1046	950	934	976	979	1145	1098	717	539	10879
TA	25.1	25.2	32.9	44.8	54.6	64.6	68.7	67.5	61.4	51.6	40.1	29.1	47.1
D50	772	694	530	173	22	1	0	0	2	53	300	648	3197
D55	927	834	685	309	83	4	1	1	12	137	448	803	4244
D60	1082	974	840	457	184	21	5	8	54	266	597	958	5448
D65	1237	1114	995	606	336	80	24	43	141	415	747	1113	6851
D70	1392	1254	1150	756	478	178	98	119	263	571	897	1268	8424

HARRISBURG, PENNSYLVANIA — LAT = 40.2 — ELEV = 348

	JAN	FEB	MAR	APR	MAY	JUN	JUL	AUG	SEP	OCT	NOV	DEC	YEAR
HS	536	771	1083	1410	1652	1805	1764	1550	1267	934	579	447	1150
VS	932	1076	1129	1024	901	866	890	984	1143	1177	947	822	11890
TA	30.1	32.3	41.0	52.8	63.1	72.0	76.1	73.9	67.0	55.8	43.8	32.6	53.4
D50	617	496	288	48	3	0	0	0	1	23	205	540	2221
D55	772	636	436	122	12	0	0	0	4	77	340	695	3093
D60	927	776	589	231	46	0	0	0	16	165	487	849	4086
D65	1082	916	744	370	128	0	0	0	51	293	636	1004	5224
D70	1237	1056	899	517	230	58	21	38	136	442	786	1159	6579

PHILADELPHIA, PENNSYLVANIA — LAT = 39.9 — ELEV = 30

	JAN	FEB	MAR	APR	MAY	JUN	JUL	AUG	SEP	OCT	NOV	DEC	YEAR
HS	555	794	1108	1434	1660	1811	1758	1574	1281	958	619	470	1169
VS	957	1099	1145	1032	897	862	879	990	1145	1198	1004	857	12065
TA	32.3	33.9	41.9	52.9	63.2	72.3	76.8	74.8	68.1	57.4	46.2	35.2	54.6
D50	549	452	262	46	2	0	0	0	0	14	150	460	1935
D55	704	591	408	119	11	0	0	0	2	53	273	614	2775
D60	859	731	562	227	44	0	0	0	11	132	416	769	3749
D65	1014	871	716	367	122	0	0	0	38	249	564	924	4865
D70	1169	1011	871	514	227	53	16	29	115	393	714	1079	6190

PITTSBURGH, PENNSYLVANIA — LAT = 40.5 — ELEV = 1224

	JAN	FEB	MAR	APR	MAY	JUN	JUL	AUG	SEP	OCT	NOV	DEC	YEAR
HS	424	625	943	1317	1602	1762	1689	1510	1209	895	505	347	1069
VS	743	879	991	966	881	853	859	967	1100	1138	833	643	10853
TA	28.1	29.3	38.1	50.2	59.8	68.6	71.9	70.2	63.8	53.2	41.3	30.5	50.4
D50	679	580	372	80	6	0	0	0	2	42	269	605	2635
D55	834	720	525	170	27	2	1	1	8	115	413	760	3574
D60	989	860	679	300	89	8	3	5	35	226	561	915	4669
D65	1144	1000	834	444	208	26	7	16	98	372	711	1070	5930
D70	1299	1140	989	594	321	105	58	83	203	521	861	1225	7399

WILKES-BARRE-SCRANTON, PENNSYLVANIA LAT = 41.3 ELEV = 948

	JAN	FEB	MAR	APR	MAY	JUN	JUL	AUG	SEP	OCT	NOV	DEC	YEAR
HS	455	689	991	1339	1591	1760	1746	1513	1199	897	490	368	1086
VS	815	991	1066	1006	896	870	908	993	1117	1165	826	698	11352
TA	26.0	27.3	36.0	48.5	58.9	67.9	72.2	70.0	62.9	52.6	40.8	29.1	49.4
D50	744	636	435	104	7	0	0	0	2	46	282	648	2904
D55	899	776	589	209	32	2	0	1	9	123	427	803	3871
D60	1054	916	744	348	100	9	2	5	41	241	576	958	4994
D65	1209	1056	899	495	219	28	7	18	116	391	726	1113	6277
D70	1364	1196	1054	645	347	114	51	82	225	540	876	1268	7762

PROVIDENCE, RHODE ISLAND LAT = 41.7 ELEV = 62

	JAN	FEB	MAR	APR	MAY	JUN	JUL	AUG	SEP	OCT	NOV	DEC	YEAR
HS	506	738	1032	1374	1655	1775	1695	1499	1209	907	538	418	1112
VS	917	1073	1122	1045	944	888	892	996	1140	1191	917	801	11926
TA	28.4	29.4	36.9	47.3	56.9	66.4	72.1	70.4	63.4	53.7	43.3	31.5	50.0
D50	670	577	406	108	5	0	0	0	0	19	207	574	2566
D55	825	717	561	235	37	1	0	0	3	85	352	729	3543
D60	980	857	716	381	120	6	0	1	21	202	501	884	4669
D65	1135	997	871	531	259	36	0	10	93	350	651	1039	5972
D70	1290	1137	1026	681	406	127	35	58	204	505	801	1194	7464

CHARLESTON, SOUTH CAROLINA LAT = 32.9 ELEV = 39

	JAN	FEB	MAR	APR	MAY	JUN	JUL	AUG	SEP	OCT	NOV	DEC	YEAR
HS	744	995	1339	1732	1860	1844	1799	1585	1394	1193	934	721	1345
VS	1058	1135	1128	1006	832	753	759	808	1010	1226	1251	1083	12049
TA	48.6	50.5	56.5	64.6	72.1	77.9	80.2	79.6	75.2	66.1	56.3	49.3	64.7
D50	120	81	23	2	0	0	0	0	0	2	24	108	360
D55	222	161	75	10	1	0	0	0	0	7	75	205	756
D60	360	275	157	36	5	0	0	0	0	26	156	339	1355
D65	521	419	300	69	5	0	0	0	0	74	271	487	2146
D70	664	547	422	192	66	16	9	10	31	165	414	642	3178

COLUMBIA, SOUTH CAROLINA LAT = 33.9 ELEV = 226

	JAN	FEB	MAR	APR	MAY	JUN	JUL	AUG	SEP	OCT	NOV	DEC	YEAR
HS	762	1020	1355	1747	1895	1947	1842	1703	1439	1211	921	722	1380
VS	1114	1197	1176	1046	868	809	793	894	1075	1280	1268	1115	12634
TA	45.4	47.6	54.2	64.1	72.1	78.8	81.2	80.2	74.5	64.2	53.8	46.0	63.5
D50	185	129	47	4	0	0	0	0	0	4	49	173	590
D55	310	227	116	14	2	0	0	0	0	14	118	294	1094
D60	456	353	212	46	7	0	0	0	0	47	214	438	1772
D65	608	493	360	83	12	0	0	0	0	112	341	589	2598
D70	763	628	492	207	72	15	8	11	42	212	488	744	3683

GREENVILLE-SPARTANBURG, SOUTH CAROLINA LAT = 34.9 ELEV = 971

	JAN	FEB	MAR	APR	MAY	JUN	JUL	AUG	SEP	OCT	NOV	DEC	YEAR
HS	730	982	1328	1697	1839	1918	1830	1699	1406	1180	880	670	1347
VS	1097	1184	1187	1047	864	812	806	918	1082	1283	1245	1063	12590
TA	42.3	44.4	50.9	61.0	69.1	75.9	78.3	77.5	71.7	61.7	51.0	42.9	60.6
D50	248	173	68	3	0	0	0	0	0	3	64	232	791
D55	395	300	156	16	1	0	0	0	0	13	149	377	1409
D60	549	437	288	64	6	0	0	0	2	56	276	531	2210
D65	704	577	450	144	29	0	0	0	9	145	420	685	3163
D70	859	717	592	276	96	16	8	10	55	265	570	840	4304

HURON, SOUTH DAKOTA LAT = 44.4 ELEV = 1289

	JAN	FEB	MAR	APR	MAY	JUN	JUL	AUG	SEP	OCT	NOV	DEC	YEAR
HS	488	745	1114	1530	1871	2101	2183	1892	1418	988	577	405	1276
VS	955	1166	1307	1263	1158	1135	1245	1366	1445	1397	1060	839	14336
TA	12.5	17.9	29.0	45.8	57.0	67.1	73.7	72.1	60.7	49.6	32.4	19.2	44.8
D50	1163	899	652	169	22	1	0	0	8	107	529	955	4506
D55	1318	1039	806	288	71	6	1	2	30	201	678	1110	5549
D60	1473	1179	961	429	151	21	4	6	87	332	828	1265	6735
D65	1627	1319	1116	576	273	72	9	13	169	482	978	1420	8054
D70	1783	1459	1271	726	408	144	50	70	291	633	1128	1575	9537

PIERRE, SOUTH DAKOTA LAT = 44.4 ELEV = 1726

	JAN	FEB	MAR	APR	MAY	JUN	JUL	AUG	SEP	OCT	NOV	DEC	YEAR
HS	530	795	1206	1614	1966	2195	2278	1992	1496	1052	623	442	1349
VS	1037	1244	1415	1332	1217	1186	1299	1438	1524	1488	1145	916	15241
TA	15.6	20.4	29.8	46.3	57.4	67.4	75.2	73.9	62.1	62.1	33.8	21.5	46.2
D50	1068	832	641	239	86	22	7	9	45	47	512	888	4396
D55	1222	970	789	332	151	44	15	18	86	89	649	1041	5405
D60	1377	1110	940	447	228	83	31	37	150	155	792	1195	6544
D65	1531	1249	1091	561	267	74	6	10	152	451	936	1349	7677
D70	1686	1389	1247	720	434	221	112	129	315	326	1087	1504	9171

RAPID CITY, SOUTH DAKOTA LAT = 44.0 ELEV = 3169

	JAN	FEB	MAR	APR	MAY	JUN	JUL	AUG	SEP	OCT	NOV	DEC	YEAR
HS	542	826	1229	1589	1887	2131	2223	1963	1518	1064	647	476	1341
VS	1048	1279	1426	1296	1154	1138	1252	1400	1529	1489	1176	975	15161
TA	21.9	25.8	31.2	44.6	55.2	64.2	72.6	71.6	60.5	50.0	35.4	26.5	46.6
D50	871	678	585	202	43	5	1	1	13	110	443	729	3681
D55	1026	818	738	325	107	17	2	3	39	200	589	884	4749
D60	1181	958	893	466	196	52	8	10	100	325	738	1039	5965
D65	1336	1098	1048	612	319	134	13	17	191	474	888	1194	7324
D70	1491	1238	1203	762	463	211	73	87	301	621	1038	1349	8837

SIOUX FALLS, SOUTH DAKOTA LAT = 43.6 ELEV = 1427

	JAN	FEB	MAR	APR	MAY	JUN	JUL	AUG	SEP	OCT	NOV	DEC	YEAR
HS	533	802	1152	1543	1894	2100	2150	1844	1410	1005	607	441	1290
VS	1019	1228	1322	1243	1144	1109	1197	1299	1404	1391	1091	893	14339
TA	14.2	19.4	30.0	46.1	57.7	67.6	73.3	71.8	60.9	50.2	33.1	20.0	45.4
D50	1110	857	621	165	20	2	0	1	9	100	509	930	4323
D55	1265	997	775	282	65	6	1	2	31	190	657	1085	5355
D60	1420	1137	930	421	141	20	5	7	87	316	807	1240	6531
D65	1575	1277	1085	567	259	65	10	18	165	465	957	1395	7838
D70	1730	1417	1240	717	388	138	57	77	287	615	1107	1550	9322

CHATTANOOGA, TENNESSEE LAT = 35.0 ELEV = 689

	JAN	FEB	MAR	APR	MAY	JUN	JUL	AUG	SEP	OCT	NOV	DEC	YEAR
HS	630	859	1176	1550	1732	1831	1735	1630	1335	1108	773	580	1245
VS	949	1039	1055	960	816	777	765	883	1031	1208	1096	923	11503
TA	40.2	42.9	49.8	60.5	68.5	76.0	78.8	78.0	71.9	60.8	48.9	41.2	59.8
D50	314	218	102	8	1	0	0	0	0	8	113	286	1050
D55	461	344	195	30	4	0	0	0	1	29	209	431	1705
D60	614	480	325	88	15	0	0	0	6	87	340	584	2539
D65	769	625	483	165	51	0	0	0	9	182	483	738	3505
D70	924	759	627	296	123	27	13	17	69	297	633	893	4677

KNOXVILLE, TENNESSEE LAT = 35.8 ELEV = 981

	JAN	FEB	MAR	APR	MAY	JUN	JUL	AUG	SEP	OCT	NOV	DEC	YEAR
HS	621	863	1191	1599	1803	1902	1804	1666	1383	1121	759	569	1273
VS	956	1067	1093	1015	868	821	811	925	1094	1250	1100	925	11926
TA	40.6	42.8	49.9	60.3	68.4	75.5	78.2	77.3	71.6	60.9	49.2	41.5	59.7
D50	302	219	98	8	1	0	0	0	0	7	106	277	1018
D55	449	346	191	30	3	0	0	0	1	27	201	422	1671
D60	602	483	322	89	14	0	0	0	6	83	331	574	2504
D65	756	630	484	173	47	0	0	0	10	175	474	729	3478
D70	911	762	624	300	123	29	15	19	71	294	624	884	4654

MEMPHIS, TENNESSEE LAT = 35.0 ELEV = 285

	JAN	FEB	MAR	APR	MAY	JUN	JUL	AUG	SEP	OCT	NOV	DEC	YEAR
HS	683	945	1278	1639	1885	2045	1972	1824	1471	1204	817	629	1366
VS	1029	1143	1146	1015	888	868	870	989	1136	1313	1159	1001	12556
TA	40.5	43.8	51.0	62.5	70.9	78.6	81.6	80.4	73.6	63.0	50.9	42.7	61.6
D50	312	207	99	9	1	0	0	0	1	8	97	255	988
D55	455	324	182	27	4	0	0	0	2	25	178	391	1588
D60	606	457	299	75	13	0	0	0	7	70	292	539	2357
D65	760	594	457	131	22	0	0	0	7	142	423	691	3227
D70	915	734	591	252	100	21	11	14	61	248	575	847	4368

NASHVILLE, TENNESSEE LAT = 36.1 ELEV = 591

	JAN	FEB	MAR	APR	MAY	JUN	JUL	AUG	SEP	OCT	NOV	DEC	YEAR
HS	580	824	1130	1544	1825	1963	1891	1737	1398	1114	711	521	1270
VS	900	1027	1047	989	885	853	856	973	1116	1253	1039	854	11793
TA	38.3	41.0	48.7	60.1	68.5	76.6	79.6	78.5	72.0	60.9	48.4	40.4	59.4
D50	369	263	119	9	1	0	0	0	0	7	120	308	1195
D55	519	395	220	33	4	0	0	0	1	27	220	455	1874
D60	673	533	357	93	14	0	0	0	5	84	354	608	2720
D65	828	672	524	176	45	0	0	0	10	180	498	763	3696
D70	983	812	661	306	122	22	10	14	66	294	648	918	4856

ABILENE, TEXAS LAT = 32.4 ELEV = 1752

	JAN	FEB	MAR	APR	MAY	JUN	JUL	AUG	SEP	OCT	NOV	DEC	YEAR
HS	924	1183	1576	1843	2037	2209	2139	1956	1598	1315	1008	863	1554
VS	1296	1331	1308	1054	901	895	894	984	1140	1332	1331	1279	13744
TA	43.7	47.9	54.5	65.2	72.4	80.3	83.9	83.6	76.1	66.1	54.1	46.4	64.5
D50	236	138	58	6	1	0	0	0	0	5	60	180	683
D55	364	230	127	17	4	0	0	0	0	15	129	292	1177
D60	510	349	218	49	11	0	0	0	0	42	219	430	1828
D65	660	479	354	104	11	0	0	0	0	89	336	577	2610
D70	816	620	486	197	84	17	8	8	41	185	482	732	3675

FORT WORTH, TEXAS — LAT = 32.8, ELEV = 538

	JAN	FEB	MAR	APR	MAY	JUN	JUL	AUG	SEP	OCT	NOV	DEC	YEAR
HS	805	1069	1409	1616	1890	2153	2155	1983	1621	1293	938	766	1475
VS	1142	1216	1184	935	907			1008		1325	1253	1148	13009
TA	44.8	48.7	55.0	65.2	72.5	80.6	84.8	84.9	77.7	67.6	55.8	47.9	65.5
D50	202	106	43								16	102	242
D55	475	325	198	12						23	60	203	530
D60	626	456	335	88						60	155	383	999
D65	781	597	469	187	71	11		4	22	147	287	530	1618
D70											430	686	2382

HOUSTON, TEXAS — LAT = 30.0, ELEV = 108

	JAN	FEB	MAR	APR	MAY	JUN	JUL	AUG	SEP	OCT	NOV	DEC	YEAR
HS	772	1034	1297	1522	1775	1898	1828	1686	1471	1276	924	730	1357
VS	1014	1087	1002	814	746	795	873	795	975	1142	1018	885	11357
TA	51.5	55.3	60.9	69.1	75.8	81.0	83.0	83.0	79.0	70.1	61.8	54.1	68.9
D50	71	31	12								8	41	161
D55	150	87	31	3						8	82	108	409
D60	263	168	89	12						24	155	201	825
D65	416	294	189	23	31	8		4	13	88	281	333	1434
D70	556	448	298	107							480		2285

LAREDO, TEXAS — LAT = 27.5, ELEV = 518

	JAN	FEB	MAR	APR	MAY	JUN	JUL	AUG	SEP	OCT	NOV	DEC	YEAR
HS	979	1195	1516	1727	1952	2073	2131	2009	1705	1408	1041	885	1550
VS	1179	1170	1085	856	786	795	829	890	1046	1237	1201	1152	12202
TA	56.5	60.2	67.3	76.3	81.2	86.0	87.9	87.7	82.9	75.5	65.5	58.6	73.9
D50	36	15									5	23	79
D55	93	37	28							1	15	64	219
D60	174	92	87	11						8	45	138	482
D65	299	177	154	36	12	4		3	44	74	193	231	876
D70	426	273										365	1522

LUBBOCK, TEXAS — LAT = 33.6, ELEV = 3241

	JAN	FEB	MAR	APR	MAY	JUN	JUL	AUG	SEP	OCT	NOV	DEC	YEAR
HS	1095	1342	1762	2166	2306	2494	2412	2209	1827	1468	1116	990	1766
VS	1468	1517	1516	1286	1090	1051	1032	1144	1347	1539	1523	1430	16007
TA	39.1	43.5	48.9	60.0	68.5	77.1	79.7	78.4	71.0	61.0	48.8	41.3	59.7
D50	348	218	108							5	106	280	1069
D55	494	485	211	24					2	52	206	427	1739
D60	648	624	349	87	21			11	76	162	341	580	2582
D65	803	764	480	190	115	16	8	11	73	288	486	735	3545
D70	958		654	307							636	890	4720

LUFKIN, TEXAS — LAT = 31.2, ELEV = 315

	JAN	FEB	MAR	APR	MAY	JUN	JUL	AUG	SEP	OCT	NOV	DEC	YEAR
HS	1078	1069	1376	1886	1807	2055	2005	1804	1844	1522	963	903	1639
VS	1298	1349	1105	996	867	858	820	907	1052	1320	1231	1108	12292
TA	48.8	52.6	58.1	67.3	74.1	80.0	82.3	83.1	77.0	68.1	57.2	50.8	66.7
D50	125	60									24	93	331
D55	223	237	62	23				6	19	71	147	179	684
D60	356	348	138	56						52	256	300	1220
D65	509	371	209	145	50	11	6		22	134	390	596	1940
D70	658		379										2897

MIDLAND-ODESSA, TEXAS — LAT = 31.9, ELEV = 2858

	JAN	FEB	MAR	APR	MAY	JUN	JUL	AUG	SEP	OCT	NOV	DEC	YEAR
HS	1196	1268	1504	2192	2430	2560	2389	2210	1884	1522	1176	1000	1802
VS	1496	1534	1504	1235	1062	1030	989	1096	1295	1520	1532	1462	15755
TA	47.8	52.2	54.3	64.3	72.3	79.0	82.3	81.8	75.4	65.8	53.3	45.9	63.9
D50	225	124	44							13	54	173	627
D55	361	222	113	13				6	31	71	125	296	1137
D60	510	347	209	43						81	296	441	1806
D65	663	482	349	98	68	11	6	7	33	176	356	592	2621
D70	819		489	202							503	747	3682

PORT ARTHUR, TEXAS — LAT = 29.9, ELEV = 23

	JAN	FEB	MAR	APR	MAY	JUN	JUL	AUG	SEP	OCT	NOV	DEC	YEAR
HS	800	1123	1042	1601	1881	2017	1840	1736	1527	1321	953	750	1404
VS	1048	1121	1042	854	785	787	740	811	1009	1245	1175	1043	11667
TA	43.6	48.4	60.1	68.9	75.0	80.3	83.0	83.1	78.9	69.9	60.1	54.2	68.5
D50	78	37	41							6	12	50	193
D55	157	95	105	15				6	13	35	39	120	462
D60	269	176	183	33						42	101	215	897
D65	420	302	320	121	42	10		10	17	108	184	307	1518
D70	560											493	2412

AMARILLO, TEXAS — LAT = 35.2, ELEV = 3602

	JAN	FEB	MAR	APR	MAY	JUN	JUL	AUG	SEP	OCT	NOV	DEC	YEAR
HS	960	1243	1631	2019	2212	2393	2280	2103	1760	1403	1033	872	1659
VS	1454	1512	1471	1258	1048	1020	1010	1147	1367	1539	1473	1395	15694
TA	36.0	39.7	45.6	56.5	65.6	74.6	78.0	77.6	69.8	59.5	46.3	38.5	57.4
D50	437	296	174	2					2	27	155	362	1457
D55	590	430	302	16		2				137	273	513	2225
D60	744	569	469	171	28	10			20	206	413	662	3136
D65	894	708	601	302	81	35	2		95	333	561	822	4183
D70	1054	848	757	408	174			17			711	977	5421

AUSTIN, TEXAS — LAT = 30.3, ELEV = 620

	JAN	FEB	MAR	APR	MAY	JUN	JUL	AUG	SEP	OCT	NOV	DEC	YEAR
HS	864	1125	1429	1605	1834	2072	2105	1931	1606	1333	987	825	1476
VS	1144	1193	1114	862	759	815	848	917	1074	1271	1231	1174	12399
TA	49.7	53.3	59.1	68.6	75.2	81.6	84.6	84.7	78.9	70.1	59.1	52.3	68.1
D50	16	6	1								14	31	79
D55	216	150	58	6							53	122	602
D60	333	216	130	20						14	205	289	1088
D65	483	304	215	57		6				39	231	339	1737
D70	631		339	158						109		551	2649

BROWNSVILLE, TEXAS — LAT = 25.9, ELEV = 20

	JAN	FEB	MAR	APR	MAY	JUN	JUL	AUG	SEP	OCT	NOV	DEC	YEAR
HS	913	1135	1458	1737	1927	2115	2212	2027	1694	1439	1054	862	1548
VS	1071	1060	993	825	775	805	849	867	990	1205	1163	1089	11657
TA	60.3	63.8	67.7	74.9	79.3	82.8	84.4	84.6	81.6	75.1	68.1	62.8	73.8
D50	5										6	31	82
D55	51	24	11							5	28	80	127
D60	116	65	31	6						14	122	145	325
D65	225	151	89	20						39	205	231	650
D70	321	220	158	71	22	10		7	18	109	339	258	1263

CORPUS CHRISTI, TEXAS — LAT = 25.9, ELEV = 43

	JAN	FEB	MAR	APR	MAY	JUN	JUL	AUG	SEP	OCT	NOV	DEC	YEAR
HS	94	47	1630	1842	1966	2894	2186	1993	1687	1439	1054	862	1657
VS	1187	1030	825	1088	1035	1041	1032	1090	990	1205	1163	1089	12570
TA	56.3	59.6	64.9	72.8	77.9	82.4	85.0	85.1	81.0	73.1	64.9	58.1	71.9
D50	36	16									6	28	82
D55	94	47	13							6	16	71	232
D60	176	108	49	6						21	47	128	515
D65	304	199	120	16						51	81	219	930
D70	431	304	205	75	26	9		3	12	140	198	351	1676

DALLAS, TEXAS — LAT = 32.8, ELEV = 489

	JAN	FEB	MAR	APR	MAY	JUN	JUL	AUG	SEP	OCT	NOV	DEC	YEAR
HS	198	1187	1458	1627	1888	2115	2054	1936	1587	1305	1054	1100	1548
VS	1164	1218	1195	942	888	835	817	898	1030	1308	1250	1180	12988
TA	45.4	49.8	55.8	66.4	73.8	81.6	85.7	86.1	78.6	68.0	55.9	48.3	66.2
D50	189	106	95								16	137	505
D55	312	190	181	30				3	21	71	45	239	943
D60	457	307	314	71						179	110	374	1543
D65	608	437	445	163						296	184	521	2290
D70	763	578			55	9			59	140	428	676	3282

DEL RIO, TEXAS — LAT = 29.4, ELEV = 1027

	JAN	FEB	MAR	APR	MAY	JUN	JUL	AUG	SEP	OCT	NOV	DEC	YEAR
HS	1161	1268	1580	1699	1827	2024	2054	1936	1030	1307	1288	1100	1616
VS	1238	1246	1198	889	759	788	817	898	1030	1263	1288	1233	12649
TA	50.8	55.7	62.7	72.0	78.2	84.3	86.7	86.1	80.2	71.1	59.6	53.1	70.0
D50	95	33									14	74	223
D55	180	87	23							21	45	152	492
D60	301	165	69	16						34	110	261	924
D65	449	283	163	49						88	184	394	1523
D70	596	404	254	75	20	9		3	12	199	323	551	2335

EL PASO, TEXAS — LAT = 31.8, ELEV = 3917

	JAN	FEB	MAR	APR	MAY	JUN	JUL	AUG	SEP	OCT	NOV	DEC	YEAR
HS	1260	1680	1908	2363	2601	2682	2450	2284	1987	1581	1244	1084	1900
VS	1553	1637	1557	1327	1135	1076	1012	1130	1391	1632	1624	1503	16569
TA	43.6	49.4	54.4	63.9	72.2	80.3	82.3	80.5	74.0	64.0	51.6	43.4	63.4
D50	210	91	21							1	50	188	561
D55	355	194	81	21					1	38	131	331	1072
D60	509	326	183	69						92	257	484	1610
D65	663	465	328	183	42	10		3	23	199	402	639	2618
D70	818	605	478	195							552	794	3714

SAN ANGELO, TEXAS — LAT = 31.4 — ELEV = 1909

	JAN	FEB	MAR	APR	MAY	JUN	JUL	AUG	SEP	OCT	NOV	DEC	YEAR
HS	962	1208	1606	1851	2031	2186	2123	1966	1607	1337	1044	895	1568
VS	1313	1321	1294	1027	878	872	871	962	1112	1316	1342	1290	13599
TA	46.4	50.4	57.1	67.2	74.5	81.6	84.7	84.5	76.8	67.2	55.5	48.3	66.2
D50	178	100	33	3	0	0	0	0	0	3	45	145	508
D55	291	178	86	10	0	0	0	0	0	11	106	244	927
D60	429	286	165	31	0	0	0	0	0	32	189	375	1509
D65	577	413	287	74	0	0	0	0	0	73	298	518	2240
D70	732	551	409	158	56	12	6	6	34	164	441	674	3244

SAN ANTONIO, TEXAS — LAT = 29.5 — ELEV = 794

	JAN	FEB	MAR	APR	MAY	JUN	JUL	AUG	SEP	OCT	NOV	DEC	YEAR
HS	895	1154	1450	1612	1894	2069	2121	1947	1638	1350	1009	847	1499
VS	1160	1196	1103	846	788	807	845	906	1069	1258	1230	1159	12367
TA	50.7	54.5	60.8	69.6	76.0	82.2	64.7	84.7	79.3	70.5	59.7	53.2	68.8
D50	93	39	9	1	0	0	0	0	0	1	12	58	213
D55	179	100	32	3	0	0	0	0	0	3	40	132	490
D60	302	185	91	12	0	0	0	0	0	10	104	236	941
D65	451	310	194	31	0	0	0	0	0	32	179	373	1570
D70	599	436	299	106	31	6	3	3	13	96	319	523	2435

SHERMAN, TEXAS — LAT = 33.7 — ELEV = 764

	JAN	FEB	MAR	APR	MAY	JUN	JUL	AUG	SEP	OCT	NOV	DEC	YEAR
HS	794	1037	1366	1610	1852	2114	2077	1932	1580	1268	919	744	1441
VS	1154	1210	1179	958	845	875	891	1008	1173	1333	1258	1142	13025
TA	41.7	45.9	52.3	63.7	71.2	79.4	83.6	83.7	76.0	65.8	53.4	44.8	63.5
D50	269	149	59	2	0	0	0	0	0	1	44	190	715
D55	415	263	137	10	1	0	0	0	0	6	114	323	1271
D60	568	397	253	41	5	0	0	0	0	24	217	473	1977
D65	722	535	411	114	13	0	0	0	0	90	353	626	2864
D70	877	675	549	209	74	9	3	2	22	167	499	781	3869

WACO, TEXAS — LAT = 31.6 — ELEV = 509

	JAN	FEB	MAR	APR	MAY	JUN	JUL	AUG	SEP	OCT	NOV	DEC	YEAR
HS	833	1096	1427	1612	1774	2112	2130	1958	1601	1301	957	803	1467
VS	1143	1206	1157	900	771	845	877	963	1114	1288	1237	1164	12664
TA	47.0	50.9	57.2	67.3	74.5	81.9	85.6	85.7	78.9	69.1	57.5	49.8	67.1
D50	156	84	25	2	0	0	0	0	0	1	22	109	399
D55	269	160	74	7	0	0	0	0	0	4	68	201	782
D60	409	269	153	23	0	0	0	0	0	16	143	328	1340
D65	558	401	280	56	0	0	0	0	0	51	241	471	2058
D70	713	536	403	146	46	8	3	3	16	121	381	627	3003

WICHITA FALLS, TEXAS — LAT = 34.0 — ELEV = 1030

	JAN	FEB	MAR	APR	MAY	JUN	JUL	AUG	SEP	OCT	NOV	DEC	YEAR
HS	862	1123	1472	1763	2017	2221	2166	1969	1602	1291	957	799	1520
VS	1263	1321	1282	1059	927	925	935	1036	1200	1369	1321	1237	13873
TA	41.5	45.9	52.5	64.3	72.3	81.3	85.8	85.5	77.0	66.0	52.9	44.2	64.1
D50	284	164	74	5	1	0	0	0	0	3	67	218	816
D55	425	271	152	17	2	0	0	0	0	11	140	347	1365
D60	575	400	259	51	8	0	0	0	0	36	241	493	2063
D65	729	535	409	112	13	0	0	0	0	92	369	645	2904
D70	884	675	545	209	77	10	4	4	28	180	516	800	3931

BRYCE CANYON, UTAH — LAT = 37.7 — ELEV = 7588

	JAN	FEB	MAR	APR	MAY	JUN	JUL	AUG	SEP	OCT	NOV	DEC	YEAR
HS	914	1236	1685	2133	2454	2655	2424	2157	1920	1465	1015	818	1739
VS	1483	1610	1635	1435	1244	1196	1142	1268	1608	1723	1550	1402	17297
TA	19.8	23.2	28.7	37.7	46.2	46.2	61.6	59.9	52.9	42.8	30.7	22.4	40.0
D50	936	750	660	370	141	137	1	2	31	230	579	856	4693
D55	1091	890	815	519	276	268	8	16	102	379	729	1011	6106
D60	1246	1030	970	669	428	415	47	72	220	533	879	1166	7675
D65	1401	1170	1125	819	583	330	128	176	363	688	1029	1321	9133
D70	1556	1310	1280	969	738	714	265	315	513	843	1179	1476	11159

CEDAR CITY, UTAH — LAT = 37.7 — ELEV = 5617

	JAN	FEB	MAR	APR	MAY	JUN	JUL	AUG	SEP	OCT	NOV	DEC	YEAR
HS	882	1180	1636	2092	2467	2706	2503	2241	1968	1460	992	785	1743
VS	1431	1537	1587	1407	1251	1219	1180	1317	1648	1717	1515	1346	17156
TA	28.7	33.1	38.4	47.1	56.2	65.0	73.2	71.3	63.2	51.5	38.8	30.8	49.8
D50	660	474	364	134	20	1	0	0	2	67	340	596	2658
D55	815	613	515	249	71	6	0	1	11	150	487	750	3669
D60	970	753	670	390	156	27	0	4	43	274	636	905	4829
D65	1125	893	825	537	281	86	0	6	114	424	786	1060	6137
D70	1280	1033	980	687	430	177	45	70	220	574	936	1215	7647

SALT LAKE CITY, UTAH — LAT = 40.8 — ELEV = 4226

	JAN	FEB	MAR	APR	MAY	JUN	JUL	AUG	SEP	OCT	NOV	DEC	YEAR
HS	639	989	1454	1894	2362	2561	2590	2254	1843	1293	788	570	1603
VS	1129	1403	1542	1401	1311	1249	1328	1457	1692	1657	1310	1065	16546
TA	28.0	33.4	39.6	49.2	58.3	66.2	76.7	74.5	64.8	52.4	39.1	30.3	51.0
D50	683	467	334	116	20	3	0	0	4	72	337	612	2648
D55	837	605	481	208	61	9	0	1	13	150	480	766	3612
D60	992	745	633	334	135	31	0	4	43	259	628	921	4725
D65	1147	885	787	474	237	88	0	5	105	402	777	1076	5983
D70	1302	1025	942	625	371	167	29	47	195	548	927	1231	7409

BURLINGTON, VERMONT — LAT = 44.5 — ELEV = 341

	JAN	FEB	MAR	APR	MAY	JUN	JUL	AUG	SEP	OCT	NOV	DEC	YEAR
HS	385	607	940	1296	1574	1729	1721	1475	1122	740	375	283	1021
VS	755	953	1106	1073	977	937	984	1068	1146	1050	691	588	11329
TA	16.8	18.6	29.1	43.0	54.8	65.2	69.8	67.4	59.3	48.8	37.0	22.6	44.4
D50	1029	879	648	220	22	1	0	0	5	98	391	849	4142
D55	1184	1019	803	362	81	3	1	2	24	206	540	1004	5230
D60	1339	1159	958	510	180	18	4	9	87	350	690	1159	6464
D65	1494	1299	1113	660	331	63	20	49	191	502	840	1314	7876
D70	1649	1439	1268	810	472	165	81	122	324	657	990	1469	9447

NORFOLK, VIRGINIA — LAT = 36.9 — ELEV = 30

	JAN	FEB	MAR	APR	MAY	JUN	JUL	AUG	SEP	OCT	NOV	DEC	YEAR
HS	678	932	1281	1677	1887	2000	1853	1680	1396	1083	811	624	1325
VS	1076	1188	1214	1101	936	884	856	964	1142	1246	1212	1046	12864
TA	40.5	41.4	48.1	57.8	66.7	74.5	78.3	76.9	71.8	61.7	51.6	42.3	59.3
D50	300	247	112	9	0	0	0	0	0	2	55	248	974
D55	450	382	226	40	2	0	0	0	0	13	136	395	1646
D60	605	521	371	114	13	0	0	0	2	56	259	549	2489
D65	760	661	532	226	53	0	0	0	9	141	402	704	3488
D70	915	801	679	368	139	25	8	12	53	265	552	859	4674

RICHMOND, VIRGINIA — LAT = 37.5 — ELEV = 164

	JAN	FEB	MAR	APR	MAY	JUN	JUL	AUG	SEP	OCT	NOV	DEC	YEAR
HS	632	877	1210	1566	1762	1872	1774	1601	1348	1033	733	567	1248
VS	1019	1136	1167	1047	889	839	832	935	1122	1208	1113	967	12276
TA	37.5	39.4	46.9	57.8	66.5	74.2	77.9	76.3	70.0	59.3	49.0	39.0	57.8
D50	390	301	140	11	1	0	0	0	0	7	100	345	1296
D55	543	438	262	46	4	0	0	0	1	32	199	497	2021
D60	698	577	408	119	17	0	0	0	6	98	334	651	2909
D65	853	717	569	226	64	0	0	0	21	203	480	806	3939
D70	1008	857	716	369	148	32	11	18	84	336	630	961	5170

ROANOKE, VIRGINIA — LAT = 37.3 — ELEV = 1175

	JAN	FEB	MAR	APR	MAY	JUN	JUL	AUG	SEP	OCT	NOV	DEC	YEAR
HS	660	899	1236	1581	1764	1882	1796	1620	1358	1080	765	591	1269
VS	1059	1158	1185	1051	885	840	838	941	1124	1256	1155	1002	12494
TA	36.4	38.1	45.3	55.9	64.4	71.7	75.2	74.1	68.0	57.8	46.7	37.4	55.9
D50	423	336	171	17	1	0	0	0	0	10	136	393	1486
D55	577	474	306	67	6	0	0	0	2	43	257	546	2277
D60	732	613	457	152	28	0	0	0	9	119	401	701	3211
D65	887	753	611	283	101	0	0	0	32	235	549	856	4307
D70	1042	893	766	424	193	56	22	30	112	381	699	1011	5627

OLYMPIA, WASHINGTON — LAT = 47.0 — ELEV = 200

	JAN	FEB	MAR	APR	MAY	JUN	JUL	AUG	SEP	OCT	NOV	DEC	YEAR
HS	269	503	845	1255	1632	1693	1913	1549	1157	636	339	221	1001
VS	567	846	1065	1119	1095	989	1181	1211	1269	966	671	494	11472
TA	37.2	41.0	43.2	48.2	54.0	58.9	63.6	62.8	58.6	50.6	43.3	39.5	50.1
D50	398	255	219	97	21	3	1	1	4	61	209	327	1595
D55	552	392	367	211	86	22	4	5	24	155	352	481	2652
D60	707	532	521	355	196	85	25	32	90	294	501	636	3974
D65	862	672	676	504	341	197	89	103	198	446	651	791	5530
D70	1017	812	831	654	496	334	207	230	343	601	801	946	7273

SEATTLE-TACOMA, WASHINGTON — LAT = 47.4 — ELEV = 400

	JAN	FEB	MAR	APR	MAY	JUN	JUL	AUG	SEP	OCT	NOV	DEC	YEAR
HS	262	495	849	1293	1714	1802	2248	1616	1148	656	337	211	1053
VS	559	841	1082	1166	1164	1066	1405	1278	1273	1007	674	478	11994
TA	38.2	42.3	44.1	48.7	54.9	59.8	64.5	63.8	59.6	52.2	44.6	40.5	51.1
D50	367	220	192	85	13	2	0	0	2	36	173	297	1386
D55	521	356	339	197	68	14	2	3	15	116	313	450	2393
D60	676	496	493	340	171	67	16	20	71	246	462	605	3662
D65	831	636	648	489	313	167	80	82	170	397	612	760	5185
D70	986	776	803	639	468	308	181	200	313	552	762	915	6903

MADISON, WISCONSIN

LAT = 43.1   ELEV = 860

	JAN	FEB	MAR	APR	MAY	JUN	JUL	AUG	SEP	OCT	NOV	DEC	YEAR
HS	515	804	1136	1398	1743	1948	1934	1708	1299	1244	504	389	13064
VS	971	1214	1285	1109	1037	1014	1061	1185	1275	893	893	776	11191
TA	16.8	20.3	30.2	45.3	56.0	65.1	70.0	68.7	59.7	49.8	34.7	21.9	44.9
D50	1029	832	614	167	19	1	0	2	6	86	460	871	4086
D55	1184	972	769	297	157	79	5	8	87	182	609	1026	5143
D60	1339	1112	924	442	157	72	14	39	173	318	759	1181	6352
D65	1494	1252	1079	591	297	132	83	106	314	623	909	1336	7730
D70	1649	1392	1234	741	436	156					1059	1491	9284

MILWAUKEE, WISCONSIN

LAT = 42.9   ELEV = 692

	JAN	FEB	MAR	APR	MAY	JUN	JUL	AUG	SEP	OCT	NOV	DEC	YEAR
HS	479	736	1089	1443	1768	1977	1962	1719	1310	1219	525	378	12876
VS	898	1106	1225	1138	1045	1023	1070	1185	1278	908	925	750	12191
TA	19.4	22.5	31.4	45.7	54.2	64.5	69.0	69.2	61.1	51.0	36.5	24.2	45.7
D50	949	770	577	177	27	5	4	1	3	65	406	800	3774
D55	1104	910	732	313	92	24	15	4	61	153	555	955	4833
D60	1259	1050	887	460	196	90	13	36	140	285	705	1110	6045
D65	1414	1190	1042	609	348	182	81	92	273	480	855	1265	7844
D70	1569	1330	1197	759	490					589	1005	1420	9886

CASPER, WYOMING

LAT = 42.9   ELEV = 5289

	JAN	FEB	MAR	APR	MAY	JUN	JUL	AUG	SEP	OCT	NOV	DEC	YEAR
HS	683	1013	1441	1847	2204	2501	2535	2225	1749	1219	765	594	17282
VS	1280	1522	1621	1457	1303	1294	1382	1534	1707	1655	1348	1179	17559
TA	23.2	26.8	31.0	41.8	52.7	61.9	71.0	67.6	58.7	47.7	33.9	26.2	45.4
D50	831	650	589	234	53	5	0	0	3	129	484	738	3723
D55	986	790	744	373	92	61	4	8	10	242	633	893	4850
D60	1141	930	899	523	208	147	7	12	100	385	783	1048	6131
D65	1296	1070	1054	669	388	255	13	18	229	538	933	1203	7665
D70	1451	1210	1209	819	537		76	98	344	691	1083	1358	9131

CHEYENNE, WYOMING

LAT = 41.1   ELEV = 6142

	JAN	FEB	MAR	APR	MAY	JUN	JUL	AUG	SEP	OCT	NOV	DEC	YEAR
HS	766	1068	1433	1822	1995	2258	2230	1966	1667	1306	823	671	16204
VS	1365	1527	1532	1322	1117	1111	1154	1283	1584	1605	1380	1265	15620
TA	29.0	29.0	31.6	40.1	50.4	58.9	68.2	66.1	56.4	44.7	35.5	29.2	45.0
D50	785	588	571	230	49	20	2	1	10	118	436	645	3375
D55	940	728	726	299	62	83	7	9	38	233	585	800	4507
D60	1035	868	851	447	152	156	18	49	130	385	585	955	5531
D65	1190	1008	1035	659	300	268	98	141	225	538	735	1155	7255
D70	1345	1148	1190	819	546				357	685	1035	1265	8880

ROCK SPRINGS, WYOMING

LAT = 41.6   ELEV = 6745

	JAN	FEB	MAR	APR	MAY	JUN	JUL	AUG	SEP	OCT	NOV	DEC	YEAR
HS	735	1089	1530	1944	2344	2574	2547	2240	1832	1306	826	651	17559
VS	1328	1579	1659	1474	1333	1284	1337	1488	1722	1711	1404	1245	15161
TA	23.4	25.9	28.9	40.1	50.4	58.9	68.2	66.1	56.4	44.7	30.7	22.6	42.5
D50	955	745	654	299	62	20	4	1	8	176	579	849	4330
D55	1110	885	809	447	158	83	8	9	46	321	729	1004	5531
D60	1265	1025	964	587	300	198	18	49	130	475	879	1159	6889
D65	1420	1165	1119	747	448	334	98	141	408	629	1029	1314	8810
D70	1575	1305	1274	897	608					784	1179	1265	10073

SHERIDAN, WYOMING

LAT = 44.8   ELEV = 3966

	JAN	FEB	MAR	APR	MAY	JUN	JUL	AUG	SEP	OCT	NOV	DEC	YEAR
HS	517	788	1205	1594	1883	2156	2329	2006	1502	1005	591	441	15161
VS	1023	1247	1429	1284	1180	1179	1344	1466	1548	1437	1098	925	15161
TA	21.0	25.9	31.0	44.0	53.1	61.1	70.4	69.2	57.9	47.8	33.4	25.5	45.0
D50	899	675	590	217	57	27	2	3	17	137	500	760	3860
D55	1054	815	744	349	137	91	3	11	57	245	648	915	4991
D60	1209	955	898	494	237	168	28	31	131	384	798	1070	6279
D65	1364	1095	1053	642	387	280	94	113	254	536	948	1225	7708
D70	1519	1235	1209	792	526				369	689	1098	1380	9303

SPOKANE, WASHINGTON

LAT = 47.6   ELEV = 2365

	JAN	FEB	MAR	APR	MAY	JUN	JUL	AUG	SEP	OCT	NOV	DEC	YEAR
HS	315	605	1041	1495	1681	2083	2357	1942	1435	881	398	255	13064
VS	676	1036	1334	1357	1310	1239	1482	1546	1601	1298	801	581	14261
TA	25.4	32.2	37.5	46.1	54.0	61.5	69.7	68.0	59.6	47.8	35.5	29.0	47.3
D50	763	499	391	153	30	21	2	12	30	125	437	651	3061
D55	918	639	543	276	94	65	7	47	92	238	585	806	4150
D60	1073	778	698	419	190	144	21	144	196	382	735	961	5411
D65	1228	918	853	567	327	265	94		318	533	885	1116	6835
D70	1383	1058	1008	717	476					688	1035	1271	8433

YAKIMA, WASHINGTON

LAT = 46.6   ELEV = 1066

	JAN	FEB	MAR	APR	MAY	JUN	JUL	AUG	SEP	OCT	NOV	DEC	YEAR
HS	365	746	1122	1598	2008	2169	2358	1975	1608	891	444	295	14687
VS	761	1107	1399	1408	1330	1252	1438	1525	1608	1338	868	652	14687
TA	27.5	33.7	41.8	49.5	56.2	64.5	70.7	68.0	61.3	50.1	38.4	31.3	49.8
D50	698	402	265	93	12	7	0	0	18	86	352	580	2494
D55	853	541	412	188	48	30	2	10	49	180	499	735	3482
D60	1008	681	567	315	133	94	10	37	147	267	648	890	4653
D65	1163	820	722	465	283	188	35	100	248	462	798	1090	6009
D70	1318	960	874	615	378					617	948	1200	7557

CHARLESTON, WEST VIRGINIA

LAT = 38.4   ELEV = 951

	JAN	FEB	MAR	APR	MAY	JUN	JUL	AUG	SEP	OCT	NOV	DEC	YEAR
HS	498	706	1009	1356	1639	1776	1682	1514	1272	972	613	440	11047
VS	823	938	999	932	848	814	807	909	1088	1166	954	769	11047
TA	34.5	36.5	44.3	55.9	64.5	72.0	75.0	73.6	67.5	57.1	46.2	36.2	55.2
D50	483	381	202	27	3	1	0	0	1	21	176	431	1726
D55	636	519	340	83	30	10	0	0	8	69	298	590	2540
D60	791	659	495	207	113	67	0	0	69	176	438	738	3488
D65	946	799	650	355	238	167	35	49	187	267	588	894	4524
D70	1101	938	791	426	378					407	738	1048	5938

HUNTINGTON, WEST VIRGINIA

LAT = 38.4   ELEV = 837

	JAN	FEB	MAR	APR	MAY	JUN	JUL	AUG	SEP	OCT	NOV	DEC	YEAR
HS	526	757	1067	1448	1710	1844	1769	1580	1306	1004	638	467	11585
VS	870	1005	1056	995	885	845	849	949	1117	1204	993	816	12912
TA	34.3	36.1	44.3	55.7	64.3	72.4	75.3	73.9	67.1	57.1	47.0	36.0	55.2
D50	489	393	208	30	18	1	0	0	1	22	175	438	1759
D55	642	519	346	87	52	12	0	0	5	70	296	593	2574
D60	797	758	581	207	123	41	1	9	36	175	446	738	3522
D65	952	809	683	293	293	156	14	54	202	265	596	894	4524
D70	1107	938	791	432	203	64	78		336	407	735	1048	5961

EAU CLAIRE, WISCONSIN

LAT = 44.9   ELEV = 896

	JAN	FEB	MAR	APR	MAY	JUN	JUL	AUG	SEP	OCT	NOV	DEC	YEAR
HS	452	746	1090	1426	1681	1872	1886	1621	1196	826	450	341	11132
VS	897	1184	1297	1194	1057	1027	1092	1189	1236	1184	839	717	12912
TA	11.7	15.4	27.1	44.3	56.2	66.1	70.5	68.4	58.7	48.7	32.0	18.0	43.1
D50	1187	969	704	187	18	0	0	1	36	107	540	992	4714
D55	1342	1109	859	320	68	18	1	9	213	540	695	1147	5790
D60	1497	1209	1014	616	293	91	14	37	198	505	990	1302	8111
D65	1652	1389	1169	615	293	151	78	112	343	660	990	1457	8888
D70	1807	1529	1324	765	430						1140	1612	9951

GREEN BAY, WISCONSIN

LAT = 44.5   ELEV = 702

	JAN	FEB	MAR	APR	MAY	JUN	JUL	AUG	SEP	OCT	NOV	DEC	YEAR
HS	451	725	1104	1439	1719	1908	1888	1622	1218	821	465	350	12862
VS	885	1138	1299	1191	1068	1034	1080	1175	1245	1164	857	727	14348
TA	15.4	18.0	28.6	47.6	56.4	64.5	69.2	67.0	58.9	48.7	35.6	20.9	44.9
D50	1073	896	664	202	28	2	0	1	32	97	478	902	4348
D55	1228	1036	818	339	92	18	3	9	73	199	627	1057	5437
D60	1383	1209	973	486	192	65	10	22	167	339	777	1212	6808
D65	1538	1316	1128	636	338	151	52	97	303	505	927	1367	8088
D70	1693	1456	1283	786	481					645	1077	1522	9684

LA CROSSE, WISCONSIN

LAT = 43.9   ELEV = 673

	JAN	FEB	MAR	APR	MAY	JUN	JUL	AUG	SEP	OCT	NOV	DEC	YEAR
HS	481	765	1101	1426	1713	1905	1900	1666	1242	863	494	369	12953
VS	928	1181	1274	1159	1044	1014	1067	1185	1247	1204	895	754	11161
TA	16.1	20.0	31.1	47.6	57.9	68.5	72.8	71.4	61.3	51.8	35.4	21.8	46.4
D50	1050	847	586	127	10	2	0	0	15	65	440	874	3998
D55	1206	980	746	247	57	10	1	5	42	154	587	1029	4987
D60	1361	1120	896	375	163	66	3	17	130	266	738	1184	6130
D65	1516	1260	1051	522	224	127	10	52	258	421	888	1339	7417
D70	1671	1400	1206	672	346					565	1038	1494	8884

C A N A D A

EDMONTON, ALBERTA — LAT = 53.6 — ELEV = 2220

	JAN	FEB	MAR	APR	MAY	JUN	JUL	AUG	SEP	OCT	NOV	DEC	YEAR
HS	324	649	1080	1541	1731	1939	2005	1570	1109	719	376	236	1095
VS	856	1314	1330	1662	1584	1387	1516	1493	1161	1310	905	650	15748
D65	1810	1520	1330	765	400	222	-	180	411	738	1215	1603	10268
TA	6.6	10.7	22.1	39.5	49.3						24.5	13.3	36.9

SUFFIELD, ALBERTA — LAT = 50.3 — ELEV = 2549

	JAN	FEB	MAR	APR	MAY	JUN	JUL	AUG	SEP	OCT	NOV	DEC	YEAR
HS	420	863	1180	1692	1943	1983	2226	1832	1198	767	487	346	1242
VS	977	1591	1628	1661	1442	1282	1521	1581	1441	1275	1061	856	16316
D65	1497	1291	1159	696	403	213	56	112	318	611	1011	1277	8644
TA	16.7	18.9	27.6	41.8	46.3					45.3	31.3	23.8	41.3

NANAIMO, BRITISH COLUMBIA — LAT = 49.2 — ELEV = 60

	JAN	FEB	MAR	APR	MAY	JUN	JUL	AUG	SEP	OCT	NOV	DEC	YEAR
HS	299	464	870	1570	1990	1913	2396	1799	1098	711	391	206	1176
VS	673	829	1165	1493	1428	1195	1582	1502	1281	1147	825	493	13613
D65	862	723	676	501	310	156	81	87	219	456	657	787	5515
TA	37.2	39.2	43.2	48.3							43.1	39.6	49.9

VANCOUVER, BRITISH COLUMBIA — LAT = 49.3 — ELEV = 310

	JAN	FEB	MAR	APR	MAY	JUN	JUL	AUG	SEP	OCT	NOV	DEC	YEAR
HS	295	383	686	1261	1721	1777	2005	1463	925	586	346	203	1025
VS	666	686	1126	1602	1239	1252	1388	1285	1082	468	752	787	11563
D65	862	728	676	507	310	156	81	87	219	456	752	787	5515
TA	37.2	39.2	43.2	48.3							43.1	39.6	49.9

WINNIPEG, MANITOBA — LAT = 49.9 — ELEV = 820

	JAN	FEB	MAR	APR	MAY	JUN	JUL	AUG	SEP	OCT	NOV	DEC	YEAR
HS	468	840	1338	1596	1869	1961	2105	1780	1183	774	420	328	1216
VS	1076	1531	1826	1549	1370	1252	1421	1518	1407	1273	904	802	15928
D65	2008	1719	1465	813	405	147	38	71	322	683	1251	1751	10679
TA	.2	3.6	17.7	37.9							43.0	23.3	8.5	35.7

DARTMOUTH, NOVA SCOTIA — LAT = 44.6 — ELEV = 136

	JAN	FEB	MAR	APR	MAY	JUN	JUL	AUG	SEP	OCT	NOV	DEC	YEAR
HS	417	715	1017	1309	1589	1570	1710	1823	1253	840	461	402	1076
VS	820	1125	1200	1087	990	853	981	1034	1284	1195	852	838	12258
D65	1213	1122	1030	742	487	237	58	51	180	457	710	1074	7361
TA	25.9	24.9	31.8	40.3	49.3						41.3	30.4	44.8

MOOSONEE, ONTARIO — LAT = 51.3 — ELEV = 34

	JAN	FEB	MAR	APR	MAY	JUN	JUL	AUG	SEP	OCT	NOV	DEC	YEAR
HS	358	734	1128	1449	1482	1725	1655	1286	973	553	280	258	951
VS	859	1392	1600	1464	1134	1150	1166	1143	1203	945	628	659	13343
D65	2037	1735	1562	978	580	222	74	171	405	756	1245	1807	11572
TA	-7	3.0	14.6	32.4	46.3					40.6	23.5	6.7	33.3

OTTAWA, ONTARIO — LAT = 45.5 — ELEV = 377

	JAN	FEB	MAR	APR	MAY	JUN	JUL	AUG	SEP	OCT	NOV	DEC	YEAR
HS	534	826	1312	1489	1854	2018	2024	1769	1327	826	450	394	1224
VS	1078	1332	1587	1270	1187	1138	1193	1321	1395	1204	853	843	14402
D65	1624	1441	1231	708	341	90	25	81	222	567	936	1469	8735
TA	12.6	13.5	25.3	41.4						46.7	33.8	17.6	41.1

TORONTO, ONTARIO — LAT = 43.7 — ELEV = 443

	JAN	FEB	MAR	APR	MAY	JUN	JUL	AUG	SEP	OCT	NOV	DEC	YEAR
HS	501	722	1109	1463	1847	1935	2005	1629	1301	829	453	365	1194
VS	961	1109	1276	1182	1119	1024	1119	1151	1299	1150	816	741	12949
D65	1233	1013	1013	616	298	62	7	18	151	439	760	1111	6827
TA	25.2	25.0	32.3								39.7	29.2	46.3

NORMANDIN, QUEBEC — LAT = 48.8 — ELEV = 450

	JAN	FEB	MAR	APR	MAY	JUN	JUL	AUG	SEP	OCT	NOV	DEC	YEAR
HS	424	785	1294	1434	1762	1629	1640	1360	1073	601	372	328	1006
VS	943	1387	1714	1348	1249	1005	1070	1122	1238	959	775	775	13586
D65	1879	1619	1407	891	521	231	102	136	327	682	1074	1659	10528
TA	4.4	7.2	19.6	35.3	48.2					43.0	29.2	11.5	36.2

Appendix 3

Design
Data

R-VALUES OF AIR FILMS				
Type and Orientation of Air Film	Direction of Heat Flow	R-value for Air Film On:		
		Non-reflective surface	Fairly reflective surface	Highly reflective surface
Still air:				
Horizontal	up	0.61	1.10	1.32
Horizontal	down	0.92	2.70	4.55
45° slope	up	0.62	1.14	1.37
45° slope	down	0.76	1.67	2.22
Vertical	across	0.68	1.35	1.70
Moving air:				
15 mph wind	any*	0.17	—	—
7½ mph wind	any†	0.25	—	—

*Winter conditions.
†Summer conditions.
SOURCE: ASHRAE, *Handbook of Fundamentals*, 1972. Reprinted by permission.

R-VALUES OF AIR SPACES				
Orientation & Thickness of Air Space	Direction of Heat Flow	R-value for Air Space Facing: [‡]		
		Non-reflective surface	Fairly reflective surface	Highly reflective surface
Horizontal ¾"	up [*]	0.87	1.71	2.23
4"		0.94	1.99	2.73
¾"	up [†]	0.76	1.63	2.26
4"		0.80	1.87	2.75
¾"	down [*]	1.02	2.39	3.55
1½"		1.14	3.21	5.74
4"		1.23	4.02	8.94
¾	down [†]	0.84	2.08	3.25
1½"		0.93	2.76	5.24
4"		0.99	3.38	8.03
45° slope ¾"	up [*]	0.94	2.02	2.78
4"		0.96	2.13	3.00
¾"	up [†]	0.81	1.90	2.81
4"		0.82	1.98	3.00
¾"	down [*]	1.02	2.40	3.57
4"		1.08	2.75	4.41
¾"	down [†]	0.84	2.09	3.34
4"		0.90	2.50	4.36
Vertical ¾"	across [*]	1.01	2.36	3.48
4"		1.01	2.34	3.45
¾"	across [†]	0.84	2.10	3.28
4"		0.91	2.16	3.44

[‡] One side of the air space is a non-reflective surface.

[*] Winter conditions.

[†] Summer conditions.

SOURCE: ASHRAE, *Handbook of Fundamentals*, 1972. Reprinted by permission.

U-VALUES OF WINDOWS AND SKYLIGHTS		
Description	U-values[1]	
	Winter	Summer
Vertical panels:		
Single pane flat glass	1.13	1.06
Insulating glass—double[2]		
3/16" air space	0.69	0.64
1/4" air space	0.65	0.61
1/2" air space	0.58	0.56
Insulating glass—triple[2]		
1/4" air spaces	0.47	0.45
1/2" air spaces	0.36	0.35
Storm windows		
1-4" air space	0.56	0.54
Glass blocks[3]		
6 X 6 X 4" thick	0.60	0.57
8 X 8 X 4" thick	0.56	0.54
same, with cavity divider	0.48	0.46
Single plastic sheet	1.09	1.00
Horizontal panels:[4]		
Single pane flat glass	1.22	0.83
Insulating glass—double[2]		
3/16" air space	0.75	0.49
1/4" air space	0.70	0.46
1/2" air space	0.66	0.44
Glass blocks[3]		
11 X 11 X 3" thick, with cavity divider	0.53	0.35
12 X 12 X 4" thick, with cavity divider	0.51	0.34
Plastic bubbles[5]		
single-walled	1.15	0.80
double-walled	0.70	0.46

[1] in units of $Btu/hr/ft^2/°F$

[2] double and triple refer to the number of lights of glass.

[3] nominal dimensions.

[4] U-values for horizontal panels are for heat flow *up* in winter and *down* in summer.

[5] based on area of opening, not surface.

SOURCE: ASHRAE, *Handbook of Fundamentals,* 1972. Reprinted by permission.

Thermal Properties of Typical Building and Insulating Materials—(Design Values)[a]

(For Industrial Insulation Design Values, see Table 3B). These constants are expressed in Btu per (hour) (square foot) (degree Fahrenheit temperature difference). Conductivities (k) are per inch thickness, and conductances (C) are for thickness or construction stated, not per inch thickness. **All values are for a mean temperature of 75 F, except as noted by an asterisk (*) which have been reported at 45 F.** The SI units for Resistance (last two columns) were calculated by taking the values from the two Resistance columns under Customary Unit, and multiplying by the factor 1/k (r/in.) and 1/C (R) for the appropriate conversion factor in Table 18.

Description	Density (lb/ft³)	Conductivity (k)	Conductance (C)	Resistance[b] (R) Per inch thickness (1/k)	For thickness listed (1/C)	Specific Heat, Btu/(lb) (deg F)	SI Unit Resistance[b] (R) (m·K)/W	(m²·K)/W
BUILDING BOARD								
Boards, Panels, Subflooring, Sheathing Woodboard Panel Products								
Asbestos-cement board	120	4.0	—	0.25	—	0.24	1.73	0.005
Asbestos-cement board ....0.125 in.	120	—	33.00	—	0.03			0.01
Asbestos-cement board ....0.25 in.	120	—	16.50	—	0.06			0.06
Gypsum or plaster board ....0.375 in.	50	—	3.10	—	0.32			0.06
Gypsum or plaster board ....0.5 in.	50	—	2.22	—	0.45			0.08
Gypsum or plaster board ....0.625 in.	50	—	1.78	—	0.56	0.26		0.10
Plywood (Douglas Fir)	34	0.80	—	1.25	—	0.29	8.66	0.05
Plywood (Douglas Fir) ....0.25 in.	34	—	3.20	—	0.31			0.05
Plywood (Douglas Fir) ....0.375 in.	34	—	2.13	—	0.47			0.08
Plywood (Douglas Fir) ....0.5 in.	34	—	1.60	—	0.62			0.11
Plywood (Douglas Fir) ....0.625 in.	34	—	1.29	—	0.77			0.19
Plywood or wood panels ....0.75 in.	34	—	1.07	—	0.93	0.29		0.16
Vegetable Fiber Board								
Sheathing, regular density ....0.5 in.	18	—	0.76	—	1.32	0.31		0.23
.......0.78125 in.	18	—	0.49	—	2.06			0.36
Sheathing intermediate density ....0.5 in.	22	—	0.82	—	1.22	0.31		0.21
Nail-base sheathing ....0.5 in.	25	—	0.88	—	1.14	0.31		0.20
Shingle backer ....0.375 in.	18	—	1.06	—	0.94			0.17
Shingle backer ....0.3125 in.	18	—	1.28	—	0.78			0.14
Sound deadening board ....0.5 in.	15	—	0.74	—	1.35	0.30		0.24
Tile and lay-in panels, plain or acoustic	18	0.40	—	2.50	—	0.14	17.33	0.22
.......0.5 in.	18	—	0.80	—	1.25			0.33
.......0.75 in.	18	—	0.53	—	1.89			
Laminated paperboard	30	0.50	—	2.00	—	0.33	13.86	
Homogeneous board from repulped paper	30	0.50	—	2.00	—	0.28	13.86	

Thermal Properties of Typical Building and Insulating Materials—(Design Values)[a] (continued)

Description	Customary Unit						SI Unit	
				Resistance[b] (R)		Specific Heat, Btu/(lb)(deg F)	Resistance[b] (R)	
	Density (lb/ft³)	Conductivity (k)	Conductance (C)	Per inch thickness (1/k)	For thickness listed (1/C)		(m·K)/W	(m²·K)/W
Hardboard								
Medium density	50	0.73	—	1.37	—	0.31	9.49	
High density, service temp. service underlay	55	0.82	—	1.22	—	0.32	8.46	
High density, std. tempered	63	1.00	—	1.00	—	0.32	6.93	
Particleboard								
Low density	37	0.54	—	1.85	—	0.31	12.82	
Medium density	50	0.94	—	1.06	—	0.31	7.35	
High density	62.5	1.18	—	0.85	—	0.31	5.89	
Underlayment....0.625 in.	40	—	1.22	—	0.82	0.29		0.14
Wood subfloor....0.75 in.		—	1.06	—	0.94	0.33		0.17
BUILDING MEMBRANE								
Vapor—permeable felt	—	—	16.70	—	0.06			0.01
Vapor—seal, 2 layers of mopped 15-lb felt	—	—	8.35	—	0.12			0.02
Vapor—seal, plastic film	—	—	—	—	Negl.			
FINISH FLOORING MATERIALS								
Carpet and fibrous pad	—	—	0.48	—	2.08	0.34		0.37
Carpet and rubber pad	—	—	0.81	—	1.23	0.33		0.22
Cork tile....0.125 in.	—	—	3.60	—	0.28	0.48		0.05
Terrazzo....1 in.	—	—	12.50	—	0.08	0.19		0.01
Tile—asphalt, linoleum, vinyl, rubber	—	—	20.00	—	0.05	0.30		0.01
vinyl asbestos						0.24		
ceramic						0.19		
Wood, hardwood finish....0.75 in.			1.47		0.68			0.12
INSULATING MATERIALS								
BLANKET AND BATT								
Mineral Fiber, fibrous form processed from rock, slag, or glass						0.17–0.23		
approx.[c] 2–2.75 in.	0.3–2.0	—	0.143	—	7[d]			1.23
approx.[c] 3–3.5 in.	0.3–2.0	—	0.091	—	11[d]			1.94
approx.[c] 5.50–6.5	0.3–2.0	—	0.053	—	19[d]			3.35
approx.[c] 6–7 in.	0.3–2.0		0.045		22[d]			3.87
approx.[d] 8.5 in.	0.3–2.0		0.033		30[d]			5.28

Material							
BOARD AND SLABS							
Cellular glass	8.5	0.38	—	*2.63*	—	0.24	*18.23*
Glass fiber, organic bonded	4–9	0.25	—	*4.00*	—	0.23	*27.72*
Expanded rubber (rigid)	4.5	0.22	—	*4.55*	—	0.40	*31.53*
Expanded polystyrene extruded							
Cut cell surface	1.8	0.25	—	*4.00*	—	0.29	*27.72*
Expanded polystyrene extruded							
Smooth skin surface	2.2	0.20	—	*5.00*	—	0.29	*34.65*
Expanded polystyrene extruded							
Smooth skin surface	3.5	0.19	—	*5.26*	—	0.29	*36.45*
Expanded polystyrene, molded beads	1.0	0.28	—	*3.57*	—	0.38	*24.74*
Expanded polyurethane[f] (R-11 exp.)	1.5	0.16	—	*6.25*	—	—	*43.82*
(Thickness 1 in. or greater)	2.5	—	—	—	—	—	—
Mineral fiber with resin binder	15	0.29	—	*3.45*	—	0.17	*23.91*
Mineral fiberboard, wet felted							
Core or roof insulation	16–17	0.34	—	*2.94*	—	0.19	*20.38*
Acoustical tile	18	0.35	—	*2.86*	—	—	*19.82*
Acoustical tile	21	0.37	—	*2.70*	—	—	*18.71*
Mineral fiberboard, wet molded							
Acoustical tile[g]	23	0.42	—	*2.38*	—	0.14	*16.49*
Wood or cane fiberboard							
Acoustical tile[g] .... 0.5 in.	—	—	0.80	—	*1.25*	0.31	*0.22*
Acoustical tile[g] .... 0.75 in.	—	—	0.53	—	*1.89*	—	*0.33*
Interior finish (plank, tile)	15	0.35	—	*2.86*	—	0.32	*19.82*
Wood shredded (cemented in preformed slabs)	22	0.60	—	*1.67*	—	0.31	*11.57*
LOOSE FILL							
Cellulosic insulation (milled paper or wood pulp)	2.3–3.2	0.27–0.32	—	*3.13–3.70*	—	0.33	*21.69–25.64*
Sawdust or shavings	8.0–15.0	0.45	—	*2.22*	—	0.33	*15.39*
Wood fiber, softwoods	2.0–3.5	0.30	—	*3.33*	—	0.33	*23.08*
Perlite, expanded	5.0–8.0	0.37	—	*2.70*	—	0.26	*18.71*
Mineral fiber (rock, slag or glass)							
approx.[e] 3.75–5 in.	0.6–2.0	—	—	—	11	0.17	*1.94*
approx.[e] 6.5–8.75 in.	0.6–2.0	—	—	—	19	—	*3.35*
approx.[e] 7.5–10 in.	0.6–2.0	—	—	—	22	—	*3.87*
approx.[e] 10.25–13.75 in.	0.6–2.0	—	—	—	30	—	*5.28*
Vermiculite, exfoliated	7.0–8.2	0.47	—	*2.13*	—	3.20	*14.76*
	4.0–6.0	0.44	—	*2.27*	—	—	*15.73*

Thermal Properties of Typical Building and Insulating Materials—(Design Values)[a] (continued)

Description	Density (lb/ft³)	Conductivity (k)	Conductance (C)	Resistance[b] (R) Per inch thickness (1/k)	Resistance[b] (R) For thickness listed (1/C)	Specific Heat, Btu/(lb)(deg F)	SI Unit Resistance[b] (R) (m·K)/W	SI Unit Resistance[b] (R) (m²·K)/W
ROOF INSULATION[h] Preformed, for use above deck Different roof insulations are available in different thicknesses to provide the design C values listed.[h] Consult individual manufacturers for actual thickness of their material.			0.72 to 0.12		1.39 to 8.33		— —	0.24 to 1.47
MASONRY MATERIALS CONCRETES								
Cement mortar.	116	5.0	—	0.20	—		1.39	
Gypsum-fiber concrete 87.5% gypsum, 12.5% wood chips.	51	1.66	—	0.60	—	0.21	4.16	
Lightweight aggregates including expanded shale, clay or slate; expanded slags; cinders; pumice; vermiculite; also cellular concretes	120	5.2	—	0.19	—		1.32	
	100	3.6	—	0.28	—		1.94	
	80	2.5	—	0.40	—		2.77	
	60	1.7	—	0.59	—		4.09	
	40	1.15	—	0.86	—		5.96	
	30	0.90	—	1.11	—		7.69	
	20	0.70	—	1.43	—		9.91	
Perlite, expanded.	40	0.93	—	1.08	—	0.32	7.48	
	30	0.71	—	1.41	—		9.77	
	20	0.50	—	2.00	—		13.86	
Sand and gravel or stone aggregate (oven dried).	140	9.0	—	0.11	—	0.22	0.76	
Sand and gravel or stone aggregate (not dried).	140	12.0	—	0.08	—		0.55	
Stucco.	116	5.0	—	0.20	—		1.39	
MASONRY UNITS								
Brick, common[i].	120	5.0	—	0.20	—	0.19	1.39	
Brick, face[i].	130	9.0	—	0.11	—		0.76	
Clay tile, hollow:						0.21		
1 cell deep . . . 3 in.	—	—	1.25	—	0.80			0.14
1 cell deep . . . 4 in.	—	—	0.90	—	1.11			0.20
2 cells deep. . . 6 in.	—	—	0.66	—	1.52			0.27
2 cells deep. . . 8 in.	—	—	0.54	—	1.85			0.33
2 cells deep. . . 10 in.	—	—	0.45	—	2.22			0.39
3 cells deep. . . 12 in.	—	—	0.40	—	2.50			0.44

Material	Density	Conductivity (k)	Conductance (C)	Resistance (1/k)	Resistance (1/C)	Specific heat		
Concrete blocks, three oval core:								
Sand and gravel aggregate .... 4 in.	—	—	1.40	—	0.71	0.22		0.13
.... 8 in.	—	—	0.90	—	1.11			0.20
.... 12 in.	—	—	0.78	—	1.28			0.23
Cinder aggregate .... 3 in.	—	—	1.16	—	0.86	0.21		0.15
.... 4 in.	—	—	0.90	—	1.11			0.20
.... 8 in.	—	—	0.58	—	1.72			0.30
.... 12 in.	—	—	0.53	—	1.89			0.33
Lightweight aggregate .... 3 in.	—	—	0.79	—	1.27	0.21		0.22
(expanded shale, clay, slate ...... 4 in.	—	—	0.67	—	1.50			0.26
or slag; pumice) .... 8 in.	—	—	0.50	—	2.00			0.35
.... 12 in.	—	—	0.44	—	2.27			0.40
Concrete blocks, rectangular core.*j								
Sand and gravel aggregate								
2 core, 8 in. 36 lb. k* ...	—	—	0.96	—	1.04	0.22		0.18
Same with filled cores†*	—	—	0.52	—	1.93			0.34
Lightweight aggregate (expanded shae,								
clay, slate or slag, pumice):								
3 core, 6 in. 19 lb. k* ...	—	—	0.61	—	1.65	0.22		0.29|
Same with filled cores†*	—	—	0.33	—	2.99			0.53
2 core, 8 in. 24 lb. k* ...	—	—	0.46	—	2.18			0.38
Same with filled cores†*	—	—	0.20	—	5.03			0.89
3 core, 12 in. 38 lb. k* ...	—	—	0.40	—	2.48			0.44
Same with filled cores†*	—	—	0.17	—	5.82	0.55		1.02
Stone, lime or sand.	—	12.50	—	0.08	—	0.21		0.22
Gypsum partition tile:								
3 × 12 × 30 in. solid	—	—	0.79	—	1.26	0.19		0.24
3 × 12 × 30 in. 4-cell	—	—	0.74	—	1.35	0.19		0.29
4 × 12 × 30 in. 3-cell	—	—	0.60	—	1.67			

METALS
(See Chapter 37, Table 3)

PLASTERING MATERIALS

Material	Density	Conductivity (k)	Conductance (C)	Resistance (1/k)	Resistance (1/C)	Specific heat		
Cement plaster, sand aggregate ...... 0.375 in.	116	5.0	13.3	0.20	0.08	0.20	1.39	0.01
Sand aggregate ...... 0.75 in.	—	—	6.66	—	0.15	0.20		0.03
Sand aggregate ...	—	—	—	—	—	0.20		
Gypsum plaster:								
Lightweight aggregate ...... 0.5 in.	45	1.5	3.12	0.67	0.32		4.64	0.06
Lightweight aggregate ...... 0.625 in.	45	—	2.67	—	0.39			0.07
Lightweight agg. on metal lath ...... 0.75 in.	—	—	2.13	—	0.47		1.25	0.08
Perlite aggregate ...	45	5.6	—	0.18	—			
Sand aggregate ...... 0.5 in.	105	—	11.10	—	0.09			0.02
Sand aggregate ...... 0.625 in.	105	—	9.10	—	0.11			0.02
Sand aggregate on metal lath ...... 0.75 in.	105	—	7.70	—	0.13			0.02
Vermiculite aggregate ...	45	1.7	—	0.59	—		4.09	

Thermal Properties of Typical Building and Insulating Materials—(Design Values)[a] (continued)

Description	Customary Unit						SI Unit	
	Density (lb/ft³)	Conductivity (k)	Conductance (C)	Resistance[b](R) Per inch thickness (1/k)	Resistance[b](R) For thickness listed (1/C)	Specific Heat, Btu/lb (deg F)	Resistance[b](R) (m·K)/W	Resistance[b](R) (m²·K)/W
ROOFING								
Asbestos-cement shingles	120	—	4.76	—	0.21	0.24		0.04
Asphalt roll roofing	70	—	6.50	—	0.15	0.36		0.03
Asphalt shingles	70	—	2.27	—	0.44	0.30		0.08
Built-up roofing .... 0.375 in.	70	—	3.00	—	0.33	0.35		0.06
Slate .... 0.5 in.	—	—	20.00	—	0.05	0.30		0.01
Wood shingles, plain and plastic film faced	—	—	1.06	—	0.94	0.31		0.17
SIDING MATERIALS (ON FLAT SURFACE)								
Shingles								
Asbestos-cement	120	—	4.75	—	0.21	0.31		0.04
Wood, 16 in., 7.5 exposure	—	—	1.15	—	0.87	0.31		0.15
Wood, double, 16-in. 12-in. exposure	—	—	0.84	—	1.19	0.28		0.21
Wood, plus insul. backer board, 0.3125 in.	—	—	0.71	—	1.40	0.31		0.25
Siding								
Asbestos-cement, 0.25 in., lapped	—	—	4.76	—	0.21	0.24		0.04
Asphalt roll siding	—	—	6.50	—	0.15	0.35		0.03
Asphalt insulating siding (0.5 in. bed.)	—	—	0.69	—	1.46	0.35		0.26
Hardboard siding, 0.4375 in.	40	1.49	—	0.67	0.79	0.28	4.65	0.14
Wood, drop, 1 × 8 in.	—	—	1.27	—	0.81	0.28		0.14
Wood, bevel, 0.5 × 8 in., lapped	—	—	1.23	—	1.05	0.28		0.18
Wood, bevel, 0.75 × 10 in., lapped	—	—	0.95	—	1.05	0.28		0.18
Wood, plywood, 0.375 in., lapped	—	—	1.59	—	0.59	0.29		0.10

Material	Density (lb/ft³)	k	C	1/k	1/C		Sp. Heat	
Aluminum or Steel[m], over sheathing								
Hollow-backed	—	—	1.61	—	0.61		0.29	0.11
Insulating-board backed nominal 0.375 in.	—	—	0.55	—	1.82		0.32	0.32
Insulating-board backed nominal 0.375 in., foil backed	—	—	0.34	—	2.96		0.20	0.52
Architectural glass	—	—	10.00	—	0.10			0.02
WOODS								
Maple, oak, and similar hardwoods	45	1.10	—	0.91	—	6.31	0.30	0.17
Fir, pine, and similar softwoods	32	0.80	—	1.25	—	8.66	0.33	0.33
Fir, pine, and similar softwoods	32	—	—	—	—		0.33	
0.75 in.			1.06		0.94			0.60
1.5 in.			0.53		1.89			0.75
2.5 in.			0.32		3.12			
3.5 in.			0.23		4.35			

Notes

[a] Representative values for dry materials were selected by ASHRAE TC4.4, Insulation and Moisture Barriers. They are intended as design (not specification) values for materials in normal use. For properties of a particular product, use the value supplied by the manufacturer or by unbiased tests.

[b] Resistance values are the reciprocals of C before rounding off C to two decimal places.

[c] Also see Insulating Materials, Board.

[d] Does not include paper backing and facing, if any. Where insulation forms a boundary (reflective or otherwise) of an air space, see Tables 1 and 2 for the insulating value of an air space for the appropriate effective emittance and temperature conditions of the space.

[e] Conductivity varies with fiber diameter. (See Chapter 20, Thermal Conductivity section, and Fig. 1) Insulation is produced by different densities; therefore, there is a wide variation in thickness for the same R-value among manufacturers. No effort should be made to relate any specific R-value to any specific thickness. Commercial thicknesses generally available range from 2 to 8.5.

[f] Values are for aged board stock. For change in conductivity with age of expanded urethane, see Chapter 19, Factors Affecting Thermal Conductivity.

[g] Insulating values of acoustical tile vary, depending on density of the board and on type, size, and depth of perforations.

[h] The U. S. Department of Commerce, *Simplified Practice Recommendation for Thermal Conductance Factors for Preformed Above-Deck Roof Insulation*, No. R 257-55, recognizes the specification of roof insulation on the basis of the C-values shown. Roof insulation is made in thicknesses to meet these values. When density is different from that shown, there will be a change in thermal conductivity.

[i] Face brick and common brick do not always have these specific densities. When density is different, there will be a change in thermal conductivity.

[j] Data on rectangular core concrete blocks differ from the above data on oval core blocks, due to core configuration, different mean temperatures, and possibly differences in unit weights. Weight data on the oval core blocks tested are not available.

[k] Weights of units approximately 7.625 in. high and 15.75 in. long. These weights are given as a means of describing the blocks tested, but conductance values are all for 1 ft² of area.

[l] Vermiculite, perlite, or mineral wool insulation. Where insulation is used, vapor barriers or other precautions must be considered to keep insulation dry.

[m] Values for metal siding applied over flat surfaces vary widely, depending on amount of ventilation of air space beneath the siding; whether air space is reflective or nonreflective; and on thickness, type, and application of insulating backing-board used. Values given are averages for use as design guides, and were obtained from several guarded hotbox tests (ASTM C236) or calibrated hotbox (BSS 77) on hollow-backed types and types made using backing-boards of wood fiber, foamed plastic, and glass fiber. Departures of ±50% or more from the values given may occur.

Appendix 4

Sample
Building
Heat Loss
Determination

The example shown on pages 212 and 213 is the town-house organization shown in Fig. 6.7 by Teamworks of Cambridge, Mass. The plans are shown to scale here. The heat loss rate is calculated for the entire building, so a unit's loss is one-half the listed value.

WALLS

2 x 4 construction with R-11 batt insulation and 1" Styrofoam[R] cladded with shingles.

COMPONENTS	R VALUES
Outside air film	0.17
Wood bevel siding lapped	0.81
1" styrofoam	5.00
3½" fiberglass	11.00 x 90%
(10% derating for thermal bridging through studs)	
½" gypsum board	0.45
Inside air film	0.68
	17.01

$$U = 1/R = 0.059 \text{ BTU/hr}°\text{Fft}^2$$

$$\text{Area} = 968 \text{ ft}^2$$

$$U \times A = 0.059 \times 968 = 56.91 \text{ BTUH/}°\text{F}$$

ROOF

Truss roof with R19 fiberglass batt and foil covered 1" Thermax

COMPONENTS	R VALUES
Outside air film	0.17
Asphalt shingles	0.44
Felt building membrane	0.06
Plywood sheathing, 0.625"	0.78
6" fiberglass batt	19.00
1" thermax with foil-faced air space	11.00
½" gypsum board	0.45
Inside air film	0.68
	32.58

$$U = 1/R = 0.031 \text{ BTU/hr }°\text{F ft}^2$$

$$\text{Area} = 1380 \text{ ft}^2$$

$$U \times A = 0.031 \times 1380 = 42.36 \text{ BTUH/}°\text{F}$$

FOUNDATION WALLS

3½" of urethane insulation over block walls: R = 21

$$U = 1/R = 0.048$$

$$\text{Area} = 160 \text{ ft}^2$$

$$U \times A = 0.048 \times 160 = 7.6 \text{ BTUH/}°\text{F}$$

DOORS

Partially insulated wood doors: R = 2.32

$$U = 1/R = 0.43$$

$$\text{Area} = 20 \text{ ft}^2$$

$$U \times A = 0.43 \times 20 = 8.6 \text{ BTUH/}°\text{F}$$

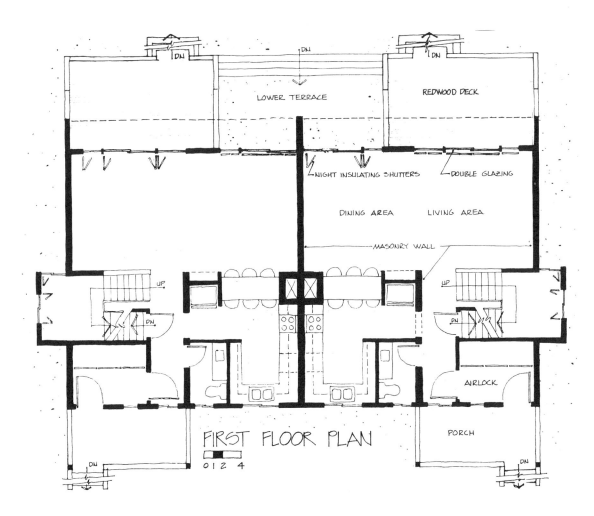

FIRST FLOOR PLAN

GLAZING

Double glazed with ¼" air space

U = 0.65

Area = 470 ft

U x A = 0.65 x 470 = 305.5 BTUH/°F

Total skin conductance   420.97 BTU/hr°F

Infiltration (Because of the continuous vapor barrier inside, and insulation board sheathing on the outside, one can conservatively assume the air change rate is 0.5 ac/hr.)

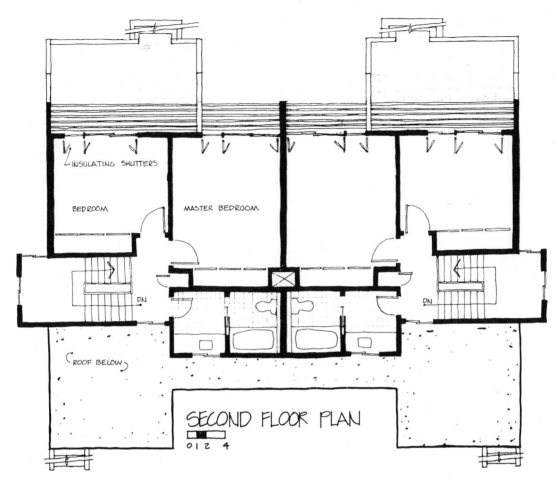

INSULATING SHUTTERS

BEDROOM

MASTER BEDROOM

DN

DN

ROOF BELOW

SECOND FLOOR PLAN

0 1 2 4

VOLUME		SPECIFIC HEAT		ACH		
20,600 ft³	x	0.018	x	0.5	=	185.40 BTU/hr°F

Total Heat Loss Rate = 606.37 BTU/hr°F

VALUES FOR SELECTIVE PROPERTIES

Property (Typical Values)	Specific Heat (Btu/lb-°F)	Density (lb/ft³)	Thermal Conductivity (Btu-ft/hr-ft²-°F)
Air	0.24	0.076	0.015
Aluminum	0.214	171	128
Concrete	0.156	144	0.54
Hardwood	0.55	50	0.1
Water	1.0	52.3	0.348

METRIC CONVERSIONS

LENGTH

1 m	=	1.09361 yd	(0.9144)*
	=	3.28084 ft	(0.3048)
1 cm	=	0.3937 in	(2.54)
1 mile	=	1.6093 km	(0.6214)

AREA

1 m^2	=	1.19591 yd^2	(0.8362)
	=	10.7636 ft^2	(0.0929)
1 cm^2	=	0.155 in^2	(6.4516)
1 hectare	=	2.47 acres	(0.4049)
1 acre	=	43.560 ft^2	(2.2957 x 10^{-5})

VOLUME

1 m^3	=	1.30795 yd^3	(0.7646)
	=	35.3147 ft^3	(0.0283)
1 cm^3	=	0.061 in^3	(16.3934)
1 liter	=	0.0354 ft^3	(28.3170)
	=	0.2642 gal.	(3.7854)
1 barrel (bb1)	=	42 gallons	(0.0238)

MASS

1 kg	=	2.2046 lb.	(0.4536)

TEMPERATURE

t $^\circ$C	=	0.556 (t $^\circ$F–32)	
t $^\circ$F	=	1.8 t $^\circ\Delta \cong {}^{32}$	
t $^\circ$F	=	1.8 t $^\circ$C + 32	
Y $^\circ$F	=	1.8 Y $^\circ$C	(0.5556)
t $^\circ$K	=	t $^\circ$C + 273	
t $^\circ$R	=	t $^\circ$F + 460	

DENSITY

1 kg/m^3	=	0.0624 lb/ft^3	(16.0256)

ENERGY, HEAT

1 MJ	=	0.2778 kWh	(3.600)
1 kJ	=	0.9478 BTU	(1.0551)
1 J	=	0.7376 ft-lbf	(1.3557)
1 kWh	=	3412.4 BTU	(2.93 x 10^{-4})

FLOW

1 liter/s	=	2.1189 ft^3/min (CFM)	(0.4719)

HEAT STORAGE

1 KJ/°C	=	0.5269 BTU/°F	(1.8979)
1 Wh/°C	=	1.8969 BTU/°F	(0.5272)
1 kJ/m^2-°C	=	0.04895 x 10^{-3} BTU/ft^2-°F	(20.4290)
1 kJ/kg-°C	=	0.2390 BTU/lb-°F	(4.1841)

HEAT TRANSFER

1 W/m-°C	=	0.5782 BTU-ft/hr-ft^2-°F	(1.7295)
	=	6.9380 BTU-in/hr-ft^2-°F	(0.1441)
1 W/m^2-°C	=	0.1762 BTU/hr-ft^2-°F	(5.6745)
1 W/°C	=	1.8956 BTU/hr-°F	(0.5275)
1 W/m^2	=	0.3172 BTU/hr-ft^2	(3.1526)

POWER

1 W	=	3.4144 BTU/hr	(0.2929)
	=	0.7380 ft-lbf/sec	(1.3550)
1 kW	=	1.3423 hp	(0.7450)

PRESSURE

1 Pascal	=	0.1450 x 10^{-3} psi	(6894.759)
	=	0.0040 in water	(250.00)

VELOCITY

1 m/s	=	196.85 ft/min	(0.0051)
	=	2.2369 mph	(0.4470)

BUILDING HEAT LOSS

1 Wh/DD$_{(°C)}$	=	3.600 kJ/DD$_{(°C)}$
	=	1.896 BTU/DD$_{(°F)}$
1 Wh/m^2-DD$_{(°C)}$		3.6 kJ/m^2-DD$_{(°C)}$
	=	30.4 BTU/ft^2-DD$_{(°F)}$

ILLUMINANCE

1 lux	=	0.0929 lm/ft^2 (foot candle)

Index